THE CHURCH STRUGGLE
IN SOUTH AFRICA

THE CHURCH
STRUGGLE
IN SOUTH AFRICA

Second Edition

by
John W. de Gruchy

WILLIAM B. EERDMANS PUBLISHING COMPANY
DAVID PHILIP

Copyright © 1979, 1986 by Wm. B. Eerdmans Publishing Co.

First published 1979
Second edition jointly published 1986 by Wm. B. Eerdmans Publishing Co.,
255 Jefferson Ave. SE, Grand Rapids, Mich. 49503,
Wm. Collins Sons & Co., 8 Grafton St., London W1X 3LA, England, and
David Philip Publisher (Pty) Ltd, PO Box 408, Claremont 7735, South Africa

Library of Congress Cataloging-in-Publication Data

De Gruchy, John W.
    The church struggle in South Africa.

    Bibliography: p. 279.
    Includes index.
    1. South Africa — Race relations.   2. Race relations —
Religious aspects — Christianity.   3. South Africa —
Church history.   I. Title.
DT763.D397   1986   261.8′348′′00968   86-19820

ISBN 0-8028-0243-5

Collins ISBN 0 00 599954 5

David Philip ISBN 0-86486-069-2

Contents

Foreword

FOR THE MAJORITY of Christian believers the church is both
a divine and a human institution. Jesus said, "You are
Peter, and on this rock I will build my church, and the gates
of hell shall not prevail against it." More than 1900 years
later, Father Trevor Huddleston, whose life has been given
to the service of Christ and the church, wrote an article
called "The Church Sleeps On." He made it worse by adding,
"though it occasionally talks in its sleep." Huddleston's article greatly displeased his bishop, the great Geoffrey Clayton
of Johannesburg. For Clayton the church was the creation of
Christ, whatever its human manifestation. And how could
one write of a sleeping church when the Holy Spirit was
alive and working through it? He thought Huddleston's
words reprehensible.

This conflict is indeed one of the themes that runs
throughout John de Gruchy's book, *The Church Struggle in
South Africa.* The believer is buoyed up by his confidence in
the power of the Holy Spirit, who rules and sustains the
universe. But he is cast down by the knowledge that so often
the power of the Spirit does not seem to manifest itself in the
church, so that theologians must find evidences of his action
in other agencies and instruments, some of them wholly
antagonistic to the church.

A second theme also runs throughout Dr. de Gruchy's

book, namely, that the church, although it is a divine institution, is affected by, and often corrupted by, the society in which it is placed. In Britain, which in 1914 and 1939 was a less divided country than it is today, the church had little difficulty in identifying itself with the cause of the nation. But South Africa in 1978 is a highly fragmented society. The Afrikaner churches identify themselves very closely with the maintenance of Afrikaner identity in an extremely hostile world. The black churches identify themselves more and more with the cause of black liberation, and the hard fact must be faced that the cause of black liberation and the cause of Afrikaner survival are often incompatible. The so-called English-speaking churches, with their multiracial character, are in no such simple position as the Afrikaner and the black churches.

More and more the non-Dutch Reformed, non-black churches are struggling with the agonizing tension between the demands of white security and those of black liberation. Thus, in these multiracial churches there is a tremendous tension between white conservatives and black liberationists. This tension can be seen very clearly in the South African Council of Churches, which in the past has been under white leadership, but which has recently appointed Bishop Desmond Tutu, who might be called a black liberationist, as its General Secretary. The tension can be seen as well in the rift between the Dutch Reformed churches of South Africa and the Dutch Reformed churches in the rest of the world, and in the widening gulf between the biggest white Dutch Reformed Church and its "daughter" or "sister" churches, the African, Coloured, and Indian churches, which have totally rejected apartheid as unscriptural and immoral. There is also a gulf between the white Dutch Reformed churches of South Africa and what one might call the other historic churches, the Anglican, Catholic, Methodist, Presbyterian, and others, and this too is a further proof of the rift between white conservatives and white not-so-conservatives, though it must not be concluded that all white conservatives are to be found in the Dutch Reformed churches, or all white not-so-conservatives in the other historic churches. There are also tensions inside the Dutch Reformed churches themselves, and the most notable evidence of these is the way in which Dr. Beyers Naudé, once a powerful moderator, has not only been rejected by his church, but has also been silenced by the state.

The tension between church-in-Christ and church-in-society is inevitable, we humans being what we are. It can to a large extent be avoided by exceptional bodies such as the Quakers or Jehovah's Witnesses, but not by the larger churches. The important matter from the Christian point of view is to acknowledge the tension, and to use it as fruitfully as we are able.

The tension between the church-of-Christ and the church-of-the-nation is another matter. Throughout history the church has never found great difficulty in rallying to the nation in times of war. But as I have pointed out, the situation in South Africa in 1978 is much more complex than the situation in Britain in 1939. What is the nation in South Africa? The Afrikaner Nationalist always refers to the Afrikaners as a nation, but it is notable that the English-speaking South Africans never refer to themselves as such. That is why in the present situation, which is more or less a war situation, many young English-speaking South Africans are not enthusiastic about taking up arms. What are they fighting for? Are they fighting for the government or for the National party (the governing party) or for Afrikanerdom? They can hardly say they are fighting for any of these; therefore, many are compelled to say they are fighting against Communism, or for white civilization, or for law and order; and some maintain that they are fighting to give white South Africa its last chance to create a just society. But some will not fight at all, maintaining that their consciences will not allow them to fight for the maintenance of white supremacy. Dr. de Gruchy deals with this most difficult problem in an illuminating manner.

There is yet another way to deal with the tension between church-of-Christ and church-of-the-nation. That is to assert that the tension does not exist, that love of Christ and love of nation are in fact identical. It is to assert that it is only when a person is a member of a nation, and finds pride and meaning and self-realization in that membership, that he or she is obeying the will of God for mankind. This is one of the most striking characteristics of Afrikaner Nationalism—it distrusts and indeed despises any person who values lightly his or her membership in a nation. This is why Afrikaner Nationalism is bitterly hostile towards liberalism. The Afrikaner liberal finds that he or she has more in common with the American liberal and the British liberal and the fellow South African liberal, than with his or her fellow Afrikaner. This accounts also for the (up-till-now) monolithic nature of the ruling National party.

This fusion of love of nation with love of Christ is called Christian nationalism. It would perhaps be going too far to say that it *replaces* Christianity. Rather, it is fairer to say that for the Afrikaner Nationalist it *is* Christianity. For him, every child in South Africa—and in the world for that matter—is being robbed of his very birthright if he is not brought up as a member of a nation.

It remains only to say that the fusion of love of nation with love of Christ produces an unstable compound. One of the supreme values of love of nation is survival, and it is hard to reconcile this with the teachings of the gospel. The true believer gives his supreme loyalty to Christ, not to the nation. If he claims that the two loyalties are identical, then he must close his mind to all reason and indeed to all theological argument except that which he himself manufactures. This is the position of many Afrikaner churchmen. But it is clear that after thirty years of government, many Afrikaners are questioning the basic principles of their political creed. And quite apart from moral and theological considerations, one must ask if it is really possible to have ten separate "civilizations," ten separate autonomies, within the confines of one piece of land?

The struggle between the church-in-Christ and the church-in-society first revealed itself with the advent of the missionaries from Europe. The society was essentially a white supremacist society, and the customs of the white settlers have finally come to rule us. But it was the missionaries who first challenged the customs. That is why the original Dutch settlers and their descendants came to distrust intensely the interfering missionaries, a distrust that eventually came to be shared to a lesser or greater degree by the British settlers and their descendants more than a century and a half later. It persists today, though it is now less evident, owing to the removal of school and hospital control from missionary hands during the last twenty-five years, and owing to the much greater part now played in missionary work by the Afrikaner churches.

There is also the struggle between the philosophies (and the moralities and the theologies) of the Afrikaner churches and the other historic churches, what I have called (not altogether accurately) the conservative and the not-so-conservative churches. This struggle continues today, especially as the other historic churches are striving, sometimes heroically and sometimes not, to make themselves more representative of a multiracial society. As a result, communication between the Afrikaner churches and the others has never been worse.

Finally, there is the tension between black Christian and white Christian, which continues unabated. Yet one must record that when Dr. Verwoerd, our redoubtable Minister of Native Education, tried in 1957 to bring "mixed" worship to an end, he was astonished by church reaction, and for the only time in his career, he withdrew. He later tried to do the same thing by another method, but for some unknown reason, the law was never invoked. Today, in 1978, it appears that the National party government would not attempt to carry race separation into the churches. In fact, the Minister of Plural Relations has announced that the government will not require permits for one-day gatherings, but only for those that continue longer, which means those that continue overnight. This provision has, to me, an unmistakable sexual connotation, whether conscious or unconscious.

Dr. de Gruchy deals with the phenomena of black consciousness, black power, and black theology, all of which have an integral relationship, but each of which must also be distinguished from the others. One can hardly exaggerate the intensity of the crisis that confronts the Christian church in South Africa. Black theology is saying to white Christians, "Make up your minds. Do you belong to the church-of-Christ or the church-of-the-nation?" And one cannot ask a harder question than that. That is not to say that black Christians do not also have a church-of-the-nation. But their church-of-the-nation has moral arguments superior to those of white Christians, namely, those of social and economic and political justice.

Nor must one leave out of account the possibility that black power, if it receives what it considers to be an inadequate response to its moral demands, will withdraw from Christianity altogether. There is unfortunately abundant evidence that many black radicals regard Christianity as a white exploitative religion, and the Christian missionaries, whose beliefs deeply influenced people like Lutuli,* Z. K. Matthews, Sobukwe, and many others, as responsible for the destruction of the ancestral beliefs, a destruction which has left so many black people rudderless, faithless, purposeless, lost to the cause of liberation.

All these strains and stresses within the church are discussed with great skill and perception by Dr. de Gruchy in his book *The Church Struggle in South Africa.* His closing chapter on "The Kingdom of God in South Africa" is a masterly one and a fitting conclusion. I can also add that he has that knowledge of our racial and political history which is indispensable for the proper discussion of a theme such as this. It is with pleasure that I write a foreword to his penetrating work.

ALAN PATON

---

*While Chief Albert Lutuli's name is usually spelled "Luthuli," the spelling adopted here is the way the chief preferred.

Preface to
the Second Edition

FOR SOME TIME now I have been working on a sequel to
The Church Struggle in South Africa, which will update the
story and reflect upon its significance. In the meantime the
publishers have expressed their desire to keep *The Church
Struggle* in print, a decision which is, for me, both gratifying
and problematic. I am gratified to know that the book has met
a need and continues to do so both in South Africa and elsewhere. It is, evidently, a helpful introduction to the church situation in South Africa for the general reader as well as a useful
textbook for students. My problem derives from the fact that
not only have ten years of tumultuous events passed since it
was first conceived, profoundly affecting both church and society, but also during this decade a large and growing amount of
research has been done on the church in South Africa which
needs to be taken into account. Moreover, while my own theological convictions have not altered a great deal, some of my
social perceptions and theological insights have changed and
developed.

In the light of this problem I have considered two alternatives. The first was a complete rewriting of *The Church Struggle,* which would not only bring the story up to date but would
also reflect throughout the text the changes in my own analysis. After consultation with colleagues, however, I have decided
against this. *The Church Struggle* belongs to the period in

which it was first written and remains, I believe, a substantially accurate account of the story as far as it goes. This is confirmed, for me at any rate, by a rereading of the reviews the book received, and by references to it in more recent literature. At the same time the book is by no means beyond criticism, and it would be both unhelpful and foolish to reprint it without taking such criticism into account. Indeed, I believe the value of the book can only be enhanced by indicating what these criticisms are and by responding to them.

The second alternative, then, and the one I have decided to follow, is to leave the substance of the text unaltered but to provide a Postscript in which I examine the major criticisms. This will enable the reader to approach the text with some awareness of its weaknesses and their remedies. It will also indicate some of the ways in which my own thinking has developed. An extended and updated Bibliography (which is totally new to the American edition), together with a Subject Index, will also make it a more useful textbook. As already intimated, there is a considerable and growing literature on the church in South Africa, and no one who is really interested need remain uninformed. In any event, the Bibliography will enable the reader to explore the subject beyond the parameters and limitations of *The Church Struggle,* and so, in some measure, bring the story up to date.

Much has indeed happened in southern and South Africa during the past decade, not least with regard to the struggle of the church for justice and genuine reconciliation. It is now widely believed that South Africa has reached a critical moment in the struggle between those who cling to white power and dominance and the vast majority of South Africans who look toward a future without apartheid, however disguised. Unless present perceptions are totally misguided, I do not believe that the birth of a new South Africa is too far away, though it would be falsely optimistic to expect that it will be born without continuing conflict, pain, and suffering. I also do not believe that the birth of a new South Africa will usher in the kingdom of God or some utopia in which the prophetic responsibility of the church will somehow cease. In the meantime, the church struggle in South Africa has entered a new phase as the struggle for a just society has intensified. If the continued publication of this volume makes some contribution to that struggle I shall be gratified, but in any event I dedicate it to that end and to all who are committed to the birth of a just and truly free society in South Africa.

JOHN W. DE GRUCHY

Cape Town
January 1986

Preface

WHEN I RECEIVED an invitation in 1975 from Bethel College in North Newton, Kansas, to present the Menno Simons Lectures in 1977 on *The Church Struggle in South Africa,* neither those responsible for the invitation nor I had any premonition that by the time they would be given, South Africa would be so much in the news headlines of the world. In fact, the lectures were scheduled for and given within a few days of the banning of the Christian Institute, and amid the widespread publicity which surrounded the death in police detention of black student leader Steve Biko.

Prior to presenting the lectures at Bethel College, I was privileged to give them a trial run in seminars at Wesley Theological Seminary in Washington, D.C., and at the Iliff School of Theology in Denver, Colorado, as part of their summer school programs. The lectures were also given at the Canadian Mennonite Bible College in Winnipeg, and in January of this year they formed the basis for a winter inter-term seminar at the Associated Mennonite Biblical Seminaries in Elkhart, Indiana.

I am most grateful, therefore, to Bethel College, its president, Dr. Harold Schultz, and the Menno Simons lectureship committee, Drs. Alvin Beachy, Robert Kreider, and James Juhnke, for the original invitation to give the lectures. I count this a great honor and privilege. But thanks are also due to the college community as a whole, both faculty and students, for the warm welcome and friendship we experienced as a family throughout our stay during the fall semester. I am also grateful to the other institutions already mentioned, to their presidents, and to those members of their faculties responsible for the invitations and our well-being, and particularly to those students whose stimulating participation helped me to clarify many of my own thoughts.

Since returning home, I have expanded the lectures and attempted to produce a readable book. In doing so, I have benefited from the critical comments and encouragement of colleagues and friends, especially Alex Boraine, Jim Cochrane, Jo Dunstan, Jaap Durand, James Leatt, James Moulder, and Francis Wilson. In expressing my gratitude to them, I naturally absolve them from responsibility for errors of fact or judgment which may be found in the text.

In thanking Alan Paton for so willingly and graciously writing the Foreword, I wish to pay tribute to him as a man, a Christian, and a South African. His prophetic concern for justice, his dogged struggle against racism in all its forms, and his capacity for genuine hope are an encouragement to many people, both here and in other parts of the world.

At many times during the writing of this book, I have been conscious of my identity as a white, English-speaking South African, and the limitations that this inevitably means in terms of insight and perspective. I cannot speak for either Afrikaners or blacks, nor, indeed, for the English-speaking community. If I have misrepresented any, I ask for pardon. But I have written as one involved in the situation, and out of the conviction that the Christian gospel contains the word of hope for present and future South Africans, irrespective of race or culture.

Among the many people who have helped me complete my task, I would like to thank those in the Secretarial School at Bethel College, and Suzanne Lind at the Mennonite Seminary in Elkhart, who typed the first drafts of the manuscript, and especially our departmental secretary, Shaan Ellinghouse, who prepared the final draft with amazing patience and considerable skill. Professor John

Cumpsty, head of the Department of Religious Studies at the University of Cape Town, has supported and encouraged me throughout my labors, and I am most grateful to him for this. It has also been a privilege to have the help and guidance of the editorial staff at Wm. B. Eerdmans, and in particular, the confidence and support of Mr. Marlin Van Elderen, the Editor-in-Chief.

Finally, I wish to thank my wife, Isobel, and my children. As they enjoyed my sabbatical in the United States as much as I, I do not feel unduly guilty about the time devoted to these pages rather than to them. But without my wife's constant encouragement, and the badgering of Stephen, Jeanelle, and Anton, who also enthusiastically prepared the Index, I would still be writing.

JOHN W. DE GRUCHY

University of Cape Town
Pentecost, 1978

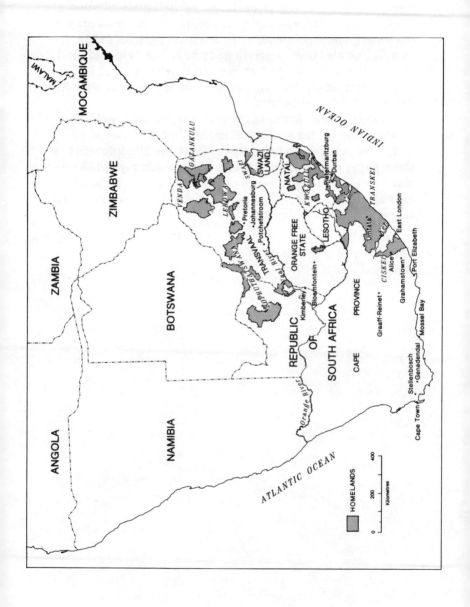

1

Historical Origins

Settler Church / Mission Church

IT HAS BEEN a failure of European colonialist historians to write about South African history as though it began with the arrival of Portuese explorers in the sixteenth century and the Dutch settlers in the next. Some recent historiography has attempted to correct this false assumption.[1] But it is true that the history of the church begins with the coming of the Dutch (1652), the French Huguenots (1668), and the early German settlers a little later. With few exceptions these settlers were Protestants, and the Dutch and French were Calvinist. Although Portuguese Catholics had predated the Dutch in landing at the Cape—a small Catholic chapel was built at Mossel Bay in 1501—by 1652 this very temporary presence had long since gone. Indeed, even though there were Catholics residing at the Cape, the Dutch East India Company forbade the practice of Roman Catholicism.[2] The Dutch Reformed Church (DRC), controlled by the classis in Amsterdam, was the established church, into which the Huguenots were soon assimilated. The German Lutherans were more successful in their struggle to retain their own identity, but it was only in 1779 that they finally obtained permission to erect their own church building.[3]

As the Cape colony expanded during the eighteenth cen-

1

tury, so the DRC grew, but its growth was almost totally confined to white settler congregations. Early attempts to evangelize the indigenous San and Khoi populations were sporadic and eventually declined, until the birth of the nineteenth-century international missionary movement provided new impetus and concern for the evangelization of the "heathen." Indeed, the first European missionary specifically sent to minister to the indigenous population at the Cape was not Dutch Reformed but a Moravian, George Schmidt, who in 1738 commenced his work at Genadendal, about a hundred miles east of Cape Town.[4] Within ten years he had to stop. One reason for this was that the evangelistic piety and gospel of universal grace proclaimed to the indigenous peoples collided with the Calvinist orthodoxy of the Dutch church. There was, at this time, considerable opposition to the Moravian Brethren in Holland itself, and this had begun to influence opinion at the Cape. But the teaching and practice of George Schmidt was not only regarded as a threat to the theology and authority of the church, it was also seen as a threat to the social life of the settler community to which the church ministered.

This conflict between "settler" church and "mission" church became a dominant issue for church and society at the Cape during the nineteenth century. When Britain finally gained occupation of the Cape in 1806, and the DRC and the small Lutheran congregations were no longer the only churches in the colony, Protestant missionaries of other persuasions arrived by the score from Europe and America "to Christianize the heathen." But they soon discovered that the white settlers were largely unconvinced about the need for and desirability of such missionary enthusiasm and endeavor. Again and again, missionaries had to answer objections to Christian missions, objections that were by no means strictly theological. Charles Brownlee, a mid-nineteenth-century missionary of the London Missionary Society, tells how he had to convince his audience that it was not true "that Christian Natives are not such good servants as the wild heathen."[5] As we proceed, we shall show how this tension between church and mission played a crucial

role in the social history of South Africa. It provides one of
the clues for understanding the struggle of the church for
faithfulness and relevance today.

By 1824 the DRC at the Cape had gained its autonomy
from the church in Holland, symbolized by the constitution
of its own synod.[6] Though it remained dependent upon its
distant mother church in many ways, this was a momentous
step for the DRC. Indeed, it was the establishment of the
first independent church in southern Africa. The church had
finally taken root, even though the soil was largely white.
What precipitated this development, however, was not simply the inevitable desire of and need for congregations to
organize and control their own affairs in a new land, but the
fact that the Cape colony was now British. It was undesirable and impractical for the established church to be controlled from an enemy country. And the DRC was the official
church even after the British took control of the Cape. Included in the terms of Dutch surrender was the stipulation
that the position and privileges of the DRC would be maintained by the new colonial administration. A somewhat
strange and anomalous situation ensued. The DRC was now
free from the Calvinist control of Amsterdam, but its synodical decisions required the sanction of the Anglican governor
at the Cape. Meanwhile, the Church of England, to which
the governor belonged, not only had little influence, it had
no parishes. It existed to serve the spiritual needs of the
colonial officials and militia. Its first sanctuary was the
Dutch Groote Kerk in Cape Town; its growth was sporadic,
and its life remained disjointed and haphazard until the
arrival of the first Anglican bishop of Cape Town, Robert
Gray, in 1848.

The cutting of the umbilical cord linking the DRC with
its mother church in Holland came at a time when the
church in the Netherlands was shedding some of its strict
Calvinist theology under the impact of the Enlightenment.
By 1817 the ultra-Calvinistic decrees of Dort were no longer
binding, and rationalism had made considerable gains in
the church. Unlike the church in the Netherlands, the DRC
did not jettison Dort, but neither did it escape these Euro-

pean developments. It was only after a protracted struggle
that it managed to curtail the influence of its more liberal
theologians and pastors.[7] Even so, in spite of official adher-
ence to Dort, the theology of the DRC during the nineteenth
century was not pure Calvinism.

After the Cape Synod was constituted, long debates were
held about the desirability of establishing a theological
seminary. This became increasingly necessary because of
the difficulties facing the church in calling Dutch pastors,
and in sending students for training in Holland. There were
those who opposed the formation of the seminary on the
grounds that it would shut the door on participation in the
important theological developments taking place in Europe
at the time. But the majority supported the move for precisely that reason.[8] With the establishment of the theological seminary at Stellenbosch in 1859, the DRC was able to
control its own theological teaching, and in spite of sporadic
attempts to introduce more liberal emphases, it was able to
plow a conservative furrow for its ministers and members to
follow.

Another decisive development in the DRC was the arrival of a number of Scottish Presbyterian ministers from
about 1820 onwards. The need for them arose because the
British disliked the calling of Dutch ministers to the colony,
and there were delays in establishing the Stellenbosch
Seminary. Thus, in the interim, the church was encouraged
by the British authorities to obtain the help of Scottish
dominees whose churchmanship was acceptable to the DRC
and whose citizenship was acceptable to the government.
Notable among these divines, some of whom had received
part of their training in Holland, was Andrew Murray, who
arrived at the Cape in 1822. More famous was his son Andrew Murray, Jr., who with his brother John went to Scotland and Holland to train for the ministry in the mid-
nineteenth century. The younger Andrew became moderator of the DRC Synod on six occasions. Together with John,
Andrew Murray, Jr. injected a new evangelical enthusiasm
into the church, profoundly shaping Dutch Reformed theology and piety at a critical moment in its development. The

Murrays had personal experience of the church-state contro-
versies which had split the Church of Scotland in 1843;
they had also encountered firsthand the rationalism of the
church in the Netherlands. Thus, they were ideally equipped
to steer the church through this crucial period when liberalism and state relations were the dominant issues. That their
evangelical piety did not logically fit pure Calvinism did not
really matter because the DRC, though conservative, was
not strictly Calvinist anyway. The astonishing revivals under the ministry of Andrew Murray, Jr., to which modern
Pentecostalism owes a great deal,[9] produced a crop of new
theological students ready to fill the desks at Stellenbosch.
The spiritual life of the church was immeasurably enriched,
and considerable impetus was given to education, especially
the training of devout Christian teachers. This evangelical
theology and revivalist piety also corresponded well with
the international missionary movement of the time, now
well into its stride at the Cape. Around 1857, the DRC
began to embark more seriously than before upon missionary work among the Coloured peoples on their doorstep,[10]
and the Murray influence gave this mission motivation,
direction, and manpower.

At the same time, Murray's influence created tension.
Although evangelicals now dominated the church, orthodox
Calvinists coexisted in an uneasy relationship. Both found a
common enemy in rationalism and liberal theology, but
there were those who were critical of the pietist and foreign
input, an influence made more suspicious by the fact that
the Murrays were of British descent. Moreover, Calvinism
was being revived in Holland. Rationalism, having split the
church there, led to various schisms, beginning in 1834 with
the founding of the Separated Christian Reformed Church,
inspired by Groen van Prinsterer. Van Prinsterer was
highly critical of the liberalism of both the state and the
established church. He was convinced that this would eventually lead to atheism and revolution. Europe was going
through revolutionary years as it was. Thus, under the ban-
ner of Christian Nationalism, and with the motto, "In isolation is our strength," van Prinsterer waged an intense polit-

ical and ecclesiastical war on behalf of his brand of Calvinism. Liberalism was the enemy.[11] Try as he did to prevent its spread, van Prinsterer failed in his lifetime. However, he profoundly influenced Abraham Kuyper, the person who did succeed to a remarkable degree in achieving his neo-Calvinist goals.

Schism in Holland stabilized with the formation of the Christelijke Gereformeerde Kerken in 1869. Kuyper was the most important influence within these new Gereformeerde Kerken. A statesman and theologian of considerable stature, Kuyper not only gave fresh expression to the strict Calvinism of Dort, but also developed van Prinsterer's idea of Calvinism as an all-embracing philosophy and lifestyle.[12] A valiant fighter for the separation of church and state, Kuyper insisted that all spheres of life exist by virtue of God's common grace, and that therefore each has a sovereignty over its own affairs under God. Education, art, economics, family life, are all spheres through which God operates directly. This common grace, as distinct from saving grace, is built into the structures of creation and provides the basis for Christian Nationalism in its various dimensions.

Kuyper eventually founded the Free University of Amsterdam, at which many Dutch Reformed theologians were trained in the course of the following century. But already by the middle of the nineteenth century, these neo-Calvinist developments were being propagated and assimilated at the Cape. An important leader in this was the Rev. S. J. du Toit, a father of Afrikaner Nationalism. Not only did this movement offer an articulate alternative to evangelical pietism, but it also laid the foundation for Christian National education, a cornerstone of later Afrikaner Nationalist policy. The pietism of Murray and the neo-Calvinism of Kuyper, the one so intensely personal, the other so much more directly socio-political in significance, never came together in a creative synthesis. On the contrary, it led to schism when S. J. du Toit left the DRC to form his own church. Later, when the Gereformeerde Kerk (the "Dopper Kerk") was established in Potchefstroom, Transvaal, in 1859 after the Great Trek, it embodied this neo-Calvinism and attracted many from the DRC who had been influenced by du Toit and others like him. It was this church, rather than the DRC, that was strictly Calvinist, at least in the Kuyperian sense, during the nineteenth century. It is important to keep this distinction in mind, for "the existence of this truly Calvinist Church alongside the Dutch Reformed Church has led many commentators to attribute Calvinist attitudes to the Dutch Reformed Church which in fact come from the Reformed Church (i.e., the Gereformeerde Kerk)."[13]

This was not the only tension heightened by evangelicalism within the DRC. Expanding missionary work produced as much, perhaps even more. In the very early days at the Cape colony, discrimination practiced between white and black, freeman and slave, was ostensibly based more on religion than race. Though racism and a European sense of cultural superiority were rife, the first Dutch commandant at the Cape issued a proclamation in which it was decreed that "everyone is . . . earnestly admonished and ordered to show all friendliness and amiability to the natives. . . ." A decisive criterion for interracial relationships was Christian baptism. A Khoi convert, Eva, who was baptized in 1661, married an influential European official, and such mixed marriages between Christians of different races, though rare, were initially tolerated. But race proved more powerful than religion. When, in the nineteenth century, missionary work met with the success it did, the DRC was confronted with a crisis similar to that which beset the early Jewish-Christian community when, to their amazement, the gospel was so readily accepted by gentiles. While baptism theoretically rendered all distinctions void, whether in church or society, a fact demonstrated at the Lord's Table, not all white settlers warmed to this theology in practice. Racial prejudice and the interests of labor and land clashed with theology.

The Synod of 1829 stood firm and undeterred. Holy Communion, it maintained, was to be administered "simultaneously to all members without distinction of colour or origin" because this was "an unshakable principle based on the infallible Word of God." This refusal to allow race to determine church practice was reaffirmed at several subsequent synods. But taking into account the great social rift that did exist between the settler community and the indigenous people, many of whom were slaves, it is not surprising that social pressures eventually proved stronger than synodical resolutions.

By 1857, the synod had to change its stance and depart from the plain sense of the Word of God. It decided that, though not desirable or scriptural, due to the weakness of some (i.e., whites), it was permissible to hold separate services for whites and blacks.[14] Its resolution read:

> The Synod considers it desirable and scriptural that our members from the Heathen be received and absorbed into our existing congregations wherever possible; but where this measure, as a result of the weakness of some, impedes the furtherance of the cause of Christ among the Heathen, the congregation from the Heathen, already founded or still to be founded, shall enjoy its Christian privileges in a separate building or institution.

This permitted separation was not allowed simply for racial reasons. Social pressures found an ally among missionary strategists such as Andrew Murray, Jr. In line with much nineteenth-century European Protestant missionary strategy, this separation was regarded as a way of facilitating mission work. Influential German missiologists such as Gustav Warneck taught that the gospel should not be proclaimed to mankind in general, but to each nation and group in ways appropriate to their culture.[15] There was, and still is, sufficient sense and biblical sanction ("a missionary to the gentiles") in the proposal to give it plausibility. But the cost was high—it was a policy that divided the church along ethnic and cultural lines. Although mixed congregations continued to exist, what was meant in 1857 to be an exception became the rule. Separate parallel congregations were formed, leading eventually to separate mission or "daughter" churches. The first of these was *Die Sendingkerk* (the Mission Church), established in 1881 for Coloured people.*

---

*For the designation of so-called "Coloured" people see the first page of the Appendix.

This was followed later by the N. G. Kerk in Africa, for blacks (Africans), and the Indian Reformed Church. Churches were also established in other African countries as a result of extensive mission work.

This separate development within the DRC, reluctantly accepted by some, had enormous ramifications for the church. While it facilitated the growth of indigenous congregations, it divided the church along racial lines in a way that was recognized even then as theologically unsound. It is debatable that what was gained by this development was of greater value for the church than what was lost. It is also debatable that it was necessary on cultural grounds, for the separation did not begin initially among black African converts, with their very different Nguni or Sotho cultures and languages, but in the western Cape, where settler and Coloured communities shared much in common. Would the church not have been more faithful and thus eventually more relevant if it had attempted to provide a bridge between people rather than serve as an instrument whereby social and racial differences were legitimized? However understandable from a cultural and evangelistic perspective, it seems to be an example of social pressure and pragmatism, custom and culture, rather than theology and Scripture, determining the life of the church. The Dutch Reformed theologian, Professor B. B. Keet, critically commenting on this, wrote: "Why could the Coloured Christian not have come into his own inside the Church of the Europeans? The answer is obvious: It is because the white man was not prepared to give him the opportunity of doing so."[16] In any event, the missionary program of the DRC as it developed during the next hundred years followed custom and culture consistently, thus providing an ecclesiological blueprint for the Nationalist policy of separate development. Thus, this separation of settler and mission churches had implications far beyond the ecclesiastical realm.

It is evident, then, that the theology and practice of the DRC has been influenced by a great deal more than the authentic teaching of John Calvin. The original Dutch Calvinism at the Cape was affected by liberalism, then transformed by the Murrays' evangelicalism. It was also profoundly influenced by the neo-Calvinism of Abraham Kuyper.[17] Even though Kuyper's theology was much more dominant in the Gereformeerde Kerk in the Transvaal, neo-Calvinism penetrated and influenced the DRC to an ever increasing extent. Kuyper's idea of separate spheres of sovereignty embedded in creation corresponded well with the Lutheran doctrine of the "orders of creation" as expounded by German missionary science and embodied in DRC policy. Together they have had considerable influence on South African social history. Indeed, it helps explain why at a later date the DRC could give its support to the Nationalist policy of separate development as being in accord with the will of God. It was this theological position which provided the religious ground for the policy. But it was a position somewhat removed from the theology propounded by the reformer of Geneva.

Throughout the nineteenth century, British administrative influence at the Cape was strengthened by the growing numbers of British immigrants. Many of these immigrants were casualties of the Napoleonic wars, escaping from severe hardships at home to start a new life in the colony. By this time, many of the Dutch settlers, most of whom were farmers (Boers) often living in remote country areas, had begun to lose touch with their own European culture and were beginning to mold a new one with its own language and traditions (Afrikaans and Afrikaner). The British colonial agents and the British settlers who came in increasing numbers after about 1820, to settle largely along the eastern Cape frontier, were a different European breed.

In particular, the British settlers were townspeople rather than farmers, though they soon had to learn to use the plow in order to survive. They were the products of working-class England. Independent-minded grocers and laborers hit by the economic recessions of the day, they were more often than not Nonconformists and Wesleyans by religious conviction and of a social class that disliked the British aristocratic establishment and its arid Anglican faith. But they were British. As the century passed and their numbers grew, they were proud to belong to an expanding empire, even though they still had to fight for their rights, especially the liberty to express their opinions in the press. They were part of the Victorian Age, an outpost of a culture which they regarded as inferior to none, and superior to most, including those they encountered at the Cape. "The Victorians," Owen Chadwick reminds us, "changed the face of the world because they were assured. Untroubled by doubt whether Europe's civilization and politics were suited to Africa or Asia, they saw vast opportunities open to energy and enterprise, and identified progress with the spread of English intelligence and English industry."[18]

The Boers were probably a little overawed, even though they had arrived to possess the land 150 years before; they were certainly apprehensive, if not of the English-speaking settlers themselves, then of the British authorities and the policies they would adopt. They had every reason to be. Rumors of English liberalism were sufficient cause for concern. Moreover, they were increasingly unhappy about the missionaries who emanated from London, and who seemed to embody such liberalism in religious guise. Their struggle against imperialism, an alien culture, liberalism, and interfering missionaries was about to begin, and it would not end until it had produced an Afrikaner Nationalism equal to the task of subduing the land and reshaping society. All of this had significant ramifications for the DRC, for if it was to be relevant to Afrikaner fears and aspirations, it could not stand aloof from the Afrikaner struggle. If it became involved, it could not but be affected by political developments. To this dilemma we must return later. For the moment let us consider the British settlers and their churches.

Whereas the DRC missionary enterprise began only after the Dutch church had taken root in the country, the British churches came to the Cape in two forms from the outset. They came to serve the needs of the colonial administrators and the 1820 settlers. But even before that, they came as part of the great nineteenth-century missionary thrust. In 1799 the first and much maligned London Missionary Society (LMS) missionary, Dr. Johannes van der Kemp, arrived in Cape Town. It is ironical that a Dutchman should have been the first English missionary to become the bane of the Afrikaner farmers. But he was. And so were many other LMS missionaries, including Robert Moffat in Kuruman, and especially Dr. John Philip, who served as the Cape superintendent of the society from 1819 until 1851, and who in that period became the best known and most hated of all.[19] Some LMS missionaries, including van der Kemp, who married a Coloured woman, were accused of immorality, and others of treason. The trouble was that they were not serving the apparent needs of the white settlers and farmers, but striving to be relevant to the conditions and struggles of the Coloureds and Africans. Not only were these "non-Europeans" regarded as inferior, the majority of settlers considered them born to be their servants. Moreover, they were often considered cattle-thieves, and the frontier wars made the Xhosas enemies of the settlers. To be sympathetic to their needs, to champion their cause, and to do so by enlisting both the authority of the British administration and overseas opinion was, to say the very least, regarded as reprehensible. Such was the opinion not only of Afrikaner Boers, but also of British settlers, and even of some English clergy. A Scottish Presbyterian, the Rev. John M'Carter of Ladysmith in Natal, wrote an apologia for the DRC in 1869 in which he exclaimed to his British readers accustomed only to the reports of missionaries: "We cannot avoid giving utterance to our impression that missionaries and their friends have sometimes overstated their case. . . . we have been astonished at the onesidedness of some. . . ."[20] Even Robert Gray, the Anglican bishop in Cape Town, charged that some LMS missionaries had been the cause, albeit unintentionally, of the Kat River Rebellion.

The problem which has continuously dogged relationships between the white community and the missionaries who have come to serve black South Africans is simply, how do you relate to the needs of both at the same time? Jane Sales sums it up well:

> There was some validity to the charge of "traitor" which the Dutch farmers had levelled at Vanderkemp when he negotiated with Klaas Stuurman in 1802, and again at James Read at the

time of the Black Circuit. The attacks which the Grahamstown merchants made on John Philip in 1838 and on Nicholas Smit, Dutch-background pastor of the Coloured LMS Church in Grahamstown in 1851, also indicated this charge of treason. To deny the charge was, in a sense, to forsake the Coloured people, the "objects" of their missionary concern. If social welfare is conceived only on a racialistic basis, then Vanderkemp, Philip, the Reads, and others, even Stockenstroom, were "traitors" to white society in South Africa.[21]

This is an interesting comment, not only for its perception of the problem we are considering, but also because it shows how the English-speaking settlers and their churches had also begun to follow the pattern established by their Afrikaner or Dutch counterparts. The "Grahamstown merchants" to whom Sales refers were British, not Boers. The London Missionary Society Church was Coloured, not multiracial—there was a separate Congregational Church in the town which served the English Independents and Presbyterians. The same was true for the Wesleyan Methodists, who were numerically the strongest among the eastern Cape settlers centered in Grahamstown.

The basic reason that Dutch and English settlers alike resented the presence of some missionaries was thus precisely because the missionaries not only evangelized the indigenous peoples, but took their side in the struggle for justice, rights, and land. The missionaries, being white, regarded themselves as the conscience of the settlers and the protectors of the "natives." A great deal of the bitterness had to do with the way the missionaries went about their task, for some, as the Rev. John M'Carter complained, were quite unwilling to listen to settler grievances and automatically presumed that their mission flock was in the right. But whatever the faults of the missionaries, from a black as well as a white perspective, it is true to say that the church's struggle against racism and injustice in South Africa only really begins in earnest with their witness in the nineteenth century.

Although Anglican chaplains served the spiritual needs of the British civil servants and soldiers, and occasional services were permitted for Congregationalists and Presbyterians alike, Methodists were less fortunate. The first Methodist minister left Cape Town for Ceylon after waiting eighteen months for permission to preach. His successor, Barnabas Shaw, who arrived in 1816, preached without permission, like John Wesley, but within ten years he left the white Methodists at Cape Town in order to pioneer missionary work in the North. Methodism really began to flourish when the 1820 settlers arrived, among whom was William Shaw, no relative of Barnabas but also a Wesleyan minister. His prime responsibility was to minister to the settlers, but he soon became restless: "There is not a single missionary between my residence and the northern extremity of the Red Sea," he wrote in a report to the Mission House in London.[22] By 1823 he had pioneered the first step in that direction by establishing a chain of mission stations from the eastern frontier towards Natal, and ensured that the Methodist Church would eventually have the most black African members of any mainline denomination. At the same time, the Methodist Church grew to be the largest English-speaking church in the country. Continual streams of Englishmen swelled the settler community. Cornish miners and Yorkshire entrepreneurs, Wesleyans to the core, were attracted by work opportunities resulting from the discovery of diamonds and gold in the Transvaal as the nineteenth century drew to a close. But though white and black Methodists belonged to the same church, they worshipped in different buildings and belonged to separate circuits. The settler/mission-church pattern was adopted by them as well.

It is perhaps strange to note that the most articulate exponents of the need for separating settler and mission churches were not always the settlers but often the missionaries, van der Kemp and John Philip leading the way. They regarded this as necessary for the sake of the indigenous peoples. One of the founders of the London Missionary Society, Thomas Love, became secretary of the Glasgow Missionary Society in 1800. From knowledge gained while with the LMS, he soon encouraged the Scots to send missionaries to the Cape. By 1824 the famous Lovedale Mission, forerunner of the University of Fort Hare, was established, and had begun what was to be a long and very distinguished ministry to black South Africans, especially the Xhosa people. Eventually, as a result of Scottish missionary work, the Bantu Presbyterian Church was born. It is interesting to read the rationale for the foundation of this church:

> The Bantu Presbyterian Church claims to be a true Church of Christ, with no barriers of colour or race, though from the circumstances of its place and service its membership will be preponderatingly of people of the Bantu races. . . . The Bantu Presbyterian Church however is in no sense a secessionist Church. It is the natural development of the hundred years of South African missionary work of the two Scottish Churches. . . . It is the declared missionary policy of that Church to work through its missions towards the formation of self-governing and self-supporting Churches. So the "mission" from overseas fosters a Native "Church", and as the latter increases in strength, the work of the "mission" reaches completion, and a time comes when the Native Church is able to take upon itself its full responsibilities.[23]

This only happened in the 1920s, but it was the goal of many Protestant missionaries of all traditions from the outset.

This question, "Should the native churches of this country develop on independent lines, or should they be brought into organic connection with the European churches of the same denominations?"[24] was widely debated by the various European missionary societies at the turn of the nineteenth century as missionary work came to fruition in South Africa. Successive missionary conferences stressed, as the DRC had earlier, the need to keep them apart for their own sake. "Christianity," pleaded the French missionary Edouard Jacottet in 1907, "is here far more foreign and exotic than it ever was among the Saxons and the Slavs. If ever it should exert on the bulk of the Native races the same attraction it did once in Europe, so as to draw them into its bosom, it must needs become thoroughly African and present itself to the Africans in such a form that they will be able to understand it and to accept it as something of their own."[25] To insist otherwise, it was argued, was to keep Christianity alien in Africa. Thus, the Scottish missionaries helped to create the Bantu Presbyterian Church; the Swiss, the Tsonga Presbyterian Church; the French, the Evangelical Church of Lesotho; the American Board missionaries, the Bantu Congregational Church among the Zulu; and the LMS, a mission church in Botswana. Each was dependent on foreign mission boards and missionary leadership, but they were independent of the settler churches.

But at the same time, there was development in the opposite direction. The Coloured congregations of the LMS joined with the white Congregationalists in the Evangelical Voluntary Union in 1864, which became the Congregational Union in 1883 and included a fair number of Africans.[26] The white Presbyterians gradually developed their own mission work and so became multiracial in principle, though, like the Congregationalists, seldom in practice, except in the higher courts of the church. The Baptists took a similar approach, with a multiracial union, but separate congregations and work. To begin with, this was not an issue for the Roman Catholics, who, though permitted to worship and have their own chaplains, were at first discouraged by both the DRC and the Anglican authorities from undertaking missionary work. When they did, it grew with amazing rapidity; there was no separate autonomous church for black Catholics. This did not mean that there was no discrimination, nor that the problem of race was resolved. In fact, the problem was far from resolved, but in principle the issue of separate churches for different ethnic groups of Catholics did not arise in the same way. Both the Roman Catholic and Anglican doctrines of the church prevented this. Separation would have meant schism.

What, then, of the Anglicans, the communion to which the governor himself belonged? We must return to 1829. There was no bishop, and the nine colonial chaplains, according to Anglican historian Peter Hinchliff, "were not, on the whole, an inspiring body of men."[27] The bishop of Calcutta performed the necessary episcopal functions as he journeyed between India and Britain! Robert Gray transformed the situation, and his coming in 1848 really marks the beginning of growth for the Anglican Church in the country. Gradually the church, with its vast diocese of about

20,000 square miles, took shape, ministering to black and white alike. By 1853 there were bishops in Grahamstown and Natal, and in 1857 Gray convened the first synod of the church, confiding in a letter to England that now he had "transplanted the system and organization of the Church of England to this land. . . . "[28]

There was, as might be expected, a certain amount of tension between the church in England and this fledgling Church of the Province of South Africa. A major issue concerned the appointment and therefore the dismissal of bishops. The tension reached its climax when Gray charged his erstwhile friend, Bishop Colenso of Natal, with heresy. The heresy trials against liberals in the DRC were being repeated by Anglicans. In the process Gray fought for the independence of the church in South Africa to decide its own affairs, and eventually won. This led, after many legal battles, to the formation of two separate autonomous churches—the Church of the Province (Gray's church), and the Church of England in South Africa. The latter was much smaller than the Church of the Province, but claimed continuity with the church in England. When Gray died in 1872, he left behind him a well-organized church, rapidly growing among all the races of the land, and recognized by Canterbury as the Anglican Church in South Africa.[29]

The deposed Bishop of Natal also left an important legacy. Not only had he introduced critical biblical scholarship to the country, and thus been found wanting by the Anglo-Catholic and conservative Gray, but he had also forced the issue, in spite of himself, which made the Anglican Church become an autonomous province within the Anglican communion. He also, as Peter Hinchliff reminds us, "advocated revolutionary and unpopular missionary policies" and "asserted very firmly that the Christian gospel possessed definite social implications."[30] With regard to his missionary policies, Colenso was convinced that the way forward was not to reject African religious traditions and customs out of hand, as other missionaries tended to do, but to leaven African culture and its social system with the gospel. What was required was the transformation of African society, not the detribalization of individuals by turning them into black Europeans. On this, as on biblical criticism, Colenso and Gray disagreed. Zonnebloem College in Cape Town, founded by Gray for the education of the sons of African chiefs, was designed to take them out of their traditional culture and turn them into good Anglicans fitted for English society.[31]

The struggle to make the Anglican Church and other churches of British origin relevant to South Africa was not easy, nor were its leading architects agreed on how it should be done. But they agreed that it must be attempted if the church was to survive and grow. One thing is tragically clear, however. Few if any black Christians were consulted on the subject. Paternalism was rife. Eventually, the English-speaking churches adopted a different way of relating settler church and mission church from that followed by the DRC. But during the nineteenth century, the pattern was similar if not always the same. The English-speaking churches were in fact divided along ethnic lines, even if this did not usually mean separate synods or denominations.

Afrikaner Church / English Church

THE DISTINCTION between settler and mission churches is only one of the cleavages that has shaped the church in South Africa. Equally significant is the division between the DRC and the so-called English-speaking churches, that is, churches of British origin. This division is integrally related to the first, for the two groups of churches eventually took different positions on the racial composition of the church. But it is also an issue of great importance in itself. Thus, we return to the history of the DRC, especially in relation to the struggles of the Afrikaner against British imperialism.

By the late 1820s, many Afrikaners along the eastern Cape frontier had grown disenchanted with the British administration. This was largely because of the promulgation of Ordinance Fifty in 1828, at the instigation of Dr. John Philip, which established the principle of equality in the sight of the law for all free persons irrespective of color or race. Disenchantment turned to disgust when, five years later in 1833, slavery was abolished. Thus, from about 1834, numbers of Boers decided to trek beyond British rule. Anna Steenkamp gave as one of her reasons for joining the Great Trek "the shameful and unjust proceedings with reference to the freedom of the slaves." "Yet," she continued, "it is not their freedom that drove us to such lengths, as their being placed on an equal footing with Christians, contrary to the laws of God and the natural distinction of race and religion, so that it was intolerable for any decent Christian to bow beneath such a yoke; wherefore we withdrew in order to preserve our doctrines in purity."[32]

Language was also an issue, for English was now the official language of the colony. But there was another reason for the trek: the economic. It is just as false to gloss over the economic factor in interpreting South African social history as it is to make this the key to everything else.[33] Analytically, it may be possible to separate the ethnic, cultural, religious, and economic aspects from each other, and claim the priority of one over the others. But this is not possible when the complexities of historical development are taken seriously and not simply interpreted in the light of later theories. From the earliest days at the Cape, the "natives" were regarded as inferior, their culture was despised, and they were mistreated. Moments of enlightenment on the part of the authorities and settlers proves the rule. And in all this, economic factors played an important part. After all, the Cape was colonized in order to facilitate trade with the East. Settlement necessitated the acquisition of land and labor. A critical development in this respect was the decision very early in the life of the colony to employ slaves. Thus, when we come to analyze the reasons for the trek, as well as the rationale for much else in the growth of racial discrimination in South Africa, the question of land and labor looms large. Was Anna Steenkamp only worried about the freedom of the slaves because this placed them on an equal footing with white Christians; was she, and was the embryonic Trekker community, not equally concerned about the economic ramifications of such liberation? Methodist church historian Leslie Hewson, in sketching the historical background to the racial problem in South Africa at a church conference in 1949, commented:

> Land and Labour! No one understands the complexities of the racial situation in South Africa until he has given due consideration to the significance of land and land hunger, until he has sought to understand the necessity for labour, and attempted to assess the exorbitant cost of what is called "cheap" labour.[34]

The Trekkers went north from the Cape, in search of a new land where they could build a republic of their own. They were devout men and women; avid readers of the family Bible, and able marksmen as well. But they went without the blessing of their church. In 1837 the Synod of the DRC denounced the trek, and refused permission for any of its ministers to leave the colony with the Trekkers. It is worth noting, then, that the Great Trek went ahead led by devout laymen, and sometimes ministered to by preachers of other traditions, but without the DRC clergy.[35] The theological interpreters of the events that were to shape Afrikaner tradition indelibly were not trained by Dutch or Scottish faculties of Calvinist theology, but by their own experience and their reading of the sacred book. As they journeyed, the pages came alive with meaning and relevance. The exodus of the people of Israel and their testing in the wilderness were happening again.[36] Any obstacle along the way to the promised land had to be overcome, by sheer grit and by the gun. Any doubt of divine providence was not only unthinkable, but blasphemy, a harbinger of disaster. The church at the Cape was no longer relevant, but the saga of Israel in the holy book was.

Once across the borders of the Cape, the Trekkers passed beyond the jurisdiction of both the British and the DRC. This was what the DRC had feared. But there was dissension among the Trekkers. In spite of what had happened, some wished to remain faithful to the Cape church, but schism became inevitable. In 1853 the Nederduitsch Hervormde Kerk (NHK) was born. This *Voortrekker* Church became the *volkskerk* of the South African Republic, founded by the Trekkers in the Transvaal. Six years later, also in the republic, a further split took place, to which we referred earlier, and the Gereformeerde Kerk was born. This division was not directly the result of the trek, but a consequence of theological controversy and schism in Holland. Centered in Potchefstroom, the Gereformeerde Kerk adopted the neo-Calvinism of Kuyper. The Cape DRC, or, to use its proper title, the "Nederduitse Gereformeerde Kerk" (NGK), eventually established its own synod in the Transvaal. The story is a complex one, but the result was three separate white Afrikaner Reformed churches: the NGK or DRC, with its autonomous synods; the NHK, which sought to be the true *volkskerk* of the Transvaal Republic; and the Gereformeerdes, with their ultra-Calvinist theology. When we refer to the Dutch Reformed Church, we mean the NGK; the other two churches will be referred to by name when appropriate.

It is worth noting that the NHK regarded the DRC as tainted by Scottish Calvinism, and saw itself as theologically more flexible in the tradition of Dutch Calvinism. However, on the question of race and mission work it was the DRC, both in the Cape and Transvaal, that took the more liberal position. DRC ministers in the Transvaal expressed concern for blacks and sometimes denounced Boer race attitudes, considering them a threat to the republic.

One reason why the DRC had been unhappy about the Great Trek was the fact that this church, after all, was the established church, and had a special relationship with the British authorities. The Anglicans were only too ready to take over in this capacity. However, by the 1860s both churches were increasingly unhappy about too close a relationship with the state. Their reasons were similar. Both churches were involved in heresy trials, the Anglicans against Bishop Colenso and the DRC against three of its theologians who were indicted on the charge of being theological liberals. In both cases, when the accused appealed to the state against the verdict of their respective churches, the state upheld their appeal. This was an intolerable situation for the leaders of the two churches, and disestablishment was the only plausible option open to them.

Thus, contrary to their traditional position on church-state connections, they both supported a Congregationalist Member of Parliament, Saul Solomon, who had been trying for some time to get Parliament to withdraw state aid from the churches.

Eventually, in 1875, following the example of the colony of Natal, the Cape Parliament conceded under pressure from the DRC and the Anglicans, and Solomon's "Voluntary Bill" was passed. Since then, there has been no established church in South Africa. Of course, this did not affect the position of the NHK, which remained the state church of the South African Republic until 1910. But all the churches in the Cape became "free churches," free to pursue their affairs in their own way. At the same time, because of the widespread strength and unique position of the DRC, it continued to fulfill many of the social roles of an established church. And, because of the peculiar relationship of the Anglican Church to the government, and despite the "Voluntary Bill," there was continued tension between the DRC and the Anglican Church concerning their respective positions in the country. A great deal depended on who was in political power.

It is, therefore, somewhat surprising to discover that in 1870 a short-lived attempt was made by the Anglicans, under the leadership of Bishop Gray, to unite with the Cape Dutch Reformed Church. Indeed, this was the first attempt at church union in the country. The DRC leaders were interested, if rather sceptical. Negotiations began, but they were soon shipwrecked on the issue of episcopacy. Of course, there was more to it than such theological issues. Michael Nuttall puts it tersely: "The Dutch found no place for themselves in the English Church any more than the English found themselves a place in the Dutch."[37] For one thing, there were very few white South-African-born priests in the Church of the Province, and even fewer who could communicate in Dutch; in this respect, the Anglicans had not taken root in the larger white Cape society. On the other hand, however, by the end of the century it was not uncommon for black priests to be members of synod, though the Anglicans

were behind the Methodists, Presbyterians, and Congregationalists in this respect. As the years passed, it became increasingly significant that these English-speaking
churches were becoming more multiracial in character,
which meant that they had less in common on this crucial
issue with the DRC and the other Afrikaner churches. This
multiracialism did not mean a great deal at the time, either
in terms of black leadership or in the life of local congregations. Discrimination abounded. Nevertheless, the principle
of multiracialism was established, and this was potentially
of great significance.

One reason for the parting of the ways between the
English-speaking churches and the DRC at the end of the
nineteenth century was the fact that tension between the
Afrikaners and the British had spread from the Cape to the
republics in the Orange Free State and the Transvaal. This
fact was related to the discovery of gold and diamonds, and
the attempt by the British authorities to annex Afrikaner
republican territory. War broke out in the late 1880s. More
significantly, a Second War of Independence, or the Anglo-
Boer War, erupted in 1899, producing a legacy of bitterness
and tragedy from which South Africa has yet to break free.
Relations between the Afrikaans churches (DRC, NHK, and
Gereformeerdes) and the English-speaking, particularly the
Anglican, were virtually non-existent, as each church generally sided with its own group. The DRC congregations
nearer the western Cape were in a particularly difficult
situation, as many of their members were of British descent.

The racial issue, as far as whites were concerned, was
tangential to this conflict between the Afrikaner republics
and Britain. While the Afrikaners wanted to retain their
independence, and while the British posed as benefactors of
the "natives," control of the newly found mineral wealth was
a much more powerful motive than either acknowledged. In
this regard, the Africans were not seen as contestants. The
general feeling was that they should be kept out of the fray
altogether. It is clear, nonetheless, that most blacks identified with the imperialist cause. They hoped that a British
victory would mean the extension of the franchisement to

include them, and the establishment of equitable land and labor rights.[38] Nevertheless, blacks became virtual spectators as the emerging Afrikaner nation took on the British imperial giant, or, perhaps more significantly for the blacks, as Christian killed Christian. Christianity could not win. Dutch Reformed ministers, like their English-speaking counterparts, found it difficult to remain neutral, and both British and Boer soldiers found appropriate moral support from within their respective ecclesiastical institutions. Perhaps this was more true of the Afrikaans churches, for their nation had its back to the wall. From their perspective they had justice on their side, a view widely held in Europe at the time. This was their country. The Boer soldiers were not alien conscripts but the fathers and sons of families who worshipped and prayed week by week in homestead and congregation throughout the land that was now a battlefield.

As we have mentioned, this civil war created much bitterness. Indeed, some Afrikaners regarded England as a horn of the apocalyptic beast. Given the "methods of barbarism," as British Liberal leader in the House of Commons, Campbell-Bannerman, himself described British military methods, this is not surprising. Twenty-seven thousand Afrikaner women and children, and many black servants, died in concentration camps, as superior British armory gradually crushed the highly mobile but ill-equipped Boer commandos. As is well known, the courageous Boers had the support not only of their own people, but also of many in Europe. An illuminating example of this is found in a sermon preached by F. C. Fleischer, a Mennonite minister in Holland. The sermon was preached in Glasgow at the end of a Conference of Christian Churches on Peace, in September, 1901, and later published and sold on behalf of the International Boer Women and Children's Distress Fund of Alcmaria.[39]

Fleischer's sermon was entitled "September 15th, A Day of Tears, Not Only in South Africa." September 15 was the day in 1901 which General Kitchener had set for the surrender of all Boer soldiers. Failing their surrender, Kitchener had decreed that they would be banished and the cost of maintaining their families charged against their property. While this had the opposite effect on the Boer soldiers than was intended, it certainly moved the Mennonite preacher of peace to understandably righteous anger:

> I think it is well, that the day begins at midnight. For the red of daybreak might seem to be the red of blushing. The beauty of sunshine is too good to welcome such a day of abomination.

> Who can imagine how the morning sun, symbol of Truth and Happiness, was greeted today in the Refugee-Camps of South-Africa? O Sunshine, they have longed for you in the calm of a sleepless night, and yet they feared for you, the 100,000 old men, women and children, crowded into cold, shivering, damp and dark tents where the helpless young can not be properly cared for and cried in vain for food.

> It would be a hideous irony if they should call this Sunday there a holiday of rest.

> Is it a mere chance or is it a cruel purpose, that for this tyrant's date the dear Lord's Day has been chosen?

> Our hearts bleed for them in their distress.

> Blood is thicker than water. Kinship in itself is something. But more than our kinship speaks our sorrow, our anger because holy justice has been violated, because might is above right, because of the Violence done to children who are not yet boys, to feeling women, mothers, wives, brides, daughters, to old men worn out with age....

Fleischer continued by lambasting the British government and war effort, and decrying war in general and this war in particular:

> ... We address the proud Government on the banks of the silvern Thames and our eyes are filled with sorrow and reproach and we say: Even entering this war for the maintenance of your Empire, even if it be undeniable that you have not been impelled by the arrogance of pride, the passion of revenge nor the lust of gold ... for God's sake! What right have you to carry on this war as you do?

> And we sum up our grievances, many and grave grievances. Have you not armed your soldiers with dum-dum bullets, an inhuman crime, condemned by civilization and martial laws? Did not your generals in the beginning of the war like Antiochus Epiphanes selecting the Lord's Day to attack the Boers

and deliberately fall upon their camps when engaged in worship? Have you not like Tiglath Pilezer Nebuchadnezzar carried off your prisoners of war into foreign regions? . . .

The sermon continues, page after page, in similar vein. The warfare is hideous. It is doubly so because it is Protestant Britain at war with Protestant Boers. In fact, Fleischer concludes, it is all beyond understanding; "at present we wander in darkness and grief."

We have quoted at length from this sermon not only to highlight the evils of the Anglo-Boer War, or the lengths to which British imperialism went to achieve its political and economic ambitions, but also because of the radical change that has taken place in international thinking about the Afrikaner in South Africa. Preachers in Holland and elsewhere today are saying things similar to the words of this older preacher, but now in support of blacks and in condemnation of the Afrikaner Nationalist government. British imperialism has a great deal to answer for; it helped spawn a nationalism whose racial policies have become as hideous to the world at large as the war Britain waged against the Afrikaner.

As far as black Africans were concerned, however, the British victory in 1902 held out promise of better things. Indeed, the executive of the South African Native Congress in 1903 not only expressed loyalty to the British government, but also indebtedness for bringing the gospel to the native peoples. The executive declared:

> The question of loyalty raises the larger question of the indebtedness of the Native races to the Government and people of Great Britain. How much is implied in the thought that out of the self-sacrificing faith of the Christian nations, foremost among whom are the people of the British Isles, the Gospel of Salvation has been brought to the people that sit in darkness and the shadow of death, cannot be adequately expressed. . . . "[40]

But black confidence in the British government gradually dwindled away during the years following the war, as the government began to create a Union of South Africa out of the British provinces and the Afrikaner republics. Time and again, black leaders, especially church leaders and Christian spokesmen such as the Rev. John L. Dube and J. Tengo Jabavu, represented black grievances and hopes before the British authorities and local commissions.[41] Every effort was made to persuade Westminster to make sure that black political and land rights were firmly established in any new constitution for a united country. But all of this was to little avail. The black voice was left crying in the wilderness, as Westminster tried to meet the conditions of the republican leaders. Moreover, it was not only the republicans who demanded segregation and white control. In fact, the roots of segregation as a political policy to ensure white supremacy and survival were part of British policy as developed by Sir Theophilus Shepstone in Natal.[42] The British settlers in that colony were strongly opposed to any kind of power-sharing and integration. The missionaries there, including Bishop Colenso, found themselves as much at odds with the colonial administration on "native policy," as did missionaries in the other regions of southern Africa.

By 1909, after years of negotiation, Afrikaner and Englishman agreed to differ within a united country. But union under one constitution, approved by both the British Parliament in Westminster and representatives of the republics and the Cape and Natal colonies, tragically meant that the franchisement of the Coloureds and blacks in the Cape remained limited and was not extended beyond that colony. This was part of the bargain demanded by the republican leaders in return for approving the union. The constitution was racially discriminatory, in order to ensure the participation of the Transvaal and the Orange Free State. The verdict of the *Oxford History of South Africa* is sharp and sobering: "In withdrawing from South Africa, Great Britain left behind a caste-like society, dominated by its white minority. The price of unity and conciliation was the institutionalization of white supremacy."[43] In 1910, the first Parliament of the Union of South Africa was convened in Cape Town, with Pretoria as the executive capital.

Interestingly, the modern ecumenical movement was also born in 1910, in Edinburgh, with the first great international missionary conference held under the inspiration of John Mott. William Carey, the father of modern Protestant missions, had suggested such a conference as long before as 1810 and, strangely enough, had recommended Cape Town as its venue. His plan came to nothing. But the events of 1910 in Edinburgh and Cape Town have both been of great significance for South Africa. As J. du Plessis, a noted Dutch Reformed historian, wrote: "Contemporary mission history and contemporary Cape history find a point of meeting in the year of grace 1910."[44]

A number of South African church leaders were inspired by the Edinburgh Conference, and as a result the South African General Missionary Conference formed in 1904 took a new lease on life. It brought together missionaries and ministers of both the English- and Afrikaans-speaking churches in a series of important conferences until 1932. Two years later, John Mott himself visited the country. With him he brought the vision which was later to take form as the World Council of Churches. But before that dream was realized in Amsterdam in 1948, it became real in South Africa in 1936, when the Christian Council of South Africa was constituted in Bloemfontein. Members of the DRC Cape and Transvaal Synods played leading roles in this development. But this fledgling attempt on the part of English and Afrikaans Christians to discover each other in fellowship and service was to be short-lived. It fell victim to the nationalist aspirations of the Afrikaner and the insensitivities of the English.

The years after 1910 were years of intense struggle for the Afrikaner people, a struggle for identity in a land which they had lost through war but which they regarded as their own, a land dominated by a foreign government, economy, and culture. In 1914 the National party was launched in Bloemfontein, with the conviction that the way to regain what had been lost by conquest was through the development of a separate nation (*volk*) within the Union, stressing its own distinct language, traditions, religion, and institutions. While the motto of the Union was "Unity is Strength," the Nationalists echoed the slogan of nineteenth-century

Dutch Nationalism, "Isolation is Strength." The story of this struggle is a relatively complex one, and does not need to be repeated here, but it is nonetheless an important factor in the history of the churches in the land. It is also important because it gave birth to what has more recently been described as Afrikaner civil religion, a phenomenon to which we will return below.

Afrikaners were by no means united in the struggle for identity and power. The other major political party, the South African Party (SAP), which later became the United Party (UP), was led by ex-Boer generals Louis Botha and Jan Smuts, and included many Afrikaans-speaking people. Smuts believed that the future depended on white unity between the Afrikaner and English-speaking South Africans; but others such as General Barry Hertzog, and later Dr. D. F. Malan, were convinced that the way into a secure future was through an Afrikaner Nationalism that carefully strove to maintain its own distinct identity, separate from the English community as well as the "non-Europeans." This division among Afrikaners had its impact upon the Afrikaans churches, especially the DRC in the Cape. Many ministers and members of this church favored co-operation with the English-speaking community and their churches. But on the whole, the Afrikaans churches could not remain aloof from the Nationalist aspirations of their people, for they were very much churches of the people. This was especially so in the area of social welfare. Many Afrikaners, especially in the cities, were very poor, and the church was their main source of solidarity and comfort. Some Dutch Reformed ministers left the pulpit and entered politics, while many others supported the struggle through social and cultural organizations. Political-ministers were as much in evidence then as political-priests have become since the National party came to power in 1948.

But quite apart from any direct involvement in political activity, the DRC held the key to the birth of Afrikanerdom. In every town and village, the DRC and its sister Afrikaner churches provided continuity with the traditions of the Afrikaner. They provided educated and articulate leadership, and offered a moral and spiritual basis for personal and social life. They were the spiritual home for the potentially great but slowly emerging Afrikaner Nationalism that was to dominate so much of contemporary South African history.

The struggle against British imperialism was more than a military one. The war with weapons had been fought and lost—for the moment. The spiritual and cultural struggle had to continue, or begin again and be sustained on other flanks: education and language, welfare and economics. Cultural and particularly language (Afrikaans) rights had to be achieved; children had to be educated in ways consonant with their Afrikaner heritage; the Afrikaner had to gain access to the growing economy of the country and find ways of adapting to the alien environment of burgeoning cities and towns. And, above all, the Afrikaner needed to develop a sense of history, a vision for the future, and a strategy which could inspire action, create an identity and solidarity, and so lay the foundations for eventual victory.

A defeated people need an interpretation of their history, a mythos, which can enable them to discover significance in what has happened to them. The continuity of the Afrikaner demanded such a world-view which would provide coherence to their shattered hopes. Such a mythos was not difficult to construct, especially for a people with such a strong belief in providence and an existential awareness of the plight of ancient Israel as it sought liberation from the Egyptian yoke. So it is not surprising that Afrikaner history, like that of other nations, took on a sacred character. This was especially true of history since the Great Trek. While such "holy history," with its vivid use of Old Testament motifs, was not official Dutch Reformed theology, it was certainly fundamental to Afrikaner self-understanding.[45]

Dr. D. F. Malan, a former minister and the Nationalist leader who became Prime Minister in 1948, described this history as follows:

> Our history is the greatest masterpiece of the centuries. We hold this nationhood as our due for it was given to us by the Architect of the universe. [His] aim was the formation of a new

nation among the nations of the world.... The last hundred
years have witnessed a miracle behind which must lie a divine
plan. Indeed, the history of the Afrikaner reveals a will and a
determination which makes one feel that Afrikanerdom is not
the work of men but the creation of God.[46]

In their struggle against British imperialism, especially in
the aftermath of the Anglo-Boer War, or the Second War of
Independence, the Afrikaners drew immense strength from
this interpretation of history. They detected a sacred thread
running through all the events of their past, beginning with
the Great Trek into the unknown (the exodus) and including
the encounter with and victory over the black nations
(Philistines), especially at the Battle of Blood River, where
they entered into a sacred covenant with God, the entry into
the promised land of the Transvaal and Orange Free State,
and the encounter with the pursuing British. Though they
believed defeat on the battlefield in 1902 was the judgment
of God calling his people back to their covenant as his
people, they knew it was not the cancellation of the call to be
his people and bring light to the dark continent. Their
struggle was not over. They still had that eschatological
vision which anticipated once again the rebirth of a republic
in which the Afrikaner would be the free and undisputed
ruler under the providence of the Almighty.

The Afrikaner churches fulfilled a central role not just in
this struggle for identity, but also in providing a theological
base upon which nationalism could flourish.[47] G. D. Scholtz,
a prominent Afrikaner author, wrote: "Without hesitation
it can be said that it is principally due to the Church that the
Afrikaner nation has not gone under.... With the dilution
of this philosophy [i.e., the unity of nation, church and par-
ty] it [the Afrikaner nation] must inevitably disap-
pear.... that is the great difference between the Afrikaner
nation and other nations."[48] Here we see the powerful impact of Dutch nationalistic thought adapted to the Afrikaner
situation. Mediated through philosophers such as Herman
Dooyeweerd in Holland, and interpreted by men such as
H. G. Stoker at the University for Christian Higher Educa-

tion at Potchefstroom, it provided the framework for and the necessary legitimation of both Afrikaner Nationalism and its racial policies:

> God willed the diversity of Peoples. Thus far He has preserved the identity of our People. Such preservation was not for naught, for God allows nothing to happen for naught. He might have allowed our People to be bastardized with the native tribes as happened with other Europeans. He did not allow it.... He has a future task for us, a calling laid away. On this I base my fullest conviction that our People will again win back their freedom as a People. This lesson of our history must always be kept before our eyes.[49]

As Dunbar Moodie says, "For Stoker, the People (*volk*) was a separate social sphere with its own structure and purpose, grounded in the ordinances of God's creation. Here Stoker's Calvinism was able to accommodate the Afrikaner civil religion, indeed to undergird it, for the Afrikaner People, too, was sovereign in its own circle, acknowledging no other master than God, whose purpose was to be seen in its structures and calling, its historical destiny."[50] What this is, in fact, is a civil religion based on a doctrine of creation, history, culture, and calling, designed to uphold the Afrikaner people in their struggle for identity, survival, and power, against all odds.

But it is also a theology which includes the corollary that every other ethnic group should also retain its identity as part of the will of God. A main drafter of the National party constitution and policy was J. D. du Toit, the son of a founding father of the Gereformeerde Kerk. Like his father, du Toit was deeply committed to Kuyper's theology and Christian National principles. Indeed, it has been cogently argued that it was the Gereformeerde Kerk rather than the DRC, Potchefstroom rather than Pretoria or Stellenbosch, that really provided the theological basis for Afrikaner Nationalism.[51] But such nationalist convictions also had a significant following within the DRC itself. It was a Dutch Reformed missionary conference in 1950 which was to recommend "territorial apartheid," and so prepare the ground not only for one of the most controversial and heartbreaking pieces of apartheid legislation, the Group Areas Act, which has caused such tremendous bitterness within the black community, but for separate development itself. It is indicative of the vast difference in perspective between Afrikaner Nationalists and those opposed to separate development that a man such as J. C. G. Kotzé, who was opposed to racial discrimination, could regard the resolution of this conference in such a positive light. Total segregation was not wrong or bad; it was right and good. Separate development was the will of God. Commenting on the recommendation, Kotzé said: "It must be remembered that no people in the world who is worth its salt, will always be content with no, or even an indirect, voice in the political and social economic organizations of the country whose decisions are taken with regard to its interests or future. To expect such a thing from the Bantu, is not only unfair to the Bantu, but it will eventually lead to the greatest disillusionment and strife."[52] It was to certain Afrikaner theologians that the National party ideologists turned for scriptural and theological justification for their racial policies and too readily obtained them, to the dismay of other Christians, including other Dutch Reformed theologians and ministers. Thus, the seeds of separate development were sown in the fertile soil of Afrikaner religious belief and fed with the conviction that a Christian National policy and way of life was fundamental to the survival and proper growth of Afrikanerdom, and therefore necessary for South Africa as a whole.

However, if some Afrikaner theologians provided the framework and justification for what eventually became apartheid, it was not they who filled the framework with its full ideological content. Those responsible for this were a group of well-educated, highly articulate Afrikaners who were gradually replacing the old Boer generals in the Afrikaner hierarchy and struggle for power. Bound together in a secret society known as the *Broederbond,* they believed that the Afrikaner nation was specifically put in this land by God to fulfill a particular calling as a nation, and that the maintenance of Afrikaner identity was essential to this task, and therefore part of the will of God. Profoundly influenced by German idealism and what Moodie calls neo-Fichteanism, this new generation of thinkers and political visionaries was able to stir the hopes and direct the steps of their people—first, in overthrowing the British yoke, and second, in developing an ideology which enabled them to meet the growing threat of the black races. These men, especially Dr. D. F. Malan, Dr. H. Verwoerd, Dr. N. Diederichs, Dr. P. J. Meyer, and Dr. Geoff Cronjé, were the pioneers of the National party as we know it today.

It is largely in connection with this ideological development that W. A. de Klerk writes: "Afrikaner politics was slowly but fatally being theologized. There was a growing urge to set the South African world aright, once and for all, to reconstruct it and redeem it in terms of a newly-defined Afrikaner 'lewens-en-wereldbeskouing'—a world view." The National party, he comments, "was itself becoming, if not a church, then a party imbued with religion—a secular religion—at its very roots."[53]

What can we now say about English-speaking South Africa? Unlike Afrikaner Nationalism, the English in South Africa had few leaders with a sense of national calling and destiny. But there were some who regarded South Africa as crucial to the designs of British imperialism. Notable among these was Cecil John Rhodes. It was the ambition of Rhodes to paint Africa red from Cape to Cairo—a somewhat ironical vision now that red no longer refers to British territory on maps of the world. Rhodes' imperial dream of political and economic power, no less than Afrikaner Nationalism, claimed religious sanction. "Only one race," he declared, "approached God's ideal type, his own Anglo-Saxon race; God's purpose then was to make the Anglo-Saxon race predominant."[54] The will-to-power was justified in the name of God, on behalf of the Queen and the empire.

Military flags and memorials in Anglican cathedrals throughout the country testify to this English civil religion that pervaded South Africa at the turn of the century. An inseparable relationship existed between God and the empire. Anglicans apparently found nothing incongruous about the Union Jack coexisting with cross and altar, even

when blood-stained from encounters with Boers and "natives." Somehow, British success in battle was ordained and
blessed by God.[55]

In his rather idealized account of English-speaking
South Africans, John Bond describes them as a community
with "restless energy, the freshness of ideas" and the inven-
tiveness needed to break into South Africa's history and
transform it.[56] They had something of that vision, commitment, and drive characteristic of Victorian England, which
inspired missionaries, public servants, and settlers all over
the world, and which made the empire what it was. But the
South African English were rather different in ethos from
their Puritan fellow-countrymen who had settled in New
England, and from their newly found Afrikaner country-
men, the "Puritans in Africa." The British settlers in South
Africa were the products of a Europe in transition. It was a
very different Europe from the one which the Puritans of
North America and those of South Africa had left two centuries before. No European could remain untouched by the
social, political, and industrial revolutions of the eighteenth
and nineteenth centuries. Moreover, the social vision that
inspired the British settlers was not theocratic Calvinism,
but the imperial dream—a sense of belonging to a mighty
empire whose will was supreme and whose ways were always just.

A concomitant of this civil religion was the tendency for
the Christian faith to become highly individualistic. And
when the full impact of the Enlightenment and revolutionary Europe finally destroyed the Christian convictions
of many, at about the same time as the imperial dream
began to fade away, all that really remained to characterize
the English as a group was secular individualism. This has
often degenerated into apathy, cynicism, and indifference
towards social and political issues, and it is precisely this
laissez-faire approach to life which the Afrikaner Calvinist
and Nationalist regard as symptomatic of their age-long
arch-enemy, "liberalism."

For the English South African, liberalism has a wide
range of meanings. Sometimes it is seen as a necessary by-

product of Christian faith, and therefore not simply to be equated with secular humanism. For the Afrikaner, liberalism has generally been regarded as the essence of unbelief.[57] It is important to keep this distinction in mind, for it is a significant example of the cultural and thus communication gap that has existed between the two major white communities in South Africa. This gap has affected the life of the English-speaking churches, giving them an image in the eyes of the Afrikaner that they have not always relished. It has dogged attempts to break out of imported theological traditions and provide a fresh theology for a new situation. A genuinely liberal tradition has a vital contribution to make to the future of South Africa, but there is also a kind of indifferent, cynical liberalism that is certainly of no value for the tasks facing either the church or the nation.

Shortly after 1910, two-thirds of the white population was English-speaking; from then on, this proportion gradually decreased.[58] English-speaking South Africa was at its zenith. It dominated the civil service, controlled finance and industry, had a firm grip on education, commanded the major cities, and was part of a larger empire that ruled the world. Yet, it should be remembered that the English could never govern South Africa alone. Their political power depended on unity with those Afrikaners who, like Jan Smuts, sought to bridge the gap between the white sections of the population. Thus, while the English could dominate much of Parliament, they were always in need of Afrikaner support. Every Prime Minister since the establishment of the union has been an Afrikaner.

Similarly, after the Anglo-Boer War and the founding of the union, the DRC still dominated the church scene in South Africa. But at the same time, the English-speaking churches benefited from the advantages which were accruing to the English-speaking community as a whole. This was particularly true for the Anglican Church, whose synods were now attended by high-ranking state officials. On more than one occasion the church was able to address the fledgling nation in the presence of the Governor General.[59] The shades of English establishment were not too far away. Indeed, throughout the period 1910-1948, the majority of the upper crust of English South Africans who held positions of power and responsibility in the country belonged to the Church of the Province. It is important, then, to inquire about the role of the Anglican Church with regard to the unfolding socio-political situation. This is particularly important in view of the criticism by both Marxist and Nationalist commentators that the English-speaking churches only became critical of racism in South Africa after 1948.

Although synodical resolutions cannot be regarded as synonymous with church action or practice, it is nevertheless striking that virtually all the resolutions of the Synod of the Church of the Province on social issues during the post-union pre-apartheid period were related to the race problem.[60] The church was outspoken on the question of justice for the African population, especially in terms of land distribution; African education; the need for effective and proper consultation with Africans on matters affecting them; and the need for better housing and living conditions. The synod in 1915 reacted to the Native Land Act of 1913 by asking that it be "immediately repealed until such a time as more generous and comprehensive legislation is forthcoming."

At the same time, the Church of the Province was ambivalent on some issues, and was not critical of all racially discriminatory legislation. By and large, the church was conservative. On occasion it intimated that it did not wish to disturb social custom, whether in the life of the church itself or the state. Yet, the Synod of 1924 stated that "the relations prevailing between Christians of different races belonging to our own Church are not what they should be" and so desired "an adjustment of the relations between groups of Christians living in the same places, without aiming at any interference with social customs." This adjustment was meant to express in an unmistakable way "the Brotherhood of all in Christ, the equality of all before God, and the unity of the Body" and to "witness to our desire for the inclusion of all races in the one Church of Christ." Similarly, in 1930, the Anglican bishops stated plainly: "We believe that rights to full citizenship in any country are not dependent on race or colour, but on men's fitness to discharge the responsibilities which such citizenship involves."[61]

It is difficult to determine the impact of these resolutions upon society at the time. That some of them were never followed up by the church itself is obvious from the fact that committees appointed for this purpose sometimes never reported back. The gap between synodical resolve and congregational involvement was as real then as it is today. But the fact that the church did try to influence the state in its pleas on behalf of African rights is also obvious. At first the state was not regarded as the enemy, but as the years passed and discrimination became more intransigent, the state appeared more and more as an opponent in the struggle for justice. The church persistently called upon the state to consult with Africans "for the well-being of the Native People and the security of the country." But like the church's other pleas, this one remained unheeded and unheard by those to whom it was addressed. On reflection, it is tragic that neither the church nor the state was finally able to work successfully for the kinds of changes that Christian insight proclaimed then as essential for the future. Yet, nothing can alter the fact that the church attempted to speak the prophetic word, and on occasion to implement it.

It is helpful in understanding the life of the Church of the Province, to remember that many of its bishops, priests, and missionaries were influenced by Anglican Christian socialism in England. The theology of F. D. Maurice, and later of William Temple, had considerable impact. As Peter Hinchliff puts it:

> The heroic crusades of Anglo-Catholic priests in the English slums had a profound effect upon the Anglican Church in this country. The ideal of the priest became that of the Christian socialist, struggling to bring the Faith to the poor and underprivileged, fighting their battles in matters of housing, of political and civic rights, striving for social justice, for fair wages, and no sweated labour. And just as the Union of South Africa came into existence the Province received its first Archbishop who possessed an Anglo-Catholic and Christian socialist background. . . . the proclamation of Union and the emergence of the Catholic-socialist ideal coincided.[62]

This social witness of the Anglican Church during the period 1910-1948 was more or less the same as that of the English-speaking churches as a whole. The basic difference was the special place which the Church of the Province had as a result of its connection with the British establishment. From a contemporary perspective, much of what it said and did was undoubtedly paternalistic. The concept of white guardianship was prevalent. There were no black Anglican bishops, and the leadership of the churches was firmly in the hands of missionaries and other whites. Yet, throughout the period, the number of black delegates to the synods of the churches increased. It was during this era that men such as Z. K. Matthews and Albert Lutuli came to prominence as dedicated Christians and articulate leaders of their people within the churches as well as the nation. Indeed, the churches and the country were blessed with increasing numbers of black leaders of Christian commitment, stature, and ability.

In spite of the tension between Afrikaner and English-speaking South Africa during the decades following Union and World War I, relations between the DRC and the English-speaking churches were cordial, and attempts were made to foster cooperation between them. These were the years of ecumenical stirring which led in 1936 to the formation of the Christian Council of South Africa. The Cape and Transvaal Synods of the DRC were foundation members, and very active as such.[63] But such co-operation was gradually undermined by the twin factors of nationalism and race, which eventually led to the departure of the DRC from participation in the Christian Council.

In 1941, in the midst of the Second World War, the Transvaal Synod of the DRC withdrew from the Christian Council. This was one of many signs that the Afrikaner wanted to go it alone. Dr. William Nicol, who was both a moderator of the DRC and the president of the Christian Council, gave three reasons for this withdrawal, all of them significant for understanding interchurch relations between the Afrikaner and the English South African. First, the council was not really bilingual, but English in its orientation; second, there were fundamental differences of opinion between the churches on the "native question"; third, the other synods of the DRC (Natal and Orange Free State) were not prepared to join the council.[64] None of these issues was ostensibly theological, though each had, and has, considerable theological implication. But they were of great consequence to the DRC Synods of the Transvaal and Cape, and caused their withdrawal. It is painfully true that the council was not very relevant to the needs of the DRC and its Afrikaans constituency. Few of those attending council meetings were able to speak or understand Afrikaans. There was also a sense of English superiority. Many of those involved were foreign missionaries, not South Africans. It is also painfully true that the members of the council could not agree on the "native question." Throughout the 1930s the DRC was more and more influenced by the concept of apartheid, for which it was partly responsible, while the other members of the council tended to be more liberal on racial issues. The DRC was primarily concerned about the plight of the Afrikaner. And, as the third point indicates, the DRC was by no means united. The Synods of Natal and the Free State were more conservative than those of the Transvaal and Cape, and wanted nothing to do with the ecumenical movement, which they believed would liberalize the church and even lead to flirtation with Rome.

It is interesting to note that when the Transvaal Synod announced its withdrawal, the Anglican Church of the Province chose to do the same because it saw no purpose for remaining in a body from which the DRC was absent. However, it was persuaded to rejoin a short while later. This nevertheless indicates how much the English-speaking churches have felt the need for co-operation with their Afrikaner counterparts. It also suggests that there was very little by way of an "English-speaking church front." Most Anglican bishops from the time of Gray were more concerned about relationships with the DRC than with the English-speaking Nonconformists. The ecclesiastical and social divisions imported from Britain were far too real to permit much ecumenical co-operation between them. Indeed, the English-speaking Nonconformists and Scottish

Presbyterians sometimes felt more affinity with the DRC than with the Anglicans. They had little in common with the latter, except language and perhaps racial attitudes. And yet, in the long term, it was their consensus on the racial issue which was of the greater significance.

Shortly after the end of the Second World War, the 1945 Anglican Synod addressed the nation on "social righteousness." It declared: "It is the duty of all Christian people to apply, consistently and unsparingly, the highest tests of Christian conduct to the social and industrial organisation of any State which claims to be, in any sense, a Christian country." Society, not just individuals, had to be transformed in terms of Christian ethics. This, too, was the conviction of the DRC and the Gereformeerde Kerk. But what the Anglicans and the other English-speaking churches envisaged was not the same, as was already evident by then and as would become more obvious within the next decade.

Black Church / White Church

THERE WERE three ecclesiastical alternatives for black Christians in South Africa by the turn of the twentieth century. They could be members of mission churches, whose membership was wholly black, but which were under the control of white missionaries and their mission boards in Europe, North America, or, in the case of the DRC, South Africa, and which would only much later achieve their autonomy. A second possibility was that they could be members of multiracial denominations, those churches largely of British origin where the line between settler and mission church had not been clearly drawn. But here, likewise, the black members were dominated by white leadership, European customs, discrimination, and a great deal of paternalism. In some respects, this was worse than belonging to the wholly black mission churches. There was a third option. They could leave the mission and the multiracial churches and initiate their own.

In the *Christian Express,* a Church of Scotland missionary journal published at Lovedale, the editorial of June, 1906 discussed the problem of the rise of what it termed independent "Native Churches" in the country:

> During the past dozen years, the South African Mission Field has unhappily witnessed a number of secessions of Native Church members. Some of these have been from Churches with both European and Native members. Others have been from Churches where the membership was entirely Native; so that these secessions have not been entirely due to racial feeling. Various reasons have been given by the seceders for the course they have followed. Most frequently the alleged cause has been difficulty of working together, a feeling of being curbed, or overshadowed, or otherwise restricted in the exercise of their activities, or a lack of mutual trust and confidence. In some cases these reasons have no doubt been sincerely believed and acted upon. In others they have been a mere pretext, cloaking less worthy motives. The number and extent of these secessions call for earnest consideration, if for no other reason than the danger they constitute to the Native Church.[65]

The editor spelled out the dangers. The schisms, he claimed, were "the occasion of much bitterness" in the native areas; they "lowered the vitality of the Native Church" and "led to great laxity of Church discipline." Moreover, the editor warned, the Christian creed itself would be affected. "Already," he declared, "there have been two Native Messiahs!" But he also recognized that the fault was not entirely on the side of the native schismatics:

> It may be that the Missionary Churches have been slow to recognise that the Native Church is quickly leaving its childhood behind, and is able to take upon itself an increased measure of self-control. It is conscious of new powers and is impatient of dictation. Because the parent has been slow to observe the development which was bound to come, and has not been quick enough to recognise the need of directing these new energies to work on useful and absorbing enterprises, the Native Church has in these separatist movements wrested from the parent's hand what it regards as its rights, and has asserted its ability to manage its own affairs.[66]

However, not all these so-called independent churches were the same, and their motives were, as the editor indicates, varied.

Something of the thinking of the founders of the independent church movement can be gathered from the following extract taken from the "Testimony of the Rev. Samuel Jacobus Brander, the Rev. Joshua Mphothleng, and Stephen Nquato of the Ethiopian Catholic Church in Zion, before the South African Native Affairs Commission" in October, 1904.[67] The answers were given by Samuel Brander:

Q. Who do you represent?
A. I represent the Ethiopian Catholic Church in Zion.

Q. What is that?
A. It is an organisation which we have commenced lately since we resigned from the A.M.E. Church.

Q. Are you the head of it?
A. Yes.

Q. What were you belonging to before?
A. To the A.M.E. Church.

Q. And before that?
A. We belonged to the Church of England before we joined the A.M.E. Church.

Q. Why did you leave that Church and start your own?
A. When we found that we could not get ahead, Makone and myself came together to raise the Church of Ethiopia, and later on we joined the A.M.E. Church of America, because we found at that time that it would go better if we joined the American Church, as they had education and other things better than we had. We considered that it would be better for us to join them, so that they could help us, being coloured people themselves.

. . . .

Q. What was your object in leaving the A.M.E. Church and starting a Church of your own?
A. We left on account of the promises they gave us when we joined them not being kept. . . .

Q. During the six years you were a minister of the American Church, did you receive any grants from America at all?
A. Not one.

Q. Was there any political teaching in the Church during the six years you were a member of it?
A. Not to my knowledge.

Q. Have you in the Church that you have just lately started no white supervision whatever?
A. No.

Q. What is your object in starting a Church independent of the white man and of white control; seeing that your first attempt at that was a failure, what is the reason that you made a second attempt?

A. We have not seen that we have become a failure as yet.

Q. Did you not say you made a mistake by joining the A.M.E. Church?

A. In joining the American Church we thought that, as they were our own colour, they would help us up, but we found they helped us down, and they took all the best positions without telling us a word, sending men from America. . . .

The inquiry turned to political questions. The black church leaders acknowledged that the "natives" were not yet ready for political control. For one thing, they lacked adequate education. But in time this would be overcome:

Q. And you would also like in time by constitutional methods, that is by lawful measures, to get yourselves into the control and management of public affairs in the Government as you have done in the Church?

A. Yes, I should think so.

Q. And where would you end; would you like the races to amalgamate?

A. Yes.

After further questioning, the Rev. Samuel Brander explained that he did not mean that the "natives" would ever have control over the whites:

Q. You recognise that the white man must always govern in this country?

A. I recognise it that way.

Q. What is it then you desire: religious freedom?

A. Yes, religious freedom.

Q. Do you in your church preach loyalty to the Government and obedience to the white man?

A. Yes.

The authorities clearly perceived something of a political threat in the rise of the independent churches.[68] And when the representations which some of the leaders made to the authorities on questions of voting rights, wages, land, and labor are carefully read, there remains little doubt that the independent churches were concerned about more than just religious freedom. They wanted the liberation of their people from all unjust bondages, including control by black Americans in the A.M.E. But, at least for the time being, they had to be content with religious freedom.

The first major study of this so-called independent church phenomenon was done by a Lutheran missionary in Zululand, Bengt Sundkler.[69] Sundkler distinguished between three types of independent churches. There were those which retained the outward forms, structure, and much of the theology of their parent body, and usually continued to use the name of that church as part of their new title. These churches Sundkler labelled "Ethiopian," a name which clearly stresses the fact that Christianity came to Africa long before any European missionary. The main reason for their breakaway was racial, the desire to control their own affairs, and sometimes the desire for prestige as well as power. Then there were those Sundkler described as "Zionist," church groups within which Christian faith and African tradition blended together in a dynamic synthesis, and sometimes syncretism. Considerable emphasis was given to ecstatic utterances, prophecy, dreams, healing, purification rites, and taboos. A third type, "Messianic," referred to those churches which apparently followed the leadership of "Native Messiahs," as the editorial in the *Christian Express* called them. Many years later Sundkler was to reject the use of this third category as pejorative, unwarranted, and misleading.[70]

There were various reasons for this separatist movement.[71] First of all, it was a rejection of white control both in the mission and the multiracial churches, especially with regard to questions concerning church discipline. Secondly, it was a rejection in many instances, and especially in the case of the "Zionists," of European culture and of the suppression of African culture in the life of the church. African culture was customarily rejected by missionaries, including men of the stature of Robert Moffat, as heathen or at least inferior. Thirdly, particularly in the multiracial churches, the cause was plainly racial discrimination and paternalism.

Fourthly, the desire for power and prestige partially explains the myriad of subsequent splinter groups within the independent church movement itself. By 1970, it included perhaps as many as 3,000 different groups with a combined total of more than three and a half million members.

Opinions have varied about the significance of this rapidly growing movement. Sundkler first regarded it negatively as a bridge across which black Africans would return from Christianity to heathenism. He discerned the danger of syncretism, the confusion of culture and Christ. This was the view of most missionaries and the mainline churches until the sixties. Later, opinions slowly changed. Sundkler's view became more and more positive. For one thing, it was recognized that every form of Christianity is in danger of syncretism, European Christianity as much as any other. One of the very reasons why the independent churches arose in the first place was because the white-dominated churches were so captive to European culture. The church cannot escape from the culture in which it is set. It has to relate to it if it is to exist and witness at all. But the exploration of this question will have to wait. All that is required here is to note that the African independent churches were increasingly recognized as legitimate expressions, by and large, of Christian faith in Africa, and as legitimate protests against many of the spiritually deadening influences in the more traditional churches.

The independent churches served another significant purpose. The rapid growth of black urbanization, stimulated by migratory labor and post-war industrialization, had radically altered the socio-cultural existence of the black community since early in the twentieth century. As a result, much of the former tribal cohesion was fragmented and many personal and social problems arose without traditional resources available to handle them. The independent churches have enabled many urban blacks to cope with this alien world of the townships.[72]

The groups vary a great deal, and some have been more successful than others in developing an indigenous Christian lifestyle. Generalizations are difficult. Whatever their faults, however, these churches stand as a legitimate protest against white racism and ecclesiastical imperialism, and in their own right as remarkable attempts to bring together Christian faith and the traditions of Africa. It was to take the mission and multiracial churches years fully to understand the theological and social significance of the movement, though the authorities were aware of its political potential very early. It is our contention that whatever the reasons given for the birth and growth of this African independent church movement, and whatever its problems and failures, it is properly understood as part of the story of the struggle of the Christian church in South Africa.

The independent churches symbolize the black revolt against European spiritual and cultural domination. However, while they soon became apolitical, their rise was coterminous with and paralleled by the awakening of black nationalism. And since Christians led the way, this development becomes part of our story. The African National Congress was born in 1912, in the same place, Bloemfontein, as the Afrikaner National party two years later. The history of African and black nationalism is as complex as that of Afrikaner Nationalism.[73] All the while the Afrikaner was struggling for power among white South Africans, black Africans saw their own rights being curtailed and denied. It was an even more burdensome task for the African to pick himself up after centuries of defeat and servitude than it was for the Afrikaner, for the African did not even have the vote. And, in one sense, this task could not truly be undertaken until after the Afrikaner had completed his own struggle for power. White politicians had continually turned black people into pawns in their own efforts to control Parliament.

It is very sobering for a contemporary white South African to read the story of the birth and struggles of the African National Congress. As during the period 1903–1909, the pleas and petitions of black leaders for the political rights of their people fell on deaf ears for most of the time from union until today. Document after document tells the story of one disappointment after another, whether in dealing with

Britain or with the South African government. And all the time, political rights dwindled, beginning with the Native Land Act of 1913, which, in the name of territorial separation, not only failed to distribute land on anything like an equitable basis, but also deprived the "natives" of basic rights regarding the acquisition of land and the freedom to sell their labor through bargaining in the open market, and thus severely limited "all opportunities for their economic improvement and independence."[74] It is interesting to note that during many of the early years of the black political struggle, the principle of separation was accepted by some black nationalist leaders, provided that, as the Rev. John Dube, president of the South African Native National Congress in 1914, put it, "it can be fairly and practically carried out." But, with reference to the Native Land Act of 1913, Dube made it clear: "We do not see how it is possible for this law to effect any greater separation between the races than obtains now. It is evident that the aim of this law is to compel service by taking away the means of independence and self-improvement. This compulsory service at reduced wages and high rents will not be separation, but an intermingling of the most injurious character of both races."[75]

Without going further into the details of the early post-union struggles of black leaders, it is important to comment on the role of the church. First of all, it is obvious that much of the leadership of the black nationalist movement was Christian, and that many of the leaders were ministers within the mission and English-speaking churches. Virtually all the leaders were trained and educated at missionary institutions, and their petitions and protests stress the fact that their motivation stemmed from Christian principles and convictions. African nationalism depended heavily on educated Christian leadership. Secondly, while the churches to which they belonged usually supported the principles for which they fought, such as those related to the land act already mentioned, the black leaders realized that the struggle was their own. They did not depend on the white-dominated churches, whether mission or "multiracial." At the same time, as Leo Kuper has correctly stated,

"The Christian missions brought Africans and whites together in new structures of relationship, and under dedication to a universal ethic, conditions which might be expected to counteract tendencies toward the expression of an exclusive nationalism."[76] Thirdly, there was no dualism between their religious convictions and their political aspirations. For them, Christianity could not be divorced from life as a whole; certainly, it could not be divorced from the plight of their fellow black people in the land. In this respect, these black Christian leaders were no different in their understanding of Christian political responsibility from the Afrikaner theologians and ministers who shared the burden of the day in the Afrikaner struggle against the British. Fourthly, and arising out of the last observation, the crux of the struggle had to do with land and political rights. It is important to see that racism was never regarded as a phenomenon on its own; it was almost always related to educational, economic, and political issues. It would be untrue to the facts to maintain that the Christian gospel, or the education provided by the missionary institutions, prevented blacks from a critical analysis of their situation. Their understanding was penetrating and sharp—it invariably went to the heart of the matter. This is shown in an address by Dr. A. B. Xuma delivered at a Conference of European and Bantu Christian student associations at Fort Hare in 1930.[77] Entitled "Bridging the Gap between White and Black in South Africa," Dr. Xuma's speech powerfully describes how racism works itself out in practice, or, more accurately, how racism is used to justify injustice in every walk of life. The only way to build bridges between white and black, Xuma maintained, was by getting rid of the "Union Native Policy" through the establishment of justice. Finally, it has been cogently argued that Christianity encouraged patience rather than angry revolt, dialogue rather than violent reaction, and that this delayed the black political advance over the years. Yet, the proponents of this hypothesis, even though partly correct, cannot deny the freedom with which blacks have espoused Christ and their willingness to be true to the gospel. Their hypothesis denies the leading and active role of black Christians in the political realm. Black Christians continued to lead the way in the black struggle for political and other rights well into the apartheid era. To mention only a few: Albert Lutuli was a Congregationalist; Robert Sobukwe, the founder of the Pan African Congress, was a devout Methodist; and Professor Z. K. Matthews, an Anglican and the first student to graduate from Fort Hare (1924), was at one time leader of the Cape branch of the African National Congress, and through his distinguished career as an academic, political leader, and ecumenical spokesman, influenced more than a generation of black leaders in Africa. He was also, towards the end of his life, Botswana's Ambassador to the United States of America. Whatever the failures of the missions, they did stress a genuinely liberal education, which in turn helped nurture articulate leaders dedicated to the service of their people. Apart from Fort Hare, there were many other fine institutions of all denominations; Healdtown (Methodist), Tigerkloof (Congregational), St. Peters (Anglican), and Mariannhill (Catholic) are but a few examples.

Over the years there has emerged what might be described as a black church in South Africa. This does not refer to a denomination, nor does it simply refer to the independent churches. Rather, it suggests a black Christian solidarity that straddles the theological confessions and the ecclesiastical divisions imported into the country with the arrival of the missionaries in the nineteenth century. Something of this has been expressed in IDAMASA, the black Interdenominational African Ministers' Association of South Africa, which began as a Transvaal organization in 1915, and in 1946 became a nation-wide movement. Many black Christians regarded, and still regard, denominationalism as another aspect of the political policy of "divide and rule." Indeed, as long ago as 1883, we find a black Christian spokesman decrying this divisiveness in the name of Christ, and for the sake of political rights:

> Anyone looking at things as they are, could even go so far as to say it was a great mistake to bring so many church denominations to the Black people. For the Black man makes the fatal

mistake of thinking that if he is an Anglican, he has nothing to do with anything suggested by a Wesleyan, and the Wesleyan also thinks so, and so does the Presbyterian. *Imbumba* must make sure that all these three are represented at the conference, for we must be united on political matters. In fighting for national rights, we must fight together. Although they look as if they belong to various churches, the White people are solidly united when it comes to matters of this nature. We Blacks think that these churches are hostile to one another, and in that way we lose our political rights.[78]

Certainly, denominationalism was, as Kuper says, "highly fragmenting and exclusive, analogous to tribalism," but the potentially unifying power of Christianity was also a basis for African nationalism.[79]

It is the contention of many blacks today, especially students in the urban townships and at the black universities, that Christianity has too often aided and abetted white power and domination in South Africa. As we have now seen, this fear was expressed almost a century ago. Yet, along with this, black Christians have also regarded the gospel of Christ, when rightly understood, as the liberating power of God for them as well as for the white and other communities in the country. At the center of the church struggle throughout South African history is the struggle of the black church to prove to its fellow blacks that Christianity is not the "opiate of the people" but the hope for the future and therefore the word of salvation for today. It is no easy task, for the white church has too often failed to be faithful to the gospel, and in the name of Christ given its support to policies and systems that oppress others.

This brief sketch has attempted to show the origin of the church struggle as we have come to experience it in South Africa today. The origins are complex; the struggle has many facets. But we have described some of the fundamental issues which bind the story together, not in a neat bundle, but hopefully in one which makes sense of the data. Our basic thesis at this point is that the church in South Africa has been, and remains, divided not only along theological and confessional lines, but also by race and culture. In this, the church in South Africa is not unique. But the problem is exacerbated in South Africa because of the social and political situation. The church cannot avoid relating to the cultural milieu in which it is set if it is to fulfill its task; neither can it simply stand aloof from the social and political aspirations of groups within society. But in some way divisions created by race and culture have to be transcended in the church so that its identity as the reconciled and reconciling community can be demonstrated. This does not deny the place of cultural diversity in the life of the church, but it rejects any captivity to culture whereby unjust social structures are reinforced and legitimated.

The next three chapters are not exhaustive treatments of church history in South Africa. They pick up some of the threads we regard as important in our discussion thus far as these emerge primarily after the advent of apartheid in 1948. The divisions we have noted provide the underlying theme; the questions we have raised about Christianity and politics, about culture and the ideological captivity of the church, become more and more urgent. The struggle against racism brings the church face to face with the human will to power, with all its demonic potential; it also confronts the church with the cry of the oppressed, the powerless, and the dehumanized. Our concluding chapter attempts to provide some gospel clues which may help us grasp the message of God's kingdom in relation to this situation and so be of service in the struggle ahead, as South Africa enters a new era of crisis, and hope.

2

Apartheid and the Churches

The Advent of Apartheid

IN 1942 the Christian Council of South Africa convened a conference at the University of Fort Hare. The purpose of the conference was to discuss the task of the churches in "Christian Reconstruction" after the war. That was an important year for those involved in the struggle against Hitler. The tide had turned, and now it seemed only a matter of time before the world would be at peace. South Africans were becoming optimistic, and that was the prevailing mood of those who gathered at Fort Hare to reflect together on the future role of the churches. Seven years later the Christian Council convened another conference, this time at Rosettenville near Johannesburg. The theme on this occasion was "The Christian Citizen in a Multi-Racial Society." By this time, however, the optimism of Fort Hare had gone. The mood was one of apprehension. Apartheid had arrived.[1]

We have seen enough already to know that racism in South Africa did not arrive when the National party came to power in 1948 with its clarion call to apartheid. But 1948 is symbolic of a dramatic change in the meaning of racism for South Africans. Although racial discrimination was entrenched in the Union Constitution and determined much of the legislation between 1910 and 1948, it did not have the rigid, ideological character that it began to assume under the apartheid slogan. A distinction can be made between the segregation policies before 1948 and the apartheid policy after that year. T. R. H. Davenport puts it succinctly: "They differed in degree and direction, rather than in kind, from the policies which had gone before."[2] We cannot go into all the details about the apartheid policy and the way it has evolved over the years into separate development. Some of this will emerge as we proceed; it is fully documented elsewhere.[3] There is no doubt, however, that the English-speaking churches and other denominations belonging to the Christian Council realized that a new political phenomenon had entered the scene, and that it contradicted the hopes which they had for the future of the churches and the country.

In September, 1948 the General Assembly of the Presbyterian Church of South Africa criticized proposed legislation aimed at depriving Africans of their limited Parliamentary representation as a retrograde step contrary to the claims of Christian responsibility. "Our earnest prayer," the General Assembly said, "is that white South Africa may be saved from the contempt in the eyes of the world which such action is bound to produce."[4] The Methodist Conference that same month stated that "no person of any race should be deprived of constitutional rights or privileges merely on the grounds of race, and morally binding contracts protecting such rights or privileges should be regarded on the high level of a pledged word. Political and social rights especially of the underprivileged groups should not be reduced but rather developed and expanded into greater usefulness."[5] Similar sentiments were expressed by the Congregational Assembly, which stated: "It is our sincere conviction that the Government's policy of 'apartheid' has no sanction in the New Testament Scriptures...."[6] The Assembly of the Baptist Union condemned "any tampering with the accepted constitutional understanding that the franchise rights of non-Europeans will continue to be entrenched as provided in the South Africa Act." Furthermore, it was "gravely concerned at the rising tide of bitterness and resentment, noncooperation and hatred, which is evident among those people concerned by any suggestion of the limitation of their existing rights and legitimate aspirations, and the Assembly resolutely dissociates itself from any policy which would restrict or reduce the present rights of representation in Parliament or Senate of any section of the community."[7] Finally, in November, 1948, the Episcopal Synod of the Church of the Province issued a lengthy statement on the race issue. The bishops identified themselves fully with the resolutions of the Lambeth Conference earlier that year which declared "that discrimination between men on the grounds of race alone is inconsistent with the principles of the Christian religion." The South African bishops then stated that human rights are not extraneous to Christianity but rooted in the Christian doctrine of man. They condemned the newly proposed apartheid legislation and stated:

> The only hope in our judgment for the future of the men, the women and the children of Southern Africa lies in the creation of harmonious relationships between our various racial groups. And harmony can only be achieved if the Europeans, who at present wield power, engender a spirit of confidence amongst the non-Europeans. But if, on the other hand, Europeans seek to preserve to themselves the exclusive benefits of Western Civilization, and to allow the non-Europeans merely its burdens, South Africans will inexorably draw apart into mutually antagonistic racial groups.[8]

The Rosettenville Conference in 1949, mentioned at the beginning of this chapter, was significant for a number of reasons. This was the first ecumenical conference since the National party came to power, and its affirmations characterize the position of the English-speaking churches of that period. With the exception of one fraternal delegate, the DRC did not participate in the conference. The participating churches have never retracted the position they took at Rosettenville:

> We affirm that the fundamental truths we shall neglect at our peril include:
>
> 1. God has created all men in His image. Consequently, beyond all differences remains the essential unity.

2. Individuals who have progressed from a primitive social structure to one more advanced should share in the responsibilities and rights of their new status.

3. The real need of South Africa is not 'Apartheid' but 'Eendrag' (i.e. unity through teamwork).

4. Citizenship involves participation in responsible government. The franchise should be accorded to all capable of exercising it.

5. Every child should have the opportunity of receiving the best education that the community can give, and for which the child has the capacity.

6. Every man has the right to work in that sphere in which he can make the best use of his abilities for the common good.[9]

In retrospect, these Rosettenville affirmations do not appear very radical; they smack a little of paternalism, but they were a direct attack on the unfolding policy of apartheid. One of the major papers at the conference was given by Chief Albert Lutuli, at that time a member of the Native Representative Council. Lutuli remarked:

The spirit of selfish exclusiveness shows itself [again] in a tendency to regard civilization as the sole possession and production of White people. Hence the plea that Africans must develop along their own lines. This claim ignores the fact that in its historical development western civilization has been indebted to many sources, ancient and modern. The tragedy of the attitude behind this claim is that white South Africa tends to forget its God-given mission to spread civilization and not to hoard it, and thus to ensure its survival and growth.[10]

Rosettenville proved to be the first of a series of ecumenical conferences assembled by the churches after 1948 to deal with the racial problem. The next major conference following Rosettenville was convened by the Federal Missionary Council of the DRC. It was held in Pretoria in November, 1953. Prior to this, the Federal Council had held five conferences on the racial situation in the country, attended by both black and white delegates from the various DRC synods. We have already referred to the important 1950 DRC Missionary Conference with its recommendation of "territorial apartheid." But the Pretoria Conference was particularly significant because the DRC invited church leaders from other denominations to attend, especially churches belonging to the Christian Council, of which the DRC was no longer a member. What is more, the addresses given were evenly distributed among speakers representing the various denominations present. These were hopeful signs.

After two days of frank but respectful interchange, during which agreement was reached on a number of matters pertaining to missionary work and to mutual understanding between the churches, the conference adopted a statement in which the following was expressed:

3. ... No effort was made to conceal or minimise differences.

4. In the words of one of the representatives, these differences divided the conference into three groups,—those who sincerely believed in a righteous racial separation in the Church based on the Scriptures; secondly, those who made no such confession but nevertheless practised some form of separation because circumstances demanded it although such separation did not correspond with the ideals of the Christian Church; thirdly, those who were convinced that separation in the Church was wrong and stood condemned according to Scripture.

5. A strong desire was felt by all present to reach solutions and some understanding; there was also a sense of urgency arising from a realisation of the seriousness of racial tensions in our country and of the unhappy effect on Non-Europeans when European Christians were at variance.[11]

A number of noteworthy points emerge from this Pretoria Conference. First of all, while nothing like the consensus at Rosettenville was achieved, it was significant that the DRC was willing to enter into such frank discussion of racial affairs at that moment in South African history with members of churches who were so strongly critical of the DRC for not condemning apartheid. Secondly, the list of 107 delegates does not appear to include any black representatives, a situation which would be unthinkable today and intolerable to the churches taking part. Thirdly, the differences dividing the delegates, so well expressed in point four of the statement, is an accurate description of the dividing lines which separate white Christians in South Africa to the present day. While the statement refers specifically to the church, it has implications for society as a whole. Some regard racial separation as scriptural, some as blatantly unscriptural, and others as pragmatically necessary but not the ideal.

It must not be supposed that all the delegates of the DRC stood firmly opposed to the position of the delegates from the other churches. The opening address given by Professor B. B. Keet of the Dutch Reformed seminary in Stellenbosch certainly suggests otherwise: "Personally, I believe that our brethren who want to maintain *apartheid* on biblical grounds are labouring under this misunderstanding. They confuse *apartheid,* which is an attitude of life, with a diversity which includes unity. Christian unity, I know, will include diversity but it must never be seen as separation; and *apartheid* is separation." For Keet, "our brethren" meant fellow members of the DRC. He went on to say:

> My Bible teaches me that God is no respecter of persons and that His compassion is for the miserable, the underprivileged, the neglected children of the human race. Surely, the Gospel, though far more than mere humanism, as founded on the compassion of Him who gave His life for all peoples and nations, cannot be inhuman. To love God above all, and your neighbour as yourself—on these *two* commandments hang all the Law and Prophets. Of a truth there is no way to God that bypasses my neighbour. . . .

After rejecting the slur of "liberalism" which so many attach to words such as these, he declared: "The relationship at present existing between white and coloured Christians can well be termed as a cynic has described it, 'Brothers in Christ, Limited'!"[12]

The Pretoria Conference Statement avoided any directly political utterance, except for the short eighth paragraph, where we find: "It was generally felt that Non-Europeans have a claim to right and justice in all matters, great and small, but that there should be no talk of rights if there were not also admittance of fundamental duties." This coupling of rights and duties appears in a number of DRC pronouncements over the years, but very seldom, if ever, do we find any elaboration on the subject. For example, what duties need to be performed or accepted before rights are conferred? What duties have whites fulfilled in order to receive the rights they have? Have blacks been given the opportunity to fulfill such duties as required for receiving rights? What duties have blacks failed to perform, seeing that rights have been taken away from them?

The reticence of the Pretoria gathering to pronounce on political issues and the meaning of rights and duties was not reflected in Parliament. By the mid-1950s, apartheid legislation was being introduced and implemented at full speed as act after act was introduced, and bill after bill adopted. At the same time, the government began to develop an increasing array of security laws by means of which it could suppress any radical opposition, black or white. The cornerstone of this legislation was the Suppression of Communism Act of 1950, amended in 1954, with its very wide definition of Communism.[13]

In spite of failures in their own fellowship, the English-speaking churches spoke out strongly against what was happening at virtually every step along the apartheid route during the first decade of National party rule. They were not alone. Quite apart from the critique of opposition politicians, academics, newspaper editors, professional and other community leaders, black and white, apartheid came in for rigorous attack by leading theologians in the DRC. Professor Ben Marais scrutinized racism with rigor and perception in his *Colour: the Unsolved Problem of the West,*[14] and Professor Keet demolished the false myths used by many in his own church to support apartheid in his brief but powerful statement *Suid-Afrika—Waarheen? (Whither, South Africa?).* Keet's profound grasp of Scripture and his incisive theological insight cut through all the racial shibboleths of the past and present. "The more one examines the case for complete, permanent apartheid," he wrote, "the less can one avoid the conclusion that its supporters are labouring under a delusion that belongs to a world of make-believe."[15]

The most provocative attack on apartheid came, however, from another quarter, and this evoked a response from the government that provided a foretaste of things to come. As of old, many missionaries continued their role of speaking out on behalf of the voiceless. No one fulfilled this role more ably than an Anglican missionary priest working in Sophiatown, outside Johannesburg. His name, Father Trevor Huddleston, was soon to reverberate around the British Commonwealth. In 1956 Huddleston published his book *Naught for Your Comfort*. In it he told the story of his parish, especially the agonies and heartbreaks caused by apartheid in the lives of his black parishioners. He concluded:

> In opposing the policies of the present Government, therefore, I am not prepared to concede that any momentary good which might conceivably emerge from them is good. Nor am I prepared to concede that the motives which inspire such policies have any quality of goodness about them. For both the acts and the motives are inspired by a desire which is itself fundamentally evil and basically un-Christian; the desire to dominate in order to preserve a position of racial superiority, and in that process of domination to destroy personal relationships, the foundation of love itself. That is anti-Christ.[16]

Huddleston was recalled to England shortly after by his order, the Community of the Resurrection. While the order supported him, they wanted him to serve elsewhere. But even though he left, his book remained behind to sear the consciences of the government and white South Africa. It was even too strongly worded for his own bishop, Geoffrey Clayton, in Johannesburg. Nonetheless, it was a sign that church-state relations were going to grow more tense, as Clayton himself soon discovered. During the years that followed, more and more foreign missionaries, especially Anglicans, were deported by the government. They were regarded not only as a source of irritation by the authorities, but also as perpetrators of unrest among the black population. The churches could do little about this except protest and accept the situation.

The first major crunch in church-state relations came in 1957 with the promulgation of Clause 29(c) of the Native Laws Amendment bill. This was a very different matter from the deportation of some missionaries. In effect, the bill made it very difficult for black people to attend worship in churches in so-called white areas. In other words, apartheid was beginning to affect the life and worship of the churches in a direct way. The bill caused an immediate outcry, even from those who felt that missionaries such as Huddleston had gone too far. Geoffrey Clayton, who was now Anglican Archbishop of Cape Town, saw the issues of the bill very clearly. In a strong letter to Dr. Verwoerd, the Minister responsible for the bill, Clayton accused the state of trespassing on the freedom of the church. He wrote: " . . . we feel bound to state that if the Bill were to become law in its present form we should ourselves be unable to obey it or counsel our clergy and people to do so."[17] Similar sentiments were expressed by other churches and by the Christian Council. The Baptist Union, generally more cautious on political matters, declared that "the proposed bill will compel law-abiding Baptists, together with members of many other Churches, to violate the law. This we do not desire to do, but where conscience and legislation conflict we must take our stand with our conscience, whatever the consequences may be."[18]

The DRC was also perturbed by the bill. The Federal Council of the Church produced an eight-point statement on the subject, of which only the first four points were initially made public. The DRC stressed the duty of the state to allow the church the freedom to fulfill its calling: "The right to determine how, when, and to whom the Gospel shall be proclaimed is exclusively in the competence of the Church."[19] The unpublished points specifically criticized the bill as going beyond the bounds of what the state, from a Christian perspective, was entitled to do. Rather than publish these specific criticisms, the DRC leaders preferred to discuss the whole matter with Dr. Verwoerd. After doing so, they felt reassured that the government would not in fact trespass on the freedom of the church, and thus the need to publish their critique fell away. But the fact remained that the state now had the power to act against multiracial worship *if* the Cabinet Minister felt that this was necessary.

As far as can be ascertained, multiracial services of worship have never been affected by this legislation. The state has acted on a few occasions against black services held in "white areas" where residents have complained about them creating a public disturbance. But multiracial services, particularly in the large cathedral churches of the cities, Catholic and Anglican, have been a regular feature of church life throughout the years. There is no sign that this pattern will change, for this is part of what the churches presently encourage where possible.[20]

Perhaps as a sign of protest against the bill, a black Dutch Reformed minister was invited to preach to a white Dutch Reformed congregation in Pinelands during the period of its debate. For although the DRC and the English-speaking churches differed in their interpretation of its significance, they all found the bill undesirable. "It would have been better," declared Dr. A. J. van der Merwe, moderator of the DRC in the Cape, "if it had not been introduced, because any practical advantage which it may have does not weigh up against its propaganda value against the minister. In arriving at our conclusions we have tried to be completely honest and sincere. We credit our brother Churches with the same sincerity in arriving at an opposite conclusion, and where we do not see eye to eye in this matter we must agree to differ in brotherly love."[21] Brotherly love between the churches was soon to be severely tested.

Cottesloe Consultation

IF THE "church clause" shocked the churches into action, the whole country was rudely awakened by Sharpeville. This name of a small town in the Transvaal rang around the world in March, 1960, signalling a dramatic turn in world-opinion against South Africa and ushering in a new era of racial discord and protest. At Sharpeville on March 21, sixty-nine blacks, mainly women, were shot and killed by the police, and 186 were wounded, according to official figures. It was a shocking and terrible event, precipitated by the discriminatory pass laws against which the blacks were protesting when fired upon. Opinions vary greatly as to what actually happened. The police claimed that the protesters were storming the police station, which was manned by a few policemen whose lives were thus endangered. The protesters maintained that the demonstration, sponsored by the recently formed Pan African Congress, was peaceful and, as the records show, the only violence done was by the police. Many of the dead were shot in the back.[22]

In the post-Sharpeville "state of emergency," thousands of blacks were arrested and many banned. The leadership of the African National Congress and the Pan African Congress, including Albert Lutuli, Nelson Mandela, and Robert Sobukwe, was arrested, and the organizations were declared illegal.[23] Many blacks fled the country to participate in anti-apartheid exile movements in Europe and North America. Others went underground. Whites, too, left the country out of fear for the future, and foreign investments in South Africa suffered severely. White morale reached an all-time low. Perhaps never before, and not again until the Soweto protests in 1976, were those struggling for justice and reconciliation in South Africa in such despair. What could the churches do amid all this bitterness and frustration, especially when, humanly speaking, all power resided in the hands of authorities who were unbending in their responses to the situation?

One powerful, emotive reaction came from Archbishop Joost de Blank, the successor to Geoffrey Clayton, who let off a furious broadside against the DRC for what he regarded as its connivance at apartheid. He went so far as to demand that the World Council of Churches expel the Cape and Transvaal Synods who, along with the Nederduitsch Hervormde Kerk, were then members. In a letter to the General Secretary of the WCC, Dr. W. A. Visser 't Hooft, de Blank stated: "The future of Christianity in this country demands our complete dissociation from the Dutch Reformed attitude.... Either they must be expelled or we shall be compelled to withdraw."[24]

The leaders of the WCC did not accede to de Blank's

harsh and hasty request. Indeed, members of the WCC executive committee were very unhappy about de Blank's ultimatum, and expressed considerable sympathy for the DRC. The Anglican Bishop of Ceylon, Ladkasa de Mel, reasoned "that the expulsion of the DRC would be in effect a kind of ecclesiastical apartheid adding one more scandal to an already scandalous situation."[25] Thus, instead of such action, and after much discussion with other member churches in South Africa, the WCC agreed to help arrange a "consultation on Christian race relations and social problems in South Africa." This in itself was a remarkable achievement. For not only did de Blank's hostile attitude towards the DRC create resentment within that church, but his aggressive and strident assault on the government and the manner in which he exercised his episcopal authority were alienating all around and were often counterproductive. Even those who agreed with him in principle found him to be an uncomfortable ally.

Before continuing the story of Cottesloe, we must comment a little on the episcopate of Joost de Blank. Without doubt, he was a major figure in the history of the confrontation between the church and apartheid. Formerly the Bishop of Stepney in London, de Blank burst on the South African scene like a latter-day van der Kemp and Thomas à Becket rolled into one. Like van der Kemp, he too was born in Holland, a fact which had some influence on those responsible for his election to the see of Cape Town. And like the missionary of the London Missionary Society, the Archbishop soon became one of the most controversial clerics in South Africa's history. He was applauded by blacks, but intensely disliked by most whites, especially those in authority. Though he started his adult life as a conservative evangelical, by the time of his enthronement as Archbishop in 1957, de Blank's views on episcopacy were more Roman than Protestant. Like a medieval lord bishop, he demanded the allegiance of his church to his person and his views as he confronted the government on apartheid. In the process, he polarized opinion in his own church, and created bitter feelings throughout the country—not always because of his ideas, but often because of the way he expressed them.

Opinions vary a great deal on de Blank's ministry. None can doubt that he had a razor-sharp, theologically incisive mind. His views commanded attention, even from his worst enemies. Further, there can be little doubt that he was an important catalyst in the Christian struggle against racism in South Africa. His trenchant criticism of apartheid went to the heart of the matter, and it was always based on Christian doctrine, especially the incarnation. His diaries reveal a man who could be highly self-critical, and along with his books and addresses, they also tell the story of a man who was totally committed to his Lord. It was this commitment which led him to attack racism with passion and zeal, sparing no person, high or low, least of all himself. But he failed during his episcopate to stem the tide of government policy and public attitudes. As his years in Cape Town drew to an end, he grew increasingly disappointed with the fruit of his ministry, and disillusioned with his own church, to say nothing of the DRC. De Blank returned to London in 1963, a disheartened and broken man. But before he left, he commented on his ministry in a final sermon: "Some people have hinted that I have tried to go too fast too quickly. But how far and how fast are you supposed to go when you are running away from sin and seeking to do God's will?"[26]

The official history of the ecumenical movement has only one passing reference to the Cottesloe Consultation, held in a Johannesburg suburb December 7 to 14, 1960.[27] But it was a gathering of great importance for the churches in South Africa. Presided over by Dr. Franklin Clark Fry of the United States, chairman of the central committee of the WCC, the consultation was attended by ten delegates from each of the eight South African member churches, and five representatives of the WCC, including its General Secretary, Dr. Visser 't Hooft. There were eighteen black participants, including Bishop Alphaeus Zulu and Professor Z. K. Matthews; there were eight laypeople, including author Alan Paton and the anthropologist Monica Wilson, the only woman delegate; and the ministers and theologians who made up the bulk included many distinguished church leaders of the country. The representatives of the Nederduitsch Hervormde Kerk, whose delegation, unlike the others, was all white, tended to keep apart. It was rumored that they were in frequent consultation with political leaders, including Prime Minister Verwoerd, during the consultation. The DRC Cape and Transvaal Synod delegations, unlike the NHK, were at the center of things, and whereas the NHK rejected the final statement out of hand, the DRC delegates were virtually unanimous in supporting it. One reason why the DRC supported the statement was that it was largely based on the preparatory documents they had produced for the consultation.

The concluding statement comprised three sections. Part One rejected all unjust discrimination. While it indicated that opinions varied on apartheid, it stated that the church had a duty "to proclaim that the final criterion of all social and political action is the principles of Scripture regarding the realisation of all men of a life worthy of their God-given vocation." In Part Two, far-reaching consensus was achieved:

> We recognise that all racial groups who permanently inhabit our country are a part of our total population, and we regard them as indigenous. Members of all these groups have an equal right to make their contribution towards the enrichment of the life of their country and to share in the ensuing responsibilities, rewards and privileges. No one who believes in Jesus Christ may be excluded from any church on the grounds of his colour or race. The spiritual unity among all men who are in Christ must find visible expression in acts of common worship and witness, and in fellowship and consultation on matters of common concern.[28]

The resolutions spoke of the need for consultation between race groups on all matters affecting them. Though some stressed the inadvisability of racially mixed marriages, the validity of such marriages was supported. Attention was drawn to the disastrous effects of migratory labor, the low wages paid to the blacks, and the inequitable system of job reservation. Delegates asked for the direct representation of Coloureds in the central Parliament. Part Three included concrete and specific resolutions on a variety of urgent matters: justice in trials, the position of the Asian community in South Africa, freedom of worship on a multiracial basis,

freedom to preach the gospel, and methods of future consultation and co-operation between the churches. The problems
of past attempts at dialogue between the DRC and the other
churches were discussed, and the consultation urged that
churches consult one another before indulging in public
criticism of each other.

It is not surprising, then, that in the closing stages of the
consultation, Archbishop de Blank expressed his regret that
he had sometimes spoken heatedly and through ignorance
wrongly criticized the DRC for not making a public stand on
racial issues. This was a clear retraction of his earlier demand for the DRC to be expelled from the WCC. In response,
Dr. A. J. van der Merwe said that the hand of friendship was
gladly accepted. He said that his church had been painfully
aware of the tension during the past few years which had
damaged not only the fellowship and co-operation between
the churches, but also the interests of God's kingdom.[29]

Cottesloe was held behind closed doors. But for outsiders
who were interested in its proceedings, it soon became evident that something momentous was happening. Finally,
the press was informed about the decisions. The delegates
knew, of course, that whatever they had decided still required the ratification of their respective churches, but
nonetheless they represented the top echelons of those
churches and had good reason to anticipate such agreement.
There was nothing in the resolutions that was new or unacceptable to the English-speaking churches. If anything, they
did not go far enough. The NHK had clearly rejected them.
Thus, the question was really: What would the DRC synods
do about the decisions? Although these were based on the
DRC preparatory documents, they questioned commonly
held assumptions, were highly critical of some aspects of
apartheid, and recommended that Coloureds should be en-
franchised—a highly contentious and embarrassing matter
for the government.

The response was dramatic. It came in the first instance,
not from the synods, but from Prime Minister Verwoerd
himself. He expressed his personal grave displeasure with
the actions of the DRC delegation. There was also strong

reaction from conservative groups within the church, notably Dr. Koot Vorster, brother of the future Prime Minister, and Dr. Andries Treurnicht, later to become a deputy-minister in the Nationalist government. In due course, the Cape and Transvaal Synods fell into line, thereby rejecting the role played by their own elected and distinguished representatives. In his autobiography, Visser 't Hooft comments: "I have always wondered whether the majority of the delegates [i.e., to the synods] realized that they were not voting against positions imported by the World Council and imposed on their Churches, but against the convictions expressed by the best minds of their Churches and submitted at Cottesloe by their own trusted leaders."[30] The DRC also decided to withdraw from membership in the WCC—there was no need for them to be expelled. De Blank had gotten what he originally wanted, but the integrity of the church and the struggle against racism had suffered a severe blow.

How, then, are we to assess the significance of Cottesloe? Afrikaner W. A. de Klerk puts it dramatically: "The ghost of Cottesloe would return to haunt the Afrikaner's wayward theologizing. There was evidence that, in spite of the silencing, recantation, bowing of heads and deep cogitation, something remained. The Church could never quite be the same again."[31] Visser 't Hooft's response to that question summed up the feelings of many outside the DRC who were disappointed by the official DRC rejection:

> The fact remains that this witness and the attitude which the World Council has taken with regard to race relations has encouraged many, particularly among the non-white Christians, who had begun to feel hopeless about the role of the Christian church. And it should be remembered in the churches of the World Council that not only in the present member churches in South Africa, but also in the churches which have left us, there are many men and women who are deeply conscious of belonging to the world community, gathered by the same Lord, whose task is to make the transcendent power of Christ tangible and visible in deeds of justice and fellowship through which the estrangement of the races can and must be overcome.[32]

Cottesloe itself represented a high point, the subsequent actions of the DRC synods the low point of relationships between the English-speaking churches and the DRC. To many, it now seemed as if the only way forward for co-operation between Christians of different churches was through personal participation in a new kind of ecumenical thrust not tied to denominational structures.

This was the conviction of at least one DRC participant at Cottesloe, Dr. Beyers Naudé, who at that time was the acting moderator of the DRC in the Transvaal. His vision eventually gave rise to the Christian Institute of Southern Africa, an ecumenical organization for promoting dialogue between Afrikaans- and English-speaking Christians and for witnessing to justice and reconciliation between the races in South Africa. It also led to his being deprived of his ministerial status by his church, and eventually to his banning by the state. But the story of Naudé must wait. For the moment we must consider his church, and seek to discover why and how the DRC, which has so clearly rejected racial discrimination in principle, still supports government policy. What is the connection between the DRC and apartheid?

The Dutch Reformed Church

THE DRC HAS a great deal of influence in South Africa. We have already seen how this came about, and how the DRC is integrally related with the Afrikaner nation, its culture, and its rise to power. Of course, not all its members are Afrikaners nor are all Afrikaners members of it, but the DRC with its million-and-a-half white members is quite clearly the dominant church in terms of its access to the policy makers of the nation. Included within its ranks are most of the members of Parliament and of the provincial councils. Its members virtually control many of the town councils throughout the land. The vast majority of people employed by the government in various capacities and in-stitutions, including the police and the military, belong to the DRC. It has also had considerable influence over the nearly one million members of its black "daughter churches." Given this impressive position within society, and the access it brings to the corridors of power at the national and local level, it can be argued that the DRC holds one of the keys to the future of South Africa.

Relations between the DRC and the English-speaking churches have been plagued over the years by misunderstanding and misrepresentation. Indeed, any discussion such as ours runs this risk. While the risk has to be taken, it is necessary to be as objective as possible, bearing in mind that many of the criticisms that can be levelled at the DRC can be levelled against the other churches as well. Fortunately, the DRC has always stated its own position clearly. Its official stand on issues is contained in resolutions adopted by its General Synod meeting every four years, and interim statements are made by its executive when necessary.[33]

The position of the DRC on race and related issues has been set forth fully in two major synodical documents. The first, *Human Relations in South Africa,* was adopted by the General Synod in 1966.[34] Its fifty-two pages of close print clearly set out the position of the DRC. The second, and now the most definitive statement, is the important document *Human Relations and the South African Scene in the Light of Scripture,* adopted by the General Synod in 1974.[35] This, in particular, is the basis for our discussion, a discussion which, in the nature of the case, will have to be simplified a great deal, without, we trust, distorting the truth. In basing our discussion on this report, however, we must not lose sight of the fact that it reflects the carefully considered opinion of the synod. It is not necessarily how the person in the pew sees things. Synodical declarations are often far removed from the "gut feelings" of the average church member.

The position of the DRC in all its major pronouncements invariably begins with a statement of principle, and it is made clear that principles must arise from Scripture. In true Reformed Church style, the Word of God is the norm by which we test our opinions and our actions. That the Bible "contains guiding principles for all spheres of life" is a constant refrain in the documents. Indeed, at least four years before Cottesloe, the DRC expressed the opinion that there is a "danger in acquiescing in race relations which possibly do not accord with the Word of God."[36] Similarly, J. C. G. Kotzé wrote: "The Scriptural principles must never be twisted to suit our practice."[37] He, like others, is quite explicit in saying that Scripture and not "traditional policy" is the court of appeal for the church and the Christian. So it is that human relations are considered by the DRC in the light of Scripture, and any critique must recognize this as the starting point.

The question then arises: How does the DRC interpret Scripture? Once again, the documents generally answer in considerable detail. The DRC is not fundamentalist in its approach to Scripture, though it is generally very conservative. Few within the Reformed tradition could take exception to the hermeneutical principles stated in *Human Relations and the South African Scene,* that is, principles which state not only how the Bible is to be interpreted but also how it is to be related to society. One of these principles states that "the Church has a prophetic function in respect of the state and society when the Scriptural norms that should apply in all spheres of life are not respected."[38]

Contrary to popular misconceptions, the DRC does not build its biblical case for its approach to race relations on such Old Testament episodes as "the curse of Ham," nor does it transpose the "people of God" motif from Israel onto the Afrikaner *volk.* But it does make a great deal of the creation narratives and the protohistory of Genesis 1–11. Two dominant themes emerge. The first is that "the Scriptures teach and uphold the essential unity of mankind and the primordial relatedness and fundamental equality of all peoples."[39] The second and subsidiary conviction is that "ethnic diversity is in its very origin in accordance with the will of God for this dispensation." Babel is the consequence not just of God's judgment on sin, but also of his preserving mercy (cf. Acts 17:27), effecting the fulfillment of his saving purposes. Thus, while the unity of mankind is always the basic reality given in creation, there is also a given differentiation in creation. Furthermore, because of human sin, the unity of mankind has been seriously affected, and can only be restored through God's redeeming grace in Christ. The ultimate restoration of this unity will only occur at the final coming of the kingdom of God. This does not mean that the message of the kingdom has no immediate social significance. On the contrary, "the church must exert itself to give concrete substance to the blessings of the gospel in the life and social structure of a people. On the other hand, the church should avoid the modern tendency to erase all distinctions among peoples. . . ."[40] Moreover, in serving human relationships, the church must regard justice as "a basic concept in the determination of such relationships," along with love, truth and peace.[41]

The theme of unity and diversity which is described initially in terms of Old Testament passages, is also developed on the basis of the New Testament:

> The New Testament upholds the equivalence of all people and nations. . . . [It] maintains the unity and solidarity of the human race. . . . [It] accepts and upholds the fact of the diversity of peoples. . . . [It] accepts the diversity of peoples as a fact, but does not elevate it to the only or highest principle.[42]

Although the diversity of peoples is relative to their underlying unity, the synod's understanding of the theme of unity and diversity leads it to declare: "In specific circumstances and under specific conditions the New Testament makes provision for the regulation on the basis of separate development of the co-existence of various peoples in one country."[43] Having said this, the synod makes it clear that the role of the church is to ensure that diversity does not lead to estrangement; that love for the neighbor "is the ethical norm for the regulation of relationships among peoples"; that such love must find expression in justice; and that the church must "exhort its members, the authorities and subjects to uphold the ethical principles which must be applied in the regulation of inter-people relationships." Within the church itself, human diversity exists but is sanctified, and thus "the most serious attention must at all times be given to the New Testament concepts of the brotherhood in Christ and of the koinonia."[44]

There is a great deal more that could be said, and certainly *Human Relations and the South African Scene* has much more to say than space permits us here. Christians of all traditions would agree with much of what it states. The report discusses the role of the church in society, the relationship between church and state, the questions of social justice, human rights, and social change, and it deals with many specifics such as migratory labor and racially mixed marriages.[45] However, enough has been said to provide a basis for fair assessment.

First of all, the DRC rejects racial injustice and discrimination in principle. Equally clearly, the DRC accepts the policy of separate development.[46] For the outsider, this appears to be a major contradiction because apartheid and separate development are usually regarded as synonymous. Failure to understand this distinction drawn by the DRC between the blatant racism of apartheid and the anticipated blessings of separate development has led to considerable confusion in assessing the position of the church. For one thing, it has led to false hopes, for whenever the DRC has spoken out against racism many people have presumed that this means an attack on government policy. That does not follow, although it could be an attack—as it sometimes is—on the way in which policy is implemented. The position of the DRC is well stated in the final paragraph of the 1974 report:

> The Dutch Reformed Church is only too well aware of the serious problems in respect of inter-people, inter-racial and inter-human relationships in South Africa. It seeks to achieve the same ideals of social justice, human rights and self-determination for peoples and individuals, based on God's Word, as do other Christian churches. It is also convinced that it is imperative for the church to fulfil its prophetic calling, to be sympathetic, to give guidance according to Scripture and to intercede on behalf of man. If the Dutch Reformed Church does differ from other churches, the difference is not due to a different view of moral concepts and values or of Christian ethics, but to a different view of the situation in South Africa and the

teachings of God's Word in this regard. There is no difference in
ideals and objectives, but merely disagreement on the best
methods of achieving these ideals.[47]

For the DRC, the policy of separate development is not contradicted by Scripture; indeed, the idea of diversity in the
Bible lends some credence to the policy. At the same time,
says the church, the policy must be "applied in a fair and
honourable way, without affecting or injuring the dignity of
the person."[48] So we find the Rev. W. A. Landman, a leading
minister of the DRC, referring in his *Plea for Understanding* to the fact that his church has often been condemned for
supporting something which "could not possibly be tolerated
by any Church or Christian worthy of the name."[49] We are
therefore faced with the question of whether separate development can be pursued according to the biblical norms of
justice and love, that is, whether or not the policy is consistent with Scripture or, at least, not contradicted by it.

Before we consider this question, let us proceed with a
second observation on the 1974 report. The black DRC
theologian Allan Boesak has heavily criticized the report as
representing a "downward spiral."[50] While we share many
of Dr. Boesak's criticisms, this one suggests far more movement than is warranted by the report. What we find in the
report is much more static—in the most important areas
there are no advances made on earlier positions adopted by
the DRC, such as that of 1966. When one reflects on developments within the country and Christian thinking generally, including that within the DRC, this is surprising. It
was certainly surprising for some Afrikaner Nationalist
newspaper editors who expressed their disappointment that
the General Synod had not been able to lead the way into
the future. Instead of lighting up the road ahead, it had provided a cautious statement of past and present positions.

When we probe behind the report, however, and consider
it in relation to the original draft presented to the synod,
something of crucial significance emerges. The original report was far bolder in its prophetic stance and was much
more consistent in its application of scriptural norms to
socio-political realities. But the synod would not have it that

way, with the result that the final report lost its teeth and cutting edge. Why? In some respects, we have here a repeat of the Cottesloe affair, where the clear and courageous thinking of some Dutch Reformed theologians and leaders was rejected for what appear to be politically pragmatic reasons. Three studies of the report, two by Dutch Reformed theologians, Professors J. Alex van Wyk and J. J. F. Durand, and the other by an English-speaking theologian, Dr. Brian Johanson, tackle this issue head on.[51] Dr. van Wyk suggests that concepts such as separate development were read into Scripture rather than out of it, and that the final result was, consciously or unconsciously, politically predetermined, supporting the status quo.

Dr. Durand discusses the biblical hermeneutics of the report. After affirming the hermeneutical principles that are stated at the beginning of the report, he asks whether the document itself remains true to its own declared method. Durand's contention is "that this does not happen, and that on one crucial point the document opts for the hermeneutical method that it expressly rejected. This happens as soon as the document deals with one of the concepts that is basic for its theological content as a whole, i.e. the idea of a diversity of peoples."[52] In fact, says Durand:

> the idea of ethnic diversity is completely stripped of its supposed salvation-historical framework and starts to function in itself as a God-given principle. The reason for this shift in argument is clear. The document is honest enough to realize that such a 'salvation-historical' application cannot be maintained on biblical grounds because that would mean that every phenomenon that runs counter to ethnic differentiation must be considered as a hindrance for the gospel and therefore as a sin against the purpose of God.[53]

The relative idea of differentiation between peoples, to which Scripture points and about which there can be little argument, has become "an *imperative* for division between peoples."[54] Thus, Dr. Johanson asks the question:

> What is the ultimate, the real, criterion which influences the decisions and recommendations of this document? What is the value, the principle, the concern which determines what action

should be taken, what attitude should be adopted? This issue is very important because this alone will explain why two groups of people, Christian people, working with the same Biblical data, with the same concerns for justice and peace, should come to almost opposite conclusions and solutions.[55]

For Johanson the answer is a sharp one. The hidden value which emerges is a "concern for the 'volk,'" for the well-being of the Afrikaner community. In other words, a principle that cannot be derived from Scripture is injected into the discussion. We are face to face with the dilemma of the DRC. It does not claim to be a *volkskerk* like the NHK, but it finds itself pushed in that direction time and again. The outsider cannot but wonder about the political pressures that are brought to bear on DRC decisions, whether at Cottesloe or the General Synod. The survival of Afrikaner identity and power seems to play such a determinative role. At all costs, the concept of separate development must not be surrendered—which means that its theological basis must be affirmed—for the future of the Afrikaner people is regarded as tied up with the success or failure of this policy.

For the moment, let us allow that separate development is defensible in principle. This is not out of keeping with at least some Christian thinking beyond the DRC. Dr. John Philip, the LMS missionary of the nineteenth century, advocated something like this for the true well-being of the natives; some African leaders such as the Rev. John L. Dube, a founding father of the African National Congress, early in the twentieth century made "no protest against the principle of separation so far as it can be fairly and practically carried out";[56] and no less a person than J. H. Oldham, a leading figure in the ecumenical movement and in the founding of the WCC, acknowledged the plausibility of such a policy in his classic study on *Christianity and the Race Problem*, published in 1924.[57] So let us examine the policy of separate development to see whether it fits in with what the DRC report says when it declares that "the Christian must at all times seek to ensure that his political thinking and actions are based on justice and righteousness."[58] In other words, let us see whether it can be morally justified in practice as the DRC maintains it is in principle.

One of the most articulate contemporary exponents of separate development, Dr. Connie Mulder, a member of the Gereformeerde Kerk and a leading Cabinet Minister in the Vorster government, expressed the opinion a few years ago that the policy is "in accordance with both the wording and the spirit of the United Nations Charter, when it speaks of the self-determination 'of peoples', in that it respects the identity and dignity of the diverse peoples of the Republic and seeks to lead them each and all to a state in which they may competently manage their own affairs."[59] Instead of a melting-pot approach in which ethnic differences are submerged in one all-embracing national identity, ethnic plurality is stressed, and this provides the basis for political structures and social development. All of this is done in order to eliminate racial friction and ultimately to do away with racial discrimination. Thus government policy seeks to establish separate independent "homeland" countries for each of the several African ethnic groups in the country, and to provide separate political structures through which Coloureds and Indians can express themselves independently of and yet alongside of the white community. All so-called petty-apartheid regulations that stress the inferiority of black people, and all discriminatory practices such as segregated post offices and park benches, will have to go. While it is contestable whether this distinction between petty-apartheid and grand apartheid can be maintained, either in principle or practice, in any event, the government, like the DRC, proclaims that it is against racism while at the same time it pursues its declared policy of separate development. The role of the DRC in all this has been to insist that the policy be implemented in a just manner. This has also been the role of the Gereformeerde Kerk, a church which is often very critical of the government, not because it regards the policy as unchristian and therefore wrong, but because the policy is not justly and properly pursued. The question, then, is whether the policy can be implemented "in a fair and honourable way without affecting or injuring the dignity of the person."[60]

Any political program or policy which promises a better future, as does separate development, but which requires considerable suffering in the present for the sake of that end, needs considerable moral justification. The question has to be faced: Who is doing the suffering, and for what end? Apart from the fact that political programs are notorious for failing to deliver what they promise, does the promised future justify present human pain and cost?[61]

First of all, what does separate development promise? In spite of all that is said about the policy of helping blacks to regain and strengthen their ethnic identities, the policy is clearly designed in the first instance to safeguard white interests—identity, privileges, land, and resources. It promises blacks their own traditional homelands, but deprives them of South African citizenship. Moreover, it offers homelands that are totally disproportionate to the population— 87% of the land will belong to whites, and with them to Coloureds and Indians to some degree, whereas 13% will belong to blacks. And yet blacks outnumber whites by five to one. Perhaps a theory of partition can be justified, but not on such an unjust basis. Land and resources are by no means equitably allocated or distributed; traditional but very inadequate boundaries are maintained. The Native Land Act of 1913, and subsequent legislation in 1936, remains the basis for the policy. Meanwhile, the rights of the vast urban black population are gradually denied on the basis that these blacks are not citizens of South Africa but foreigners in the land of their birth. Seeing that black rights are few to begin with, this is not much of a promise for the future, even if the government improves the lot of urban blacks. Indeed, a major weakness in the policy of the government has been its inability to deal with the urban black situation at all, which is part of the reason why it was in Soweto and other urban townships that protest erupted in 1976.

This failure of government policy must be emphasized, for it highlights the fact that the policy makers have yet to take seriously the industrial revolution that began in South Africa in the 1930s. Separate development is essentially a rural policy; it is totally inadequate for the demands of the rapid urbanization that has taken place during the past forty years, as millions of blacks have come to the cities in search of work. In fact, it has intensified some of the problems, notably migratory labor, which is recognized by the DRC and other churches as a cancer in South African society. But the policy is also wanting in at least one major respect in the rural areas. It has thus far been unable to deal with the political future of those blacks who live and work on white-owned farms. It is estimated that approximately one-quarter of the African and colored populations are in this group.[62]

Secondly, what does separate development cost? In terms of human suffering it has cost whites virtually nothing, except the support of the world community. It has, and continues to cost blacks a great deal. Whites stand to gain most, even though they will lose some territory presently under their control, but blacks, who are suffering the most for the sake of the policy, stand to gain far less than whites. The history of the implementation of separate development is full of human tragedy and pain. It has required legislation and action which no amount of Christian casuistry can condone. Perhaps, though we doubt it, the policy *could* have been implemented in a way that would injure neither the dignity of people nor, indeed, their physical well-being. But this has not been so. Nobody can really regard the Group Areas Act, and the racial classification procedures which lie behind it, as not violating the lives of people. We have only to think of the mass removals of people from places where they have lived for generations, and their subsequent placement in areas unprepared for human habitation. Nobody can regard what happened to the Coloureds of District Six in Cape Town as "fair," or what happened to Africans at Dimbaza or Limehill as "honorable." As Brian Johanson comments: "It [i.e., the DRC] declares that it [i.e., separate development] can be morally justified from the Scriptures. But the Scriptural justification has not been shown. The tremendous social evils that the document [i.e., the 1974 report] itself reveals, which result from the attempt to enforce separate development, would condemn any such attempt to justify the social system from the Scriptures."[63]

It can be argued that separate development has brought

some previously denied advantages to blacks in the homeland areas. For one thing, it has provided some kind of political base. But any talk of advantages is offset by the fact that
the system has not been freely chosen by blacks. After all,
such advantages as there are only confer what is normally
regarded in democratic countries as an inherent right of
people. There have been changes, but these highlight how
bad things have been in the past. Those black leaders who
have accepted the system are almost unanimous in holding
that they have had no other option. This does not mean that
they regard separate development as right or just. Separate
development has dictated what blacks should have.[64] It has
not been the result of sharing and consultation. This is true
of all sections—African, Coloured, and Indian. For many
black people, separate development is regarded as a sophisticated form of apartheid, certainly not as a means of overcoming racism. A significant indication of this attitude is
the amount of internal security legislation that is required
to prevent blacks from working for other alternatives. If
separate development really promises something for blacks,
why have they reacted so negatively against government policy in so many ways? In the light of all this, it is not surprising that the DRC advocacy of separate development on the
basis of Christian love and justice is treated with considerable disbelief and scepticism by outside critics.

On the other hand, there has been rigorous criticism by
members of the DRC itself. There were many Dutch Reformed theologians and ministers who felt deeply hurt when
their synods rejected Cottesloe. Earlier that year, nine Dutch
Reformed theologians had published an attack on apartheid
entitled *Delayed Action*. Professor Keet led the attack in
the opening essay. White South Africa was doomed, he declared, if it hoped to overcome black nationalism by force.
He wrote: "Our Afrikaans Churches are rightly blamed for
not being true to their prophetic calling with regard to the
apartheid policy and its bitter fruits."[65] The writer has vivid
memories of hearing Professor Keet preach at the centenary
of the founding of the Dutch Reformed seminary at Stellenbosch. Dr. Keet spoke on theological developments over the

past 100 years and their significance for Dutch Reformed theology. In no way could his own position be called anything but Calvinist theology of the highest order. He was no "liberal." Yet it was he, a father-figure in the DRC, who was the most fearless opponent of apartheid and the racism and injustice inherent in separate development. There have been many others. When Beyers Naudé was forced to leave the ministry of the DRC, he had considerable support from many of his former colleagues in his critique of the church. In 1965, eight Dutch Reformed theologians published an open letter, "A Call for Clarity in Confusion," in which they maintained that Dutch Reformed practice did not correspond to Dutch Reformed theology and the confessions of the Reformed tradition, but was more determined by the interests of the Afrikaner than the Word of God.[66]

More recently, while there has been an on-going internal critique, the DRC has had to face growing criticism from Reformed sources outside its own ranks. The DRC has come under increasing fire from the Gereformeerde Kerken in Holland. This church, which has stood squarely within the neo-Calvinist tradition of Abraham Kuyper, has had the longest and closest fraternal ties with the DRC of any church outside the country. But differences on the race question finally led to a break in relations in April, 1978. Though this rupture was finally precipitated by the support given by the Gereformeerde Kerken for the WCC Program to Combat Racism, this was but symptomatic of apparently irreconcilable theological and political viewpoints. In reflecting on this, the official newspaper, *DRC Africa News,* asked the question: "Is it in reality merely a case of an ideology to which the DR Church obstinately clings or is it a deep-seated Christian life-style which has crystallised in the crucible of practical co-existence over 300 years in South Africa?"[67] That is the crucial question. The answer given by the newspaper indicates once more the divergence between the DRC and most other churches on the subject: "The brethren from the Netherlands are opposed to the system as such while the representatives of the DR Church proceed from the premise: the system is not necessarily inherently wrong—it should only be implemented honestly, reasonably and justly in respect of all concerned."

What this would mean was spelled out in a penetrating statement, "The Koinonia Declaration," prepared by a group of *Gereformeerde* Calvinists in 1977.[68] If separate development has to exist, it maintained, then for it to be just requires that "the consolidation of the Black Homelands be based upon economic viability and governability and not purely upon historical grounds ... [that] the same economic opportunities, including property, business and labour rights, be extended to those individuals and families who are unable to prosper in a Black Homeland." Furthermore, the government must "take cognizance of the opinions of all responsible people (Black, White and Brown) living in South Africa and we particularly ask that all races and population groups of the country (including urban Blacks) will obtain an effective share in negotiations that concern their political future." Much more is said, and much more is asked for, but for the writers, this is the very least that must be granted if government policy can ever hope to gain any semblance of moral approval.

However, while the political partition of South Africa on a just basis may sound fine in theory, and probably could have been fairly and humanely implemented earlier this century, as John Dube, Oldham, and others acknowledged, this is no longer possible. Writing almost twenty years ago, Professor Keet said: "If the idea of total *apartheid* had arisen a hundred years ago, one might conceivably have regarded it as practicable, but at this point in our history it appears no other than the dream of Rip van Winkle."[69]

Related to the critique of the Gereformeerde Kerken in Holland has been that of the Reformed Ecumenical Synod. The RES binds together in world-wide fellowship those churches which adhere strictly to the various Calvinist confessional documents of the Reformation, including that of the Synod of Dort. The DRC and the Gereformeerde Kerken in Holland are the dominant members of the synod. The black "daughter" churches of the DRC are also members.

Although the RES has been cautious in its critique of the DRC, over the past twenty years this critique has grown in sharpness and intensity. Without doubt, the black Reformed churches in South Africa, together with the Dutch Gereformeerde Kerken, have been largely in the forefront of this challenge, but they have been supported increasingly by other members such as the Christian Reformed Church in the United States. The fact of the matter is that more and more the DRC has become isolated in its defense of separate development, even within the community of churches having the same creedal and confessional basis.

For a church committed to the Reformed dictum that the church is only the church as it continues to be reformed by God's Word, critique is vital for its well-being and mission. True Calvinism is not conservative and reactionary, as it is often made out to be. There is a revolutionary dynamic implicit in that for which it stands.[70] But there can be no doubt that Calvinism, like all other theological traditions, can be misused for maintaining the status quo. Then it is no longer what it should be. In his perceptive study on "The Decline of Calvinism," D. W. Howe shows how in eighteenth-century Europe and North America most "educated Protestants were strongly occupied with the importance of preserving social order. Many of them seem to have felt that a quiet modification of the urgent demands of Calvinism offered the most promising possibility for attaining such order."[71] But such modification always means that the cause of justice and righteousness must suffer.

As long ago as 1952, Dr. Ben Marais expressed the dilemma of the whites in South Africa—"to maintain ourselves, but not to do it in such a way that the non-whites and their aspirations will be the victims of our selfishness and self-interest."[72] The promise of the DRC is that it will enable whites to rise above such selfishness and seek to practice the love, justice, and mercy to which the gospel of Jesus Christ calls us. More than any other church, the DRC is in a position to do that. But it has somehow to resolve the dilemma in which it is placed by the very fact that it is so closely related to Afrikaner history and culture. J. C. G. Kotzé indicated the way for his church when he wrote shortly after Sharpeville:

> Self-preservation always has a tendency to drive people to self-interest and acquiescence in injustice. Fear will easily drive us to do an injustice and then to justify it. But when our goal is centred in the Kingdom of God, and His principles are the standard of our life, we shall be saved from the deviating paths of death.[73]

Overseas visitors to South Africa often express amazement at the extent of the DRC's ministry to blacks. Indeed, quite apart from the establishing of black churches, the DRC has developed a far-reaching diaconal program for the black communities throughout the country. This deserves greater recognition than it has received.[74] The DRC has also worked for a more humane implementation of government policy. Without detracting from this, however, we discern a strong tendency to use this ministry to justify support of the system. When this is done, it detracts from the ministry itself.

The DRC is not the only church in South Africa, and no church can avoid its own responsibility to witness to God's kingdom in its particular situation. The other churches know they cannot expect of the DRC anything that they are not prepared to work for as well. Different as they may be, they are all part of the church of Christ and need each other in the struggle for justice and peace. This presupposes the need for some kind of dialogue and co-operation between the DRC and the English-speaking churches. Relationships have clearly been strained over the years, and have reached a breaking-point on several occasions in recent times. A spokesman for the DRC put it candidly: "There can be no doubt about the desirability of dialogue between the Churches. ... [But] experience has shown in the past that on these two points—the lack of a common basis of belief and discussion on the one hand, and on the other a clash of basic policy standpoints—dialogue has been born and died."[75] This is certainly true, but it would be a sad day if that meant the end of the matter. Rather, we must affirm with the

South African Council of Churches that in spite of differences, Christians in South Africa must "have a common platform for the discussion of issues affecting the teaching and practice of the Christian faith in the context of the South African situation."[76] Those critical of the DRC dare not mute their criticisms—the interest of the gospel does not allow that. But the English-speaking churches must also be open to critique. The Catholic Archbishop of Durban, Dennis Hurley, put the matter into perspective when he wrote:

> The Christian standard is a terrifying one. And even as we take it upon ourselves to suggest where our brothers of the Dutch Reformed Churches may have fallen short of it, we dare not judge and condemn, for in the same circumstances, would we have done better?[77]

The English-speaking Churches

THE DESIGNATION "English-speaking churches" is a somewhat clumsy and untheological description. However, in the South African situation it seems impossible to avoid the phrase or find a satisfactory alternative. "English-speaking churches" does not refer in any primary sense to some common doctrinal or liturgical commitment and practice, nor does it include all those churches in the country who use English as their main language of communication and worship. Rather, the designation refers to those churches of British origin which have grown together over the years as a result of the ecumenical movement and their common attitude towards the racial situation in general and apartheid in particular. They have not claimed this title for themselves. It has been given to them by the mass media, politicians, other churches, and the populace in general. The English-speaking churches are regarded as those who oppose the racial policy of the Nationalist government.

In many ways, the appellation "English-speaking churches" is inaccurate and unfortunate. Each of the denominations normally included—the Anglican, Presbyterian, Methodist, and Congregational—has its own independent and distinct tradition and ethos. They are all different. While it is necessary to lump them together in the present context, this does not mean that they are some kind of monolithic alternative to the DRC. At the same time, these churches have been deeply involved in the contemporary search for the unity of the church, and for many years have sought ways and means to express this given unity in Christ in concrete forms. At present they have intercommunion, share numerous joint projects, and are working towards a covenanted relationship.[78]

"English-speaking churches" is also misleading because it may suggest that these churches are predominantly white, and culturally uniform. Nothing could be further from the truth. The majority of members in the English-speaking churches are black, and their mother-tongue is not English. For example, in the United Congregational Church at least eight languages are spoken, and probably as many members are at home in Afrikaans as in English. This language variety indicates something of the cultural plurality within the churches. English is the common language of communication beyond the local level, but racial and cultural diversity is part of the very fabric and significance of these churches.

There is a further problem. "English-speaking churches" may suggest churches which are in opposition to the Afrikaans-speaking Dutch Reformed churches, or at least, churches opposed to the Afrikaans community. This impression is understandable. The English-speaking churches all came to South Africa during the upsurge of British imperialism, and they took sides by and large with the British government in the ensuing struggle for power in South Africa. The missionaries who were most critical of the social situation in the nineteenth century belonged to these churches, and were often regarded as the bitter enemies of the Afrikaners. Furthermore, these churches have led the church attack on the apartheid policies of the Afrikaner Nationalist government. Thus, when government policies come in for attack by the English-speaking churches, this is often regarded as passing judgment on the integrity of the DRC and the Christianity of the Afrikaner. Historical legacies make it very difficult to avoid this impression. When and where the English-speaking churches have been pro-British and anti-Afrikaner for purely cultural and political reasons, they have certainly been guilty of denying the Christian faith, and need to recognize this fact. But in recent times, in spite of much disagreement, there has been very little anti-Afrikaner or anti-DRC sentiment. The churches have tried to prevent their attacks on the ideology of apartheid from becoming anti-Afrikaner. Indeed, there are many Afrikaners in the English-speaking churches. Joost de Blank's outburst against the DRC angered many and embarrassed virtually all the leaders of the churches.

A final consideration regarding the title "English-speaking churches" is its exclusive character. It should include the Baptists, but it generally does not, especially since the Baptist Union withdrew from the South African Council of Churches. It could include some of the Pentecostal churches, but their distinct character and lack of involvement till now in ecumenical groups and social issues excludes them. What of some other churches that are deeply committed to social witness and are ecumenically involved, in particular the Roman Catholic and the Evangelical Lutheran churches? In some respects, Catholics and Lutherans have been in the vanguard of Christian witness and action in South Africa. Yet, because they are not of British origin, we cannot properly refer to them as "English-speaking." These distinctions, then, must be kept in mind as we proceed.

Our discussion of the initial reaction of the churches to apartheid, and to the Cottesloe Consultation, has provided us with an insight into the basic attitude of the English-speaking churches to the race question in South Africa. When we consider the role of the South African Council of Churches in our next chapter, we will also be dealing with important aspects of the witness of the English-speaking churches, since they make up the largest segment of membership in the council. Here we take a more general and critical look at the overall attitude and the witness of the English-speaking churches during the past three decades.

Since 1948, the synods, conferences, and assemblies of the churches have protested against every piece of legislation they have considered unjust. Innumerable resolutions have been passed against everything designed to further apartheid and entrench discrimination. Countless deputations have been sent to the Prime Minister and other ministers of state to express concern and raise objections. Programs have been initiated to try to deal with racism at the local congregational level. Pastoral letters have been published, expressing the mind of the churches at the highest level. Indeed, there has been no lack at all of official protest against apartheid, in principle and sometimes in practice.[79]

The churches have spoken out against race classification; the forced removals of population groups due to the Group Areas Act; the Immorality Act and Mixed Marriages Act, designed to preserve racial purity; the various education acts which have created separate kinds of education along ethnic lines; job reservation, whereby certain occupations are reserved for one racial group, to the detriment of black people; the many security bills and acts which have allowed banning and imprisonment without trial, the deportation of church workers and missionaries, and the extension of police powers beyond normally accepted democratic limits; the pass laws, which govern the movement of Africans, and which have led to vast numbers of arrests and imprisonments over the years; the migratory labor system; and the farm prison system. The list is almost endless, since the racial policies of the government affect every aspect of social life in the country. Moreover, quite apart from legislation, the churches have protested against state action, whether it be in connection with the removal of squatters, or the banning, detention, and imprisonment of particular people who have not been brought to trial, or who have been kept in solitary confinement for extended periods, or who have died in prison. There must be few comparable instances in the history of the Christian church where such a sustained protest and battle has been waged over such a long period against state legislation and action. Naturally, this has led to considerable tension between these churches and the state.

The conflict between the English-speaking churches and the state is an underlying theme throughout our discussion. The conflict has many dimensions. To begin with, the very nature of the policy of apartheid is anathema to these churches. And for them, there is little difference between apartheid and separate development. If the distinction is made, separate development is regarded as little more than a sophisticated form of apartheid. Since government policy is to separate and divide people on the basis of ethnicity, and since the churches understand part of their task as the reconciliation of groups and the implementation of social equality, conflict between church and state is often unavoidable. Further, the implementation of government policy has directly affected many facets of the life of the churches in an adverse way. This has included everything from the owning of property on a nonracial basis to the holding of residential conferences open to all races.[80] Moreover, in pursuit of separate development, the state has taken over black church schools as well as many church hospitals and related institutions. This may be regarded as normal in modern states, but often, as in the case of the expropriation of the Federal Theological Seminary, it has been done in ways that smack of victimization of the churches.[81]

An important aspect of the church-state problem is the conviction embodied in the republic's constitution (1961) that South Africa is a Christian country. Religious persecution, as this is normally understood, does not exist. The state encourages the propagation and teaching of the Christian faith, and respects the rights of religious minority groups. Moreover, government leaders are on record as saying that the prophetic witness of the church is part of the church's responsibility, and is important for the well-being of the state. All of this reflects the country's Calvinist heritage, as it is maintained by the DRC itself. For example, the 1974 report of the DRC specifically states that part of the task of the church is "to preach the supremacy of Christ in all spheres of life, including that of the state. . . . it must warn when injustice is being done in the implementation of national policy and the application of laws."[82] However, two qualifications radically affect this position.

First of all, as the 1974 report indicates, Calvin's stress on the prophetic role of the church is tempered by Kuyper's teaching on the "sovereignty of separate spheres."[83] This means that the state is sovereign under God, and supported in its task by his "common grace" given in creation. The church is likewise sovereign in her sphere, under the lordship of Christ, and it is her responsibility to proclaim God's "special grace" to the world, and enable its members to fulfill their role as Christians in society. Thus, the church has no right to interfere in matters of government, but its members have a political vocation and responsibility as individuals. In other words, and here Kuyper differs from Calvin, the prophetic task of the church in society is not exercised by the church as church, but through its members in the world. These two positions can be reconciled, but when Kuyper's teaching is separated from Calvin's, you virtually end up with the Lutheran idea of the "two kingdoms," the separation of the spiritual and the secular realms, an idea which is far removed from Calvin. This is the direction in which the 1974 report moves. It states: "The golden rule of sovereignty for each institution in its own sphere, of justice and of love, should be sufficient to preserve the state from revolutionary chaos and political absolutism and tyranny."[84] Whether this is so is highly debatable, but this rule too often keeps the church silent when it should speak. Indeed, it prevents the church from speaking concretely and specifically for fear that in doing so it might trespass on the "sovereign sphere" of the state. Without doubt, the government's own understanding of the political role of the church is that of Kuyper—hence the insistence that the church stick to its own spiritual task and let the government get on with its secular vocation.

Secondly, the prophetic task of the DRC is qualified in terms of separate development. The church, as we pointed out above, "must warn when injustice is being done *in the implementation of national policy....*" When all is said and done, there is little difference between the position of the DRC and the English-speaking churches on the political responsibility of the church *in principle,* though ironically the latter take a more Calvinist position than the former. But the English-speaking churches see their prophetic task in a different light because they fundamentally reject national policy as unjust in itself.[85] Over the years, the English-speaking churches have been relatively free to criticize the government, even to criticize the fundamentals of separate development. They have also had reasonable access to those in authority. Yet, no matter how free they have been to speak out, or how cordially their deputations have been received by state officials, little has been achieved because of the basically different understanding of and attitude towards separate development. DRC criticism is heeded by the state, but it does not really affect the status quo. The critique of the English-speaking churches is disregarded, and sometimes leads to conflict and confrontation.

Tension between the English-speaking churches and the state, which normally means an uneasy coexistence, intensifies when words become deeds. Recent history is full of government action against church people—pastors, missionaries, leaders, and those involved in Christian agencies and projects. The reason is obvious. If the churches are against government policy, then it follows that church workers will become involved in programs that go against what the government regards as the well-being of the state. Hence there has been a spate of deportations of missionaries, and banning, detaining, and imprisoning of South Africans involved in this way.[86] In this connection it is appropriate to mention the celebrated trial of the Very Rev. Gonville ffrench-Beytagh, a former Anglican Dean of Johannesburg. Dean ffrench-Beytagh was charged by the state of engaging in "terroristic activities." On October 15, 1971, he was found guilty in the Transvaal Supreme Court, and sentenced to five years imprisonment. Later, in February, 1972, the Appellate Division of the Supreme Court rescinded this verdict, and the Dean was acquitted. But the whole trial indicated the extent to which the security police keep watch over the activities of people, especially of well-known clerical critics of the government.[87]

In reacting against Christians in this way, the state denies that it is acting against the churches. It insists that its target is individuals or quasi-religious organizations who use the cloak of religion to disguise subversive activities. The churches have responded in various ways. But in responding, they have generally affirmed their corporate nature, holding that action against individuals who seek to obey Christ is action against the church. They have also called on the government to give reasons for its actions. These are seldom forthcoming. The churches have also insisted that their words and deeds are motivated by Christian obedience and not politically pragmatic considerations, and that their witness is open to, not hidden from, public scrutiny. But how can one handle the government argument that it knows more about people and institutions than is in the public interest to declare, and that its actions are always the result of such inside information?

Government propaganda, especially the charge of being unpatriotic, has certainly sown seeds of bewilderment, and helped spawn opposition to the witness of the churches among their own members. This has been exacerbated by a lack of clear biblical teaching on the part of the churches regarding their social witness. And, of course, many white members accept government policy as right and necessary anyway. It would be wrong, then, to give the impression that in this conflict between the English-speaking churches and the state, the churches' members stand united. Indeed, the churches' struggle against apartheid and racism has been compromised in a variety of ways. First of all, there has been, and remains, a gap between synodical resolutions and congregational resolve and action. Secondly, there is something of a credibility gap between the stand of the churches and discriminatory practices in their own life. Thirdly, the churches have by and large failed to educate their constituencies in the meaning of Christian social responsibility. Let us elaborate on these points.

A major dilemma of the English-speaking churches is the chasm that exists between the prophetic utterances of the church courts and the attitudes and actions of local congregations and members. In writing about the Anglicans shortly after Cottesloe, Hinchliff remarked: "It is probably true to say that when members of the government accuse the bishops and clergy of the Province of interfering in politics, many of the laity silently agree with the accusation and wish that their own consciences and the secular authorities might both be allowed to rest in peace."[88] How are we to explain this credibility gap? In the first place we need to recognize that it is only half-true to say that there is this wide gap between synods and congregations. It is half-true because the majority of the members and congregations are black not white, and this majority is fully supportive of their churches' stand against apartheid. The gap is really between the synods and leadership on the one hand, and some white congregations and many white members on the other. This does not deny white support. The churches would have been rent asunder long ago if there was not general support from their membership, although one suspects that one reason why schism has not happened is simply the knowledge from past experience that resolutions are seldom implemented anyway. A major failure of the leaders of the churches has been their overconfidence in the power of resolutions. There has been a tendency to believe that if the right word is uttered, the task is achieved. Thus, there has been a plethora of pronouncements, but a lack of grass-roots teaching and a paucity of deeds. Reflecting on resolutions of the Presbyterian Church (PCSA), the Rev. Robert Orr told the General Assembly in 1963:

> In previous years your committee (Church and Nation) has tried, in its own stumbling fashion, to indicate some of the positive things Christians may do, considering all the circumstances. We have also done our best to study legislation and make clear its implications for the Christian. To the best of our knowledge, these statements and recommendations, piously noted by this Assembly, have had less effect than the rattling of tin cans tied to a cat's tail. In fact, we are worried that they may have had a negative effect, that they may have soothed the conscience of the Church members, who can point to them and

say "There you are—that is what my Church thinks" and then go back to their reading of the Sunday paper.[89]

While the prophetic witness of the English-speaking churches has been gravely impaired by this gap between the leadership and many white members, it has been equally affected by discriminatory practices within the life of the churches themselves. Although blacks have increasingly taken on leadership roles, many remain sceptical about the seriousness of the churches in combating racism. They point to a wide range of discriminatory practices that have existed over the years, and which are only now being slowly and painfully removed. Writing in *Pro Veritate* in the early sixties, Hinchliff remarked that "Anglicans are sometimes rather smug, sometimes rather angry, because our Church leaders are outspoken in their attacks on the Government. What they do not realise is that other (African) members of the Church feel that the practice of the Church lags a long way behind what its leaders say." This gap between word and deed has been exploited by the government as blatant hypocrisy. Many a deputation to the state has floundered on the mere fact that the churches' own lives have not been beyond reproach. Indeed, on occasion the state has exercised a prophetic ministry to the churches. For example, the churches soon learned that they could not justly criticize wage discrimination between whites and blacks in society or in state employ because there was similar discrimination in the churches. Earlier we quoted Archbishop Hurley's query as to whether the other churches in the same position would have done better than the DRC. His conclusion deserves quotation: "In the light of the behaviour of the other Churches in South Africa, we would not. For these Churches, too, have been hamstrung by their inability to break out of theory into practice. They have not suffered from an inadequate theory. They have just suffered from a paralysing incapacity to translate the right theory into practice."[90]

In more recent years, the English-speaking churches have become more aware of these gaps between resolutions and resolve, between word and deed, and have sought ways of overcoming the inherent problems. But it remains true that white members are usually opposed to change or else apathetic. The problem lies at a deeper level than simply the question of race relations. It is wrapped up in political uncertainties and fears for the future. There is also considerable reticence to oppose the government. There is a basic uneasiness, a sense of insecurity; and a lack of a sense of purpose is very evident. The problem has to do with what might be called a crisis of faith, commitment, and hope. And this has to do with the peculiar situation of the white English-speaking community and a failure on the part of the churches to meet the crisis in a creative way.

The dilemma of white English-speaking South Africans, quite apart from the church, is vividly shown by the difficulty one has in trying to define them. This was demonstrated at a conference on "English-speaking South Africans Today" held in 1974 in Grahamstown. A broad definition would include all South Africans for whom English is the language of daily discourse, irrespective of their ethnic origin. But, as many people of very different ethnic backgrounds speak English, this is not very helpful. Moreover, the British home connection no longer means a great deal. There is no distinguishing cultural life, and much of what there is, is mediocre, a pale shadow of something else. As Guy Butler said in his introductory lecture at the Grahamstown conference:

> The group is small, split among many religious denominations, secular by temperament, with very few cultural organizations; without a political party which makes it its business to look after its interests; with virtually no say in the education of its young, except when rich enough to send them to private schools; a socially mobile group, sprinkled over a large country, and alas, a predominantly white-collar group cut off from the sobering realities of manual labour and honest poverty.

And further, commented Butler: "Behind the facade of our impressive material success, what do we find? A great deal of cynicism and shoulder-shrugging, bitterness and resentment at Afrikaner power; disillusionment at Britain's diminished world-stature; fear of, and guilt towards our [sic] blacks; and a habit of buck-passing and scapegoat hunting."[91]

What we have, in fact, is a minority (English-speaking) within a minority (white) community with little historical awareness, and an individualism which has lost the ruggedness of settlers and pioneers, a morality that is either very secular and materialistic or pietist and escapist. An English-speaking white identity crisis is rampant. But the contribution of this community need not be something of the past; indeed, it would be tragic if this were so. The traditional strengths of the English-speaking community—pragmatism, tolerance towards other commitments and ideas, and a sense of fair play—while by no means theirs alone, are important. But they are inadequate to the contemporary crisis, and no match against other strong ideological options. It is this situation which calls for a rediscovery of prophetic elements within the tradition of the English-speaking churches, a tradition that has often been maintained by people who have become despondent about the apathy of the churches and have left them in order to join the struggle for human rights.

English-speaking South Africa has produced notable poets and writers, historians and social scientists, and leaders in many other disciplines and fields, but there have been very few who have had the ability and charisma to provide theological insight and leadership that is adequate for the kind of situation in which we now live. It seems that authors such as Olive Schreiner, Alan Paton, and Nadine Gordimer have engaged in far more profound reflection on our historical experience and contemporary challenges than all the churches and theologians put together. What is essential today is, of course, more than reflection and analysis, but this is still of primary importance for the life and witness of the English-speaking churches. Neither rampant liberalism nor doctrinaire fundamentalism is adequate for the task at hand, nor are they of the essence, by any means, of the traditions of the English-speaking churches. For one thing, both are far too individualistic. On the contrary, the rich Catholic and evangelical and Nonconformist heritage of the

English-speaking churches is full of tremendous potential for spiritual renewal and mission in the final decades of twentieth-century South Africa.

Roman Catholics and Lutherans

IT MAY SEEM STRANGE that Catholics and Lutherans should be placed together in our discussion. There is at least one good reason for this. Neither the Roman Catholic Church nor the various Lutheran synods have been in the forefront of the struggle against racism in South Africa until fairly recently. At least, it may be more accurate to say that they have not been as visible in this regard as the English-speaking churches. There have been good historical reasons for this.

Traditionally, the Roman Catholic Church has been in a peculiar situation in South Africa because of the strong position of the Protestant and especially the Dutch Reformed churches. Catholics were prohibited from public worship until 1804, and were only allowed their first bishop in 1837. For many years after that, obstacles were placed in the way of Catholic missions to the indigenous peoples of the land, and there has been a clearly acknowledged anti-Roman Catholic bias in the policies of the Afrikaner Nationalist government, particularly with regard to immigration. This latter bias has changed in recent years as more and more immigrants from traditionally Catholic countries have settled in South Africa. But the cry of "*Roomse-gevaar*" (Roman danger) still evokes considerable emotion from some people in the white Afrikaner community. This anti-Catholic sentiment has produced a cautious attitude within the church, and the hierarchy has been far more diplomatic in its relation to the state than the English-speaking churches have been. Maybe such diplomacy is more traditionally characteristic of Roman Catholics, but it has resulted in more caution than is normally the case.

Caution, however, has not meant indifference to the racial situation in the country. Before 1950, the Catholic bishops made few pronouncements on the subject, but since then, and particularly since Vatican II, the church has taken a clear and often bold stand on the issues. Just as the English-speaking churches reacted strongly to the apartheid policy after the National party victory in 1948, so Catholic bishops spoke out in similar terms. In September of that year, Bishop Hennemann addressed the churches of his diocese on the subject. In the course of his pastoral letter he said:

> In recent years it [i.e., segregation] has reappeared in the guise and under the name of 'apartheid'. A beginning has already been made to put into practice this noxious, unchristian and destructive policy.... To make matters worse, all this is done in the name of Christian civilization.... 'Christian civilization' is, we are asked to believe, one and the same thing as 'white civilization'. The truth is, there is no such thing as 'white civilization', and there never was. If it is 'white' exclusively, it is not Christian, and if it is Christian, it is not 'white'. The false doctrine of 'white civilization', if pursued to its logical conclusions, will open wide the doors of South Africa to the world's most formidable enemy today—Communism.[92]

The first joint pastoral letter of the Catholic bishops was issued in 1952, the tercentenary of white colonization of the Cape, on the subject of race. This was followed by seven letters solely on matters of racial harmony and social justice. An excerpt from a recent commentary on the stand taken by the bishops over these years reads:

> The content of the Joint Pastorals can be summed up as applying to our own circumstances the Gospel teaching of the universality of love and justice and the 'code' of human rights which protect man's dignity, freedom and well-being.... From the beginning they stated that the concession of these rights to all in the country in the same manner was a necessity of justice, and refused to be distracted from this when the theory of partitioning South Africa into separate states was brought up. The reason for this was and is that the majority of those who do the work of the Republic are black, and to refuse them citizen rights is injustice and inhumanity. As the inevitable rigidity of law grew, and harshness in its enforcement, they protested in 1964 against the law depriving Africans resident in the country hundreds of years of permanent residence rights, and four times in 1974–75 against methods used in administering secu-

rity laws and treatment of church institutions witnessing against injustice.[93]

The stand taken by the leadership of the Roman Catholic Church has been very similar to that of the English-speaking churches. It is not surprising, then, that after Vatican II, the Catholic Church developed its relationship with the other churches to a marked extent and became an observer of the Council of Churches. While the Roman Catholic Church remains sensitive to its peculiar position in the country, it has not let this prevent it from speaking prophetically to the situation. In some instances, such as the integration of church schools, it has led the way with some success. It is also noteworthy that Catholic analyses of the situation have paid considerable attention to labor and other economic factors. The most recent and comprehensive statements by the bishops are *A Call to Conscience Addressed to Catholics by their Bishops,* issued in 1972, and those issued in 1977 on a variety of matters arising out of the current situation.

The problem of the Catholic Church is the same as that of the English-speaking churches. Although the church is predominantly black (over one million), there has been considerable reluctance on the part of its 350,000 white members to follow the lead of their bishops. Archbishop Dennis Hurley of Durban has been a constant critic of this failure within his own diocese and the church at large, and over the past twenty years has attempted in various and creative ways to bridge the gap. But the sharpest critique has come from black priests. This has resulted in considerable tension within the church, and led on a number of occasions to confrontation situations. In some respects, black Catholic priests have taken a more militant line within their church than is true in most other denominations.[94]

With regard to the Lutheran denomination, there were German-speaking Lutherans among the early settlers at the Cape in the seventeenth century, and the white Lutheran community grew as successive groups of German and later Scandinavian settlers came to South Africa. From the middle of the nineteenth century, a number of continental and

American Lutheran missionary societies began work among the African peoples, mainly in Natal and the Transvaal. This eventually led to the formation of various synods composed of black Lutherans, which have been independent of each other and also largely separated from contact and certainly fellowship with the white Lutheran synods.[95]

In 1966, the various Lutheran churches and synods throughout South Africa and Namibia (South West Africa) joined together to form the Federation of Evangelical Lutheran Churches in Southern Africa (FELCSA). This new organization for Lutherans, and also Moravians, has done much to bring the various Lutheran communities closer to each other and closer to the other churches in South Africa. This has been particularly true of relationships between the black synods and the churches belonging to the South African Council of Churches. During the early 1970s, an attempt was made to unite white and black Lutherans in one church. However, due to white reticence, four black synods finally went their own way and formed the Evangelical Lutheran Church of South Africa in 1975. Although the black Lutherans have been highly critical of the race situation in the country, a great deal of their struggle has centered on the unity of the Lutheran Church. This struggle for unity has been extremely difficult because of the conservative position adopted by most German-speaking Lutheran congregations. In 1975, FELCSA unanimously adopted an *Appeal to Lutheran Christians in Southern Africa,* in which the following was stated:

> The confessional basis of the Lutheran churches obliges every Lutheran Christian, the individual church bodies as well as FELCSA, to withstand unanimously alien principles which threaten to undermine their faith and to destroy their unity in their doctrine, in their witness and in their practice. . . . The most dangerous of these alien principles are the following:
>
> 1. An emphasis on the loyalty to the ethnic group which induces Lutheran Christians to worship in a Lutheran church dependent on birth or race or ethnic affinities which insist that the Lutheran churches in Southern Africa remain divided into separate churches according to ethnic principles;

2. The belief that the unity of the Church is only a spiritual unity which need not be manifested;

3. The belief that the structures of society and the political and economic system of our country are to be shaped according to natural laws only, inherent in creation or merely according to considerations of practical expediency, without being exposed to the criterion of God's love as revealed in the biblical message.

Later, in the same document, FELCSA addressed the political situation more directly: "To us the political system now prevailing in the Republic of South Africa appears to be based on a number of errors and misapprehensions. We are convinced that this whole system needs to be radically reconsidered and reappraised in the light of the biblical revelation and of the general experiences of mankind." The statement also held that "the political system in force in South Africa, with its discrimination against some sectors of the population, its acceptance of the break-up of many families, its concentration of power in the hands of one race only, and the limitations it imposes on freedom, cannot be reconciled with the gospel of the grace of God in Jesus Christ."[96]

Like the English-speaking churches, as well as like some within the DRC, the black Lutherans and FELCSA have seen the direct connection between the unity of the church and the social situation in South Africa. This ecclesiological dimension to the church struggle is of the utmost importance. To regard the unity of the church largely in spiritual and "invisible" terms is to misunderstand the teaching of the New Testament, and in the end, to compromise the witness of the church as it struggles against racism and other forces that divide and separate people on the grounds of culture and ethnicity.

3

The Growing Conflict

A Confessing Movement

WORLD-WIDE OBSERVERS of the church struggle in South Africa are probably very familiar with the name of Dr. Beyers Naudé, and the work of the Christian Institute of Southern Africa, which he directed until both he and the institute were banned in October, 1977. While the witness of the CI has by no means been the sum total of Christian testimony and action against racism in South Africa, the story of the struggle of the church to confess Christ as Lord, over against the claims of race, cannot be told with any completeness if the struggle of the CI is omitted from its rightful place on center stage. And the story of the CI is also the story of Beyers Naudé, of his change, of his charismatic leadership, and of the community of people who rallied around the cause he represented.

Naudé was a distinguished minister in the Transvaal Synod of the Dutch Reformed Church. He was also a member of the *Broederbond*. His roots lay deep within Afrikaner tradition and culture, and especially within the piety of evangelical Calvinism as he experienced it in the early, formative years of his life in the Cape and at the Dutch Reformed theological seminary at Stellenbosch. At the time of the Cottesloe Consultation, to which he was a delegate, he was acting moderator of the Transvaal Synod. Although there were other factors which influenced the direction of Dr. Naudé's life, it was Sharpeville and then the failure of his church to stand by the resolutions of Cottesloe that finally led him to take a stand contrary to that officially adopted by the DRC.

Post-Sharpeville South Africa was a society in crisis. Nothing quite like it had happened before to disturb the apparent tranquility of white South Africa and the confidence of foreign investors. Nothing comparable was to take place again until Soweto erupted in protest in 1976, and evoked support from nations and peoples throughout the world. Thus, the early sixties were critical years for the church as well as society in South Africa. The question was simply: Could Christians in South Africa, irrespective of confession or race, transcend apartheid and find each other in the service of justice and reconciliation in the name of Christ?

In spite of official opposition from his own church, but with support from some ministers and members within it, in 1962 Beyers Naudé launched a journal entitled *Pro Veritate.* The following year, when the Christian Institute was founded by him and some English-speaking church leaders, he accepted the position of director. The founders of the CI hoped that the institute would enable members of all races of the Afrikaans and other churches to share together in bearing witness to the unity of the church and the lordship of Christ over society. Its first attempt to do this was through the formation of Bible study groups throughout the country, many of them led by Dutch Reformed ministers. Through its study guides and *Pro Veritate,* the CI provided material to challenge and guide Christian understanding and action. It also sought to expose South African Christians to developments taking place in the church in Europe and North America by providing study fellowships and arranging for scholarships. The emphasis in these original years was one of changing the awareness and understanding of white Christians who had never questioned the status quo, through a rediscovery of the biblical message.

The new work and witness of Naudé and the CI was unacceptable to the DRC from the outset. The church went so far as to declare that it would not allow Naudé to remain a minister if he accepted the position of director in the CI. Thus, Naudé faced a costly decision—whether to continue to work for change through his church and congregation, as some friends advised, since he was in a strong position to do so, or to resign as a minister and work through the institute in a more direct and radical way. It was an agonizing decision to make. Naudé appreciated the counsel of friends who urged him to remain a minister in the DRC, but finally decided to the contrary. He did not wish to lose his ministerial status, but he believed God was calling him to fulfill a new kind of ministry. Indeed, as he explained to his congregation in his farewell sermon, it was a matter of obedience to God rather than man.[1] The kind of witness which the CI was designed to make was a divine imperative he could not resist.

A similar decision faced other Dutch Reformed ministers who had joined the CI in support of their colleague. Some of them resigned from the DRC in protest and a few became ministers of other denominations. Catholic Archbishop Hurley, a strong supporter of the CI from its inception, describes the story of the institute in terms of radical conversion:

> Those who experienced the conversion referred to here were dedicated Christians of the Dutch Reformed faith. Fellow believers would not normally think of them as needing conversion. Yet they went through a painful transformation and emerged as men keenly aware of the demands of love in race-ridden South Africa.[2]

In 1965 the General Synod of the DRC resolved that all members of the church should resign from the CI. The congregation in Parktown, Johannesburg, to which Beyers Naudé and his family now belonged, and of which Naudé was an elder, stood by these members in support, rejecting the decision of the synod as contrary to the gospel. But the going was very difficult. The CI, and Naudé in particular, were regarded as driving a wedge down the middle of Afrikaner society. And in a very real sense, the accusation was correct. In accepting the leadership of the CI, Beyers Naudé had in effect rejected the determinative role of the *volk* in the life of the DRC. For him, confessing Christ meant rejecting the culture-Christianity of those who supported apartheid. An eventual result of this alienation from Afrikanerdom was an important change in the CI itself. Having failed to influence the DRC and Afrikaans-speaking Christians to any real or positive extent, Naudé turned more and more for support to English-speaking Christians. Here he gained some encouragement, but Naudé soon discovered that white English-speaking support was not much greater than Afrikaner support when it came to fundamental social change. As a result, he grew increasingly disenchanted with most whites and attempted to become more directly involved with blacks in their struggle.

While the English-speaking churches supported the CI, their relationship to it was seldom more than tentative and lukewarm. Many church leaders and members were committed to the CI and supportive of Naudé; if this were not so, the CI would have collapsed early on. But there was also unease. The CI was a fellowship of individuals answerable only to itself, and in no way responsible to the churches. The CI was widely and heavily financed by overseas church agencies. This meant that it was able to develop a large staff, drawn largely from the ministerial ranks of the churches, and to embark on far-reaching programs. The CI regarded these programs as supplements to the work of the churches; the churches often saw them as a threat to what they were doing—and they probably felt guilty that they were not doing all that they should. There was also an element of distrust. In order for the CI to gain and maintain overseas support, subconsciously or not, it had to project the image that it was a more significant witness against apartheid than the churches. This was not very difficult to do, but it tended to distort what the churches had done and were doing, and to minimize their potential role in the situation. These kinds of tensions are not new to Christian history, but they did compromise both the CI and the churches in their mutual struggle against apartheid.

Yet, the undoubted significance of the CI for the churches was that it provoked and challenged them in a way that had never occurred before. The growing radicalism of the CI was regarded with some trepidation, but the English-speaking churches could not dissociate themselves from the basic principles and confession for which the CI stood. And so, time and again, the CI set the agenda and forced the pace for the churches. Naudé's prophetic discernment, supported later by others such as Dr. Theo Kotzé, Director of the CI in Cape Town, probed deeply into the ills of South African society and challenged the churches to action.

The CI did more than prod the churches. It attempted to create a "confessing movement," something akin to the Confessing Church that arose in Germany during the Hitler regime, but something more adapted to the situation in South Africa.[3] Indeed, the CI was profoundly influenced by the German church struggle in its basic orientation to the state and to the churches, and in its understanding of the lordship of Christ. But despite much discussion and considerable support for the idea, a Confessing Church as such never materialized. One reason for this was that the German model was both impractical and inappropriate for South Africa, where the churches are so different in ethos, tradition, and self-understanding from those in Germany.[4] A more important reason was that a "confessing element" existed within the churches, and though many were disillusioned with their own denomination's witness, they nevertheless saw the need to work as members of their churches rather than create something new. After all, whatever the churches might do in practice, the English-speaking churches, the Catholic and Lutheran churches, were all committed in principle to the struggle against apartheid. What the CI did do, however, was to provide resources and an *ad hoc* supportive community for those who were at the cutting edge of the churches' witness. And this proved an immense strength to those involved.

It is beyond the scope of these pages to describe all the functions fulfilled by the CI before it was banned. But two are of special importance for our discussion. First of all, the CI was instrumental in bringing many of the African independent churches into relationship with each other and the wider church in South Africa and beyond. Until the mid-sixties, the "mainline" churches were sceptical of the independent churches. They shared the same kind of attitude typified by Sundkler's initial assessment of them as a bridge from Christianity back into heathendom. This opinion was shared by blacks and whites alike in the major denominations. The independent churches were equally sceptical of the other churches, for the same reasons that they had originally broken away. But they did feel the need for some kind of association, especially for theological education and training. Thus, they turned to the CI for help, and found a ready welcome. Supported by massive grants from Germany and Holland, the CI enabled the African Independent Churches Association (AICA) to come into being. Through AICA a new era dawned for the independent churches as they became more closely associated with other Christian communities in the country. The fledgling association was not without its internal problems, and after a few years it broke its ties with the CI. Later it became related to the South African Council of Churches (SACC). But whatever the failures of AICA or the CI, what they achieved together was a pioneering step of considerable consequence for the church in South Africa. Not only did it help the independent churches find a wider ecumenical fellowship and become a more integral part of the total life of the church and its witness, but it also made the other churches aware of the contribution and challenge of this rapidly growing tradition.

Secondly, the CI played a determinative role in the Study Project on Christianity in an Apartheid Society (Spro-cas I), and the action-oriented follow-up program, Spro-cas II. Spro-cas was a result of the *Message to the People of South Africa,* published by the South African Council of Churches in 1968. Later we shall examine the *Message* and Spro-cas in more detail, but some preliminary remarks are required here in order to understand the development of the CI. The *Message* was a decisive rejection of apartheid and separate development as contrary to the Christian faith in principle. Spro-cas I was an attempt by the SACC and the CI to work out alternatives to apartheid in South African society. It was run by an executive appointed by the council and the institute. By 1972 the project was complete, and a new phase began. Previously the accent had been on study, but now the emphasis shifted to action and implementation. This new program, Spro-cas II, was dominated by the CI, though also supported by the SACC. It represents a decisive turning-point in the work and witness of the CI. From this stage onward, the institute rapidly attempted to become more clearly involved in the struggle of blacks who had rejected any co-operation with the system of separate development. As part of this involvement, the CI was also beginning to offer a radical critique of the economic structures of South African society.

In his perceptive article on "The Christian Institute and the Resurgence of African Nationalism," Peter Walshe has described this change in the stance of the CI as a parting of company with "the old liberal illusion that change could be effected solely by education and moral appeals directed at the privileged." While Walshe tends to overstate the role that the CI played in the development of black consciousness, it is still basically true that the institute, as he puts it, "began to encourage the resurgence of black consciousness as a source of renewed dignity and potential for the poor. This involved the judgment that black initiatives would be crucial in pressing for change; that whites could and should no longer expect to control such initiatives; that the Institute, by increasing its black membership and witnessing to the essential human community above colour, could assist in the emergence of a new generation of black leaders."[5]

It is a massive understatement to say that the CI was never popular with the government. But however irksome it was in its critique of apartheid, the crunch only really came when the CI became involved in the black consciousness movement. In 1972 the government instituted the Schlebusch Parliamentary Commission of Inquiry to investigate the activities of the Christian Institute, the University Christian Movement (UCM), the National Union of South African Students (NUSAS), and the South African Institute of Race Relations. In the course of its labors, it also investigated the Wilgespruit Ecumenical Centre at Roodepoort, near Johannesburg, which had a long history of providing a multiracial program related to church and society issues. In 1975, now under the chairmanship of another Nationalist Member of Parliament, Mr. Le Grange, the Commission of Inquiry presented its findings to Parliament. As a consequence, the work of Wilgespruit and NUSAS was heavily censured, and both the CI and UCM were declared "affected organizations." As the UCM had already disbanded, it was only the CI that was affected. Being an "affected organization" meant that it was no longer able to receive financial aid from sources outside the country, the government rationale being that it was involved in political action rather than bona fide Christian work.

Before continuing the story, it is important to recall that the Schlebusch/Le Grange Commission was a highly contentious matter, strongly opposed in principle by the churches belonging to the South African Council of Churches, as well as by some opposition politicians and other community leaders. It was also opposed by those organizations being investigated; in fact, the CI leadership refused *en bloc* to give evidence to it, though this was an offense punishable by law. Eventually, the refusal to testify led to a series of court cases, one of which was the trial of Beyers Naudé himself.

The full story of the trial of Naudé has been told elsewhere.[6] It is certainly one of the most significant trials of any church leader in the history of the church in South Africa. Here was a former dignitary of the DRC, a former member of the *Broederbond,* on trial for refusing to give evidence to a state commission of inquiry. The penalty was not very serious (fifty rand or one month in prison), but the issue was. Does the state have the right to investigate people and institutions in secrecy beyond the normal processes of the law, especially when the investigation is conducted by party politicians appointed by a government clearly opposed to those being investigated? Impartiality was impossible under the circumstances. Naudé regarded the giving of evidence which could, as it already had in the case of people involved in NUSAS and Wilgespruit, lead to banning and deportation, as contrary to the gospel. No Christian, he maintained, could participate in a trial which could implicate others if it were so conducted that those implicated would be unable to refute any false evidence that might be forthcoming. He made it clear in his defense before the magistrate that this opposition was not a matter of scoring political points, but of evangelical conviction. Indeed, the whole of Naudé's statement before the court is a model of Christian witness, as clear as it was bold. But eventually he was found guilty. Having elected to go to prison for the month, Naudé was released soon after, when a friend paid the fine on his behalf, much against Naudé's wishes. Naudé was not a martyr. But many would echo the words of Lord Ramsey, the former Archbishop of Canterbury, who shortly after the trial wrote: "When I think of the men who have shown me what it means to be a Christian my thoughts will always go quickly to Beyers Naudé."[7]

Now that the CI was an "affected organization," it was forced to cut back on its programs and staff. At the same time, it managed to increase its financial support from within the country to a considerable extent. But the focus of the CI was concentrated in the prophetic witness of men like Naudé and Kotzé. By the time of the Soweto uprising in June, 1976, the CI was already deeply committed to black initiatives, and it became involved in providing guidance and support for those in the forefront of the black protests.

This involvement, especially the support given to black leaders, and the publicizing of allegations of police torture and brutality,[8] including protest at the death of Steve Biko in prison, eventually led to the mass bannings on October 19, 1977. The CI was declared illegal, many of its black staff were detained by the police, and the senior white staff—Beyers Naudé, Theo Kotzé, Brian Brown, Cedric Mayson, and former Spro-cas Director Peter Randall—were all banned. So was *Pro Veritate*. The Rev. David Russell, an

Anglican priest working among migrant workers, especially among the squatter communities in Cape Town, was also banned, and placed under house arrest during weekends. Russell worked closely with the CI, particularly in publicizing injustices and enabling blacks to fight for their legal rights through the courts.[9]

The end was sudden and total, though not unexpected. It was more than symbolic that it should have occurred on the same day that Percy Qoboza, editor of the mass-circulation black newspaper *The World*, was detained and his paper banned, the day newspaper editor Donald Woods was banned, and the day many black organizations working for social change were made illegal and their leaders arrested. By now the CI was fully identified with the black cause symbolized by leaders such as the dead Steve Biko. After sixteen years of courageous and often lonely witness, the CI was no more. Within a few hours, its once busy offices were empty and silent. One of the most articulate Christian witnesses to non-violent but radical social change was now out of action.

How are we to assess the significance of the institute in the church struggle in South Africa? Peter Walshe has suggested at least two major contributions.[10] First of all, he says that the CI "functioned as part of a vital matrix for the dissemination of ideas at a time when African political organisations had been systematically repressed." Secondly, he points to the CI as "another example of contemporary renewal," particularly in challenging exploitative structures in society on behalf of the poor. The CI, he writes, "can be seen as ethico-prophetic in opposition to the bourgeois cultic ethos of white-dominated churches. It can be described as helping to articulate an indigenous South African liberation theology that has its primary impulse in the struggle for identity taking place in the black community."

It would be asking too much of any institution to be without faults. Certainly the CI had its fair share. Perhaps we might simply say that it was weakest where it was strongest. It was very dependent upon overseas support, especially finance. This meant the constant need to design programs that would capture the imagination of donor agencies. Inevitably this meant taking responsibility for many tasks and programs which, however important, were tangential rather than central to the task of the CI. One rather crippling result of this was the considerable drain on the energies and resources of Beyers Naudé and others. Another was the tendency for the CI to become too centralized, even bureaucratic, thereby losing some of its dynamic as a confessing movement. (In many ways, being declared an "affected organization" proved to be liberating rather than inhibiting.) A further problem was the lack of participant support at the grass-roots level. The CI had undoubted moral support within the black community, and some encouragement from sections of the white community, but relatively few supporters were involved in its programs. Indeed, the impact of the CI was totally disproportionate to the size of its membership. But what it lacked in numbers it made up for in vision and courage. Then, of course, the CI was in many ways Beyers Naudé. Without his presence and leadership, it would never have been launched or sustained through the many years of its existence. This was central to its strength. It could be argued that it was also an inevitable weakness, for without Naudé the CI would have lost its charismatic center.

All of this was recognized by Naudé, Theo Kotzé, and others within the leadership of the CI. It was, and still is, not easy to challenge the status quo in the radical manner eventually adopted by the CI. Many of the problems and the failures of the institute were directly caused by the difficult conditions under which it had to operate. Through its insights, it bore witness to the radical implications of the kingdom of God for society. But a variety of circumstances prevented its being sustained as an on-going institution. This fact is nothing new. Church history is full of instances where prophetic movements have arisen to challenge both the church and society in ways similar to that of the CI; however, it must be confessed that the institute was more institutionalized than most similar movements have been. Possibly that was its main problem—it could be put out of action more easily. But movements like this have invariably been short-lived or else surrendered their original character. It is difficult to sustain a radical movement even in relatively open societies, let alone in situations where the state feels directly threatened by its presence.

Reflecting on this for a moment, we are inevitably brought face to face with the dilemma of the church. The church is called to bear witness to the kingdom of God in the world. That is its reason for existence. This kingdom is the antithesis of the kingdoms of this world—it constantly brings them under judgment. This being so, a faithful church will always find itself in a position of tension with society. At the same time, the church cannot escape being a social institution if it is to exist in the world. Jürgen Moltmann reminds us that a church which is simply a community of people founded on a relatively *ad hoc* basis "cannot disturb the official doings of this society and certainly cannot alter them—indeed, it is hardly any longer even a real partner for the social institutions."[11] Being an institution is not the problem—that can be both a blessing and a curse. The question is always: What kind of institution? The church loses its soul if it allows itself to become part of the system, to be used by society for its own interests, or to be neutralized in favor of the status quo. The church as an institution is called to be faithful to the kingdom of God, to be the "salt," "light," and "leaven" of the world. For this reason the church desperately needs the presence of prophetic movements like the CI, for these movements provide the critique that forces the church to a new assessment of itself. Such movements are part of God's way of renewing his church in every generation and situation. After all, the members of the CI were not outside the church, but also members of the church. The protest comes from within, and the protest and critique continues even though the doors of the CI are closed.

In the light of the CI experience, Peter Walshe raises three questions for Christian witness today.[12] First of all, is it sufficient for the churches to work at educating their constituency in moral issues without dealing with economic justice? Secondly, "in pursuing the scriptural demands for social justice, can Christians place themselves at the cutting edge of social evolution, activating protests and working with secular movements for justice, all the while seeking to arouse compassion and to limit the inevitable element of violence inherent in radical social change as it threatens the power of defensive established elites?" And finally, "can hope and a new directional morality be affirmed while maintaining an essential element of humility which recognises man's persisting venality and so avoids triumphalism?" These questions have to be faced. The CI, though banned, in one sense still speaks; yet the churches can no longer depend on it to take the risk of prophetic leadership. The churches have the full responsibility laid on themselves. They may act and speak in a different way, but they cannot avoid the questions, nor can they with integrity depart from the biblical principles to which they are committed.

A Message to the People of South Africa

LONG BEFORE the birth of the CI, the churches and missionary societies in South Africa were related to each other through the Christian Council. The council had served a very useful purpose over the years in enabling the member institutions to grapple with the issues facing South African society. A number of the conferences we have considered were the result of Christian Council initiative. By the time of Cottesloe, however, the council was a relatively ineffectual body, unprepared for the tasks that were about to come its way. It was not taken too seriously by its member churches or those in authority. It was virtually unknown to the public. In short, it was ill-suited and ill-equipped to serve the churches in a time of crisis. Partly for this reason, the CI took on many of the responsibilities that the council should have shouldered in the early sixties.

This relative ineffectiveness was recognized by church leaders for whom the council was regarded as a potentially important agent of church co-operation and witness. Thus, shortly after Cottesloe, the Christian Council began to expand its program under the Rev. Basil Brown, its first full-time General Secretary. In 1966 the council moved its head office from Cape Town to Johannesburg and, under the leadership of Bishop Bill Burnett, rapidly widened the scope of its work. In 1968 it changed its name to the South African Council of Churches (SACC) to emphasize the fact that it was established by the churches to facilitate interchurch co-operation. It was not intended to be an autonomous institution. In this respect, it was by constitution very different from the CI. During the seventies, the SACC developed at an amazing pace, with a wide range of programs, a large budget, and growing participation from the black Christian community. Much of this growth was due to the dynamic leadership and vision of Methodist layman, Mr. John Rees, who became General Secretary in 1970.

Although the SACC is widely known in South Africa today because of its opposition to the racial policies of the state, its work and witness has included much more than public pronouncements of a political nature. Its wider work is often forgotten because it seems less newsworthy to the media. This has resulted in an unbalanced view of the council in the popular mind, as though its sole vocation is to criticize the government. A great deal of its ministry on behalf of the churches has been out of the public eye. Through its Division of Inter-Church Aid, the SACC has been deeply involved in a wide variety of development and community projects throughout the country, and seeks to help in emergency-aid situations. This work has taken the largest slice of its annual budget. Related to this is its concern about such problems as migratory labor, an issue that has received serious attention from most churches, including the DRC, over the years. The SACC sponsored a definitive study of the problem, undertaken by economist Dr. Francis Wilson in the early 1970s.[13] Its scholarship program has provided both academic and technical scholarships to many black students, particularly in the rural areas. Its Dependents Conference has long cared for the dependents of political prisoners. And, quite apart from this, the council has fulfilled the more obvious ecumenical tasks—study programs, communications, and assistance in the total search for the union of the churches in life and witness.[14] In the words of its constitution, it has sought "to co-ordinate the work and witness of Churches and Missionary Societies and other Christian Organisations in South Africa in order more effectively to carry out the Church's mission in the world."[15] Part of this co-ordination has involved supporting and working alongside local councils of churches which have grown up in many centers throughout the country.

But we cannot tell the whole story of the SACC here, even though much of it is part of the total struggle of the church to be the church of Christ today in South Africa. We need to look more specifically at what launched it into public prominence in the late sixties and made it, along with the CI, an instrument of prophetic leadership.

In 1966 the World Council of Churches held its highly influential Conference on Church and Society. It was this conference which set the agenda for considerable theological debate and social action within its member churches during the next ten years. It also paved the way for the Program to Combat Racism in 1970, a most contentious and traumatic event for its South African member churches. Geneva confronted the churches with the cry of millions of people, particularly in the so-called Third World, for a just world. It was at Geneva that the question of Christian participation in the revolutionary struggles of our day was first raised at such a high level for the Christian church.[16]

There were many delegates at Geneva who were unprepared to accept the more extreme radical position adopted by some spokesmen. But few delegates were untouched by the new demands that were being made on the churches with respect to their calling to witness to the biblical demand for social justice and peace. Bishop Burnett and Beyers Naudé were among those affected. Thus, following the Geneva Conference, regional consultations were held throughout South Africa, sponsored by the council and the CI, to explore the significance of the Geneva recommendations within the South African context. Though the impact of these consultations was limited, they raised far-reaching questions for Christians in South Africa, and offered fresh insights for those seeking answers.

In the same years as the Geneva Conference, the council established a theological commission "to consider what obedience to God requires of the Church in her witness to her unity in Christ in South Africa." It was this commission which set about preparing the *Message to the People of South Africa*,[18] which, when published in 1968, would launch the SACC into national headlines and usher in a new phase in the saga of growing conflict with the state.

The *Message* was first aired at a "Conference on Pseudo-Gospels"[19] convened by the SACC in May, 1968. But it was in August that the *Message* was sent to all clergy, English and Afrikaans, throughout South Africa. At a news conference it became a public document. Seldom has a theological document brought such immediate reaction from so many sections of the populace, including the Prime Minister, Mr. John Vorster, himself. In a speech a few weeks after the publication of the *Message,* Mr. Vorster, in a clear reference to it, warned against people "who wish to disrupt the order in South Africa under the cloak of religion."[20] Expressing his own respect for the proclamation of the Word of God, he went on to warn clerics who were planning to "do the kind of thing here in South Africa that Martin Luther King did in America" to "cut it out, cut it out immediately for the cloak you carry will not protect you if you try to do this in South Africa." In a long open letter to the Prime Minister, a number of church leaders, including the president of the SACC, Archbishop Selby-Taylor, Bishop Burnett, and Beyers Naudé, set forth the reasons for criticizing government policy and expressed sorrow that the Prime Minister had reacted with a threat. They wrote:

> With all due respect, though with the greatest firmness, we must assure you that as long as attempts are made to justify the policy of apartheid by appeal to God's Word, we will persist in denying their validity; and as long as it is alleged that the application of this policy conforms to the norms of Christian ethics, we will persist in denying its validity.[21]

In his reply to this open letter, Mr. Vorster wrote:

> It is your right, of course, to demean your pulpits into becoming political platforms to attack the Government and the National Party, but then you must not be touchy when I and others react to your political speeches in the way I have done. It does not surprise me that you attack separate development. All liberalists and leftists do likewise. It is with the utmost despisal, however, that I reject the insolence you display in attacking my Church as you do. This also applies to other Churches, ministers of the Gospel and confessing members of other Churches who do in fact believe in separate development.... I again want to make a serious appeal to you to return to the essence of your preaching and to proclaim to your congregations the Word of God and the Gospel of Christ.[22]

Nothing portrays the basic dilemma of the church struggle in South Africa better than this correspondence in response to the *Message*. The church leaders appealed to the Word of God, as did the Prime Minister. The conflict concerns two fundamentally different ways of interpreting the biblical message. That is part of its tragic sadness. What was it, then, that the *Message* declared?

To begin with, it should be noted that, unlike the Barmen Declaration of the German Confessing Church, to which some have likened it, the *Message* was a six-page document which some critics, with justification, called "too wordy." The *Message* attempted to show how apartheid and separate development are contrary to the gospel of Jesus Christ. Taking as its starting-point the conviction that, in Christ, God has reconciled the world to himself and therefore made reconciliation between people both possible and essential to the Christian faith, the *Message* proceeded to draw out the implications of this atoning work of Christ in terms of South African society. It first of all made clear that "excluding barriers of ancestry, race, nationality, language and culture have no rightful place in the inclusive brotherhood of Christian disciples." But the main burden of the *Message* was that this unity within the church could not be divorced from what was happening in society itself: "A thorough policy of racial separation must ultimately require that the Church should cease to be the Church." In other words, apartheid and separate development attacked the church at its center; they denied the work of Christ. The *Message* declared,

> There are alarming signs that this doctrine of separation has become, for many, a false faith, a novel gospel which offers happiness and peace for the community and for the individual. It holds out to men a security built not on Christ but on the theory of separation and the preservation of racial identity. It presents separate development of our race groups as a way for the people of South Africa to save themselves. Such a claim inevitably conflicts with the Christian gospel, which offers salvation, both social and individual, through faith in Christ alone.

The task of the church was to demonstrate the reality of this reconciling work of God in its own life. Thus, Christians "are under an obligation to live in accordance with the Christian understanding of man and of community, even if this be contrary to some of the customs and laws of this country."

The Message aroused the feelings of white South Africa in a dramatic way because it went for the jugular vein in the body politic. For days, some English-newspaper editors came out in strong support of the council and its *Message*. Equally strongly, Afrikaans newspapers deplored it. Six hundred ministers formally signed the *Message,* indicating their commitment to what it proclaimed. But the council also received letters of criticism and condemnation. In the meantime, the member churches had to consider the *Message* at their annual synods, assemblies, and conferences. With few exceptions, the churches were warmly supportive. Some of them expressed minor criticisms of points, but none, with the exception of the Baptist Union, rejected it.

The Baptists gave the *Message* considerable attention. They did not reject the concern of the *Message,* for they too condemned racism as contrary to the gospel. But they believed that the *Message* was theologically questionable.[23] It confused man's eternal salvation with the salvation of political issues. Separate development, they maintained, is not a rival gospel, even though it may be an unjust political policy. Salvation through grace alone cannot be made contingent upon supporting or rejecting a political philosophy: "The views and attitudes of an individual in racial matters do not enter into the realm of his being justified by faith." This Baptist critique raised central issues in a clear and concise way, issues that are by no means resolved, but which are fundamental to the question of Christian confession in the world.

The difference between the Baptists and those who subscribed to the *Message* was largely a difference in understanding the nature of apartheid or separate development. For the drafters of the *Message,* apartheid was not just a political policy, but an ideological substitute for the gospel. It represented a total way of life based on racial identity. It determined all human relations, even marriage, in a way that contradicted Christian belief. As such, it denied in a fundamental sense the Christian doctrine of man, and ultimately the doctrine of God. In other words, apartheid was more than a pragmatic program, it was a heresy. And heresies do have a bearing on man's salvation.

But the Baptist response raised two other issues as well. It posed the question, on the one hand, of the meaning of salvation, and, on the other, of the relation between faith and obedience. Salvation is not merely a matter of individual redemption after death; according to the gospel, eternal life begins now. It is a way of life. It is participation in the kingdom of God. Moreover, while it is personal, it is not individualistic. The great prophetic tradition of Israel continually warned the nation not to trust in any political program, but to do, and therefore trust in, the will of God. Otherwise, judgment and disaster would befall the nation. The nation, too, could only be saved, as it were, by faith and obedience. This brings us to the final issue: Can it be said that the "views and attitudes" of people, on any issue, "do not enter into the realm of his being justified by faith"? To say this is to consign faith to a world of unreality, as though faith existed in a vacuum. Ethics cannot finally be separated from doctrine. This does not mean that moral effort saves man, but that faith must not become a metaphysical abstraction. Dietrich Bonhoeffer dealt with this question in a profound way in his *Cost of Discipleship,* when he wrote: "Only he who believes is obedient, and only he who is obedient believes."[24]

The *Message* had some serious consequences. It made dialogue between the English-speaking churches and the DRC extremely difficult, for in effect the SACC statement condemned those who were prepared to justify separate development on theological grounds. The Baptists did not attempt this, but the DRC did. The *Message* also ushered in a new and more intense phase in the relationship between the state and the churches belonging to the SACC, and, of course, between the state and the council itself. But the *Message* also raised basic questions about the life and witness of the churches and individuals who had responded positively to it. When were confessing words going to become deeds? Separate development having been rejected, what alternative consonant with Christianity could be pursued? It is one thing to speak out and criticize, it is another to respond positively amid the harsh realities of day-to-day South Africa. Perhaps it is better to remain silent if there is no answer to these questions.

Following the publication of the *Message,* some of those committed to its stand formed themselves into "obedience to God" groups. This took place as part of the growing interest in forming a Confessing Church in South Africa, a concern which was then being debated and discussed within the Christian Institute. Many of those involved in the "obedience to God" movement were members of the CI who regarded the *Message* as a confession of faith for the South African situation. While this "obedience to God" movement never managed to grow beyond a relatively small circle of predominantly white Christians centered in the Transvaal, its leaders did a great deal to stimulate thinking about the implications of the *Message,* particularly for the life of the churches. In one declaration they stated:

The Church has no right to address and accost the state except if

a) it has been preceded by a sincere confession by her of the guilt of the Church and of Christians in South Africa in neglecting to discover and combat effectively ignorance, indifference, prejudice, lack of compassion, even active opposition in racial attitudes and affairs;

b) she is willing and eager continually to put her own house in order and to take all steps through preaching, teaching and practice to be in deed the community of the redeemed.[25]

This declaration spoke directly to the credibility gap in the life of those churches which had condemned apartheid as a government policy, but whose own life was a denial of their confession. It was this concern that lay behind the production of a report jointly prepared by the SACC and the CI, *Apartheid and the Church.*[26]

Apartheid and the Church was part of a much larger program than simply relating the *Message* to the churches. After the *Message* was published, the leaders of the SACC and CI were faced with the questions: So what? What does all this mean amid the realities of South African society? Having uttered a prophetic critique of separate development, what alternative is there that could receive the support of those who believed in the *Message?* It was questions like these that led to the formation of the Study Project on Christianity in Apartheid Society (Spro-cas) under the directorship of Mr. Peter Randall. The project embraced a wide variety of people from many different disciplines— academics, politicians, lawyers, clergy, teachers, theologians. Working in six different commissions—economics, education, law, society, politics, and the church—these people met regularly over a period of two years, preparing reports on the meaning of the *Message* for each of these spheres of national life.[27] It is still difficult to assess the full impact of the reports, which were detailed and thorough not only in their analyses but also in their recommendations. But there is little doubt that they contributed to, and initiated a great deal in, the growing debate on the future of South African society.

Of particular importance for our reflections on the church and the SACC in their struggles against apartheid was the report of the church commission. *Apartheid and the Church* described how apartheid affects the life of the church through external legislative controls and through "internal ideological captivity," fear, prejudice, despair, conformism, legalism, authoritarianism, and wordiness. It showed how denominationalism, segregation, discrimination, and paternalism all undermine the witness of the church. It called upon the churches to move beyond ecclesiastical self-concern, pragmatic pietism, and clericalism, and to become faithful to the demands of the kingdom of God. In so doing, it made very specific recommendations on many matters affecting the life of the churches, including the equalization of salaries for ministers irrespective of race by 1975, the need to refuse any racial classification if required by the state for the purposes of owning property and so forth, and the demonstration that persons of all races are welcome as members and worshippers within every congregation. Other recommendations touched on the question of church investments, the need for a simplicity of lifestyle, the call for symbolic acts against racial discrimination, and the question of conscientious objection. This was the first time that this last-mentioned issue was raised in recent church history in South Africa, particularly in the context of the struggle against racism. Within a few years it was to become one of the most emotive points of contention in the growing conflict between the churches and the state.

The importance of a document such as *Apartheid and the Church* must not be overemphasized. It certainly reflected the thinking of many leaders, ministers, members, and theologians within the member churches of the SACC, but in itself all that could be hoped for was that it should contribute to the debate, challenging and enabling the churches to become more faithful. It is sobering as we reflect on the many strong and articulate statements and resolutions that have emanated from the churches to see how little they have achieved. There is a danger that confidence for renewal be placed in commissions and reports rather than in what God is seeking to do. This does not invalidate such reports or confessions of faith, but it reminds us that simply because certain things have been said or written, does not necessarily mean that they have happened or will happen.

During the years following the publication of the *Message* and *Apartheid and the Church,* the life and work of the SACC grew rapidly. We have already mentioned some of the more important aspects of its program. At the same time, however, it was entering a new phase in its existence. This new phase may be described in terms of three highly significant developments. The first was the impact of the World Council of Churches' Program to Combat Racism on the churches in South Africa; the second was the debate about violence and nonviolence, highlighted by the stand taken by the SACC on conscientious objection at its national conference in 1974; and the third, and most important, was the increasingly dominant role played by black Christians in the life of the churches. Much of what follows in this chapter and the two after it has to do with these issues. But before we turn to them, let us reflect a little on the significance of the SACC in the church struggle in South Africa.

In criticism it could be said that some of the weaknesses of the SACC are similar to those of the CI, particularly the extent to which the SACC has been dependent upon overseas funding. In a basic sense, this reflects more on the lack of support by the churches than on the SACC itself; it also reflects the tremendous needs that the SACC has tried to serve, needs often created by apartheid, and for which overseas funding is essential. At the same time, it must be remembered that the mission of the church in South Africa has been extensively supported by overseas donors for more than 150 years. This, then, is nothing new or exceptional. So it is not simply a question of failure and blame, but a question of how to generate support within the churches in South Africa for the kinds of programs which the SACC has implemented. This question has concerned the leadership of the SACC a great deal over the years. A related problem has been the relationship between the SACC and its member churches. On the one hand, the SACC only exists because the churches have created it; on the other hand, the SACC has an on-going life of its own. This dialectical relationship to the churches has inevitably led to tension between the SACC and its members, even though the leadership of the council has sought to avoid this. But given the nature of the

SACC, the diversity of its membership, and the disparity in the roles fulfilled in its life by its member churches, it is unavoidable that the SACC's policies and programs are often more acceptable to some than to others. In order for the council to do its work, it must stay close to the churches, but it must also pioneer and break fresh ground if it is to avoid becoming just another bureaucratic ecclesiastical organization. The tension between prophetic movement and social institution has been agonizingly real. In its earlier days, the SACC tended to be more ecclesiastical in the narrow sense; in the seventies, it began to develop a momentum of its own, though still in relationship with the churches.

Gradually at first, but with increasing speed, the SACC changed during the seventies from being a white-dominated institution, to becoming much more widely representative of the black Christian community. This is reflected not only in the changes that took place in the staff, culminating in the appointment of black Anglican Bishop Desmond Tutu as General Secretary in March, 1978, but also in the national executive. Past presidents, the Rev. E. E. Mahabane of the Methodist Church, the Rev. A. W. Habelgaarn of the Moravian Church, and the Rev. John Thorne, a Congregationalist, as well as the current president, Ds. Sam P. Buti, a leading minister in the Nederduitse Gereformeerde Kerk in Afrika (the black "daughter" church of the DRC), are all leaders from within the black community.

This transformation has been of tremendous significance and consequence for the SACC. It has meant that through the council, black leaders within the churches have been able to discover each other and so share their concerns, but it has also meant that white church leaders have come to know the feelings of blacks in a new and united way. It has meant that the policy and programs of the SACC have more and more reflected black Christian opinion, thereby making it more suspect in the eyes of the authorities and more removed from much white opinion in the member churches. And thus it has meant that the SACC has found itself at the center of the church struggle. Often regarded as not radical enough by overseas ecumenical bodies and some blacks, and always regarded as too radical by the South African authorities and most whites, the SACC has been a crucial catalyst in setting the agenda and tackling the issues facing the churches today.

The Program to Combat Racism

SOUTH AFRICAN CHURCHES have been closely associated with the modern ecumenical movement since its earliest beginnings in this century. Along with the English-speaking churches, the DRC Synods of the Cape and Transvaal were founding members of the World Council of Churches in Amsterdam in 1948. Although the DRC withdrew from the WCC in 1961 after Cottesloe, it has continued as a member of the World Alliance of Reformed Churches and the Reformed Ecumenical Synod. The English-speaking churches, together with the Moravian, the Tsonga Presbyterian, the Bantu Presbyterian, and the United Evangelical Lutheran Churches, are members of the WCC, and each has ecumenical links with its own world-wide confessional bodies and missionary councils. Since the founding of the All Africa Conference of Churches (AACC) in 1958, those churches belonging to the WCC have also belonged to the AACC. It is difficult to overestimate the significance of these long-standing and extensive ecumenical relationships for the struggle of the church in South Africa.

The ecumenical connection, however, has had a rather particular dimension. Since the first WCC Assembly, which was held the same year that the National party came to power, South Africa's racial policies have been high on the agenda of ecumenical debate and concern. With clear reference to South Africa, the Evanston Assembly of the WCC declared that "any form of segregation based on race, colour, or ethnic origin is contrary to the gospel."[28] This world-wide Christian concern about apartheid grew rapidly during the sixties, especially after Sharpeville and Cottesloe. Ecumenical agencies, mission boards, and confessional bodies all had direct contact with South Africa through their related organizations in the country, through the reports of missionaries and staff members, and through increasing contact with black and white South African exiles living in Europe and North America. Indeed, there was no lack of information, a great deal of contact, and an awareness of black opinion—all of which were and remain determinative for much ecumenical decision-making.

For the period 1948-1966, international ecumenical interest in South Africa was expressed in resolution after resolution, and while the resolutions became increasingly sharp, relationships remained warm and cordial. Indeed, even though the DRC had withdrawn from the WCC in 1961, it continued to have informal links with the world body. But a rather dramatic change began to occur after the Geneva Conference in 1966, and especially the Fourth Assembly of the WCC held at Uppsala in 1968. The Uppsala Assembly set in motion plans to establish a program for the elimination of racism throughout the world. A subsequent Consultation on Racism held at Notting Hill near London in 1969 proposed the formation of a Program to Combat Racism (PCR). This proposal was endorsed by the Central Committee of the WCC meeting at Canterbury that same year. Clearly, the WCC was no longer willing simply to talk about the evils of racism. Plans were being formulated to engage it head on, not just in the life of the churches, but especially at the political, economic, and social levels. This meant working for the liberation of racially oppressed people in the broadest sense.

South African Church leaders, especially those involved in the SACC and the CI, were increasingly aware of this more militant mood, particularly of the WCC, but also as it affected other ecumenical and confessional communities to which they were related. In August, 1969, the executive of the SACC responded to the proposals of the Notting Hill Consultation. In the main, it was a critical response. It was critical not because the SACC had any desire or reason to defend apartheid, nor because the WCC had decided to move beyond resolutions to deeds, but because of the means proposed to combat racism. The SACC acknowledged that "our social order in South Africa is already to a considerable extent based on the use of violence" and that "the conclusion reached by the World Council of Churches Consultation on Racism in London, that force may be resorted to by Christians in order to dislodge entrenched injustice, has been reached, at least in part, on account of the failure of the churches." But, the SACC also commented, "We are disturbed by the way in which the Churches and the World Council in section 6 are called upon to initiate the use of means usually associated with the civil power in the struggle against racism. These are the weapons of the world rather than the Church."[29] The appeal of the SACC executive to the Central Committee of the WCC was presented personally by the General Secretary, Bishop Bill Burnett. But it had little effect. The PCR was approved and began its work in January, 1970.[30] However, the real bombshell had yet to be dropped on the still largely unsuspecting South African member churches of the World Council.

In September, 1970, Dr. Eugene Carson Blake, then the General Secretary of the WCC, visited church leaders in South Africa. Not only did he meet with leaders of member churches and the SACC, he also had a cordial discussion with DRC leaders about the possibility of renewed fellowship between their churches and the WCC. He was invited to return for further discussion. Within a week, the scene changed dramatically. On his return to Europe, Dr. Blake attended the executive meeting of the WCC held at Arnoldshain in West Germany, where it was resolved at the request of the PCR to give financial aid to antiracist liberation movements fighting in southern Africa against white minority governments. Nothing apparently had been said by Dr. Blake to prepare the South African churches for this resolution. The first time they learned about it was when the decision was splashed across the headlines of the daily newspapers. Neither the church leaders nor the SACC had information at its disposal to answer questions, correct distortions in the media, or respond to the threat by the Prime Minister, Mr. Vorster, of government action against the South African member churches of the WCC. Mr. Vorster told them to get out of the WCC or face penalties for staying in.

The fact that the financial grants made by the WCC were for "humanitarian purposes consonant with the aims and policies" of the world body, was lost on the South African public. The way the news had been released, with very little attempt to make sure that it would be correctly and fully communicated to the media in South Africa—as it could have been through the member churches or SACC—meant that the WCC was now identified by most whites as a "terrorist organization" under Communist control. There was very little the churches could do to alter this first impression, and there still is very little they can do.

Of course, irrespective of the impression created by the media that the WCC was supplying guns instead of Bibles to the world, the fact remained that the WCC had committed itself to the liberation movements and their struggle. It appeared to be a sign that the leaders of the WCC had given up hope on the churches' own struggle for change through working for justice and reconciliation (although it should be pointed out that they have continued to give support to many church-related projects since then). It also meant that the WCC had identified itself with those engaged in warfare against South Africa, and therefore had taken sides in a way that placed its member churches in the country in an unenviable position. The churches could not escape either the threat of the Prime Minister or the challenge of the WCC. Even if the leaders wanted to avoid the issue, opposition within the ranks of their own churches to the WCC meant that they had to face it head on.

As already indicated, the SACC in its statement to the Canterbury meeting of the WCC Central Committee had clearly acknowledged that the social order in South Africa was to a large degree based on force and even violence. This, however, led the SACC not to an espousal of counterviolence to change the situation, but to a rejection of violence in principle, whether in support of the status quo or in fighting to change it.

In the rather heady days following the PCR recommendation to aid liberation movements, and its approval by the WCC, the leaders of the South African member churches held a series of meetings to reach a common agreement. In so doing, they strongly affirmed the position taken by the SACC. Though none of them stood in the pacifist tradition, they unanimously committed themselves, and eventually their churches, to a nonviolent stance with regard both to defending and to attacking apartheid. This stance was to have considerable consequences a few years later when the military situation in southern Africa deteriorated, and South Africa was drawn into combat. But that was still in the future. In the meantime, while the South African churches expressed their critique of the grants to liberation movements, they also expressed their support for much of the rest of the work of the Program to Combat Racism. This support needs to be underlined. The churches were unanimous in affirming the program—the only significant point of difference was on the grants made by the Special Fund to liberation movements using violence to achieve their ends. In rejecting the support, whether implicit or explicit, of violence as a way to solve racism, they were not opting for the status quo. They had long been committed to change that, at least in theory.

For the moment, however, the churches had to deal with the threat of the Prime Minister, and the growing opposition of their own membership to continued participation in the WCC. For many whites within the churches, the issue was crystal clear. The WCC had provided Christian legitimation for organizations committed to the violent overthrow of South Africa. By implication, member churches that supported such a program were anti-South African and had opted for a revolutionary course in fighting apartheid. Withdrawal of membership was the only option available. This was not just the opinion of those who might have had sympathies for the government, but also of many within the churches who had no desire to defend apartheid, but who felt that a principle was now at stake on which there could be no compromise. Furthermore, some believed that churches might gain credibility at home for their struggle against

racism if they refused to be associated with foreign interference. A less worthy motive expressed was that withdrawal would have certain financial and membership benefits.

The national synods and assemblies of the member
churches towards the end of 1970 were very tense. All eyes
were on the General Assembly of the Presbyterian Church
of Southern Africa, which met first. This church, though
multiracial, has a majority of white members, has large
congregations in Rhodesia (Zimbabwe), and is generally
more conservative than the other English-speaking
churches. It came close to withdrawal. But the majority at
the General Assembly voted to remain in the WCC, and the
church responded to the Prime Minister's threats by reminding him "that its [the church's] only Lord and Master is
Jesus Christ, that it may not serve other masters, and that
its task is not necessarily to support the politics of the Government in power but to be faithful to the Gospel of its Lord
and to seek justice for the afflicted and liberty for those who
are oppressed."[31] There was a remarkable degree of consensus in the responses made by the member churches:

1. All decided to retain their membership in the World Council.
2. All criticized the World Council for the implicit support of
   violence by making their grants to the liberation
   movements.
3. All strongly criticized racism in South Africa.
4. All desired consultation with the WCC.
5. Most decided not to send any funds to the WCC as a sign of
   protest.

An editorial in *Kairos,* a monthly periodical of the SACC,
summed it up:

> In making these decisions, the Churches have obviously re-
> fused to be forced into irresponsible action. They have been
> aware that they will be falsely accused of being unpatriotic and
> even agents of violence, and that they would perhaps lose
> members as a result. They have also been aware that their
> decisions would not please the more radical groups, both within
> and beyond our borders. But they have spoken what they be-

lieve to be the truth in the situation and have revealed a responsible maturity. People may not like where they stand—but they can do no other.[32]

In response to the WCC issue, the South African government now made it illegal for any funds to be sent from the country to the World Council. It also made it virtually impossible for people identified with the WCC to visit South Africa, thereby ending a long tradition of such direct contact within the country. It could also be argued that from this time the government took a harder line on the SACC as well as on the member churches of the WCC.

One of the decisions of the member churches of the WCC in South Africa was to request a consultation with the World Council on the subject of the grants to liberation movements made from their Special Fund. In order for this to take place in South Africa, the permission of the Prime Minister was required. This was obtained by a delegation of church leaders who met with Mr. Vorster in March, 1971. Negotiations immediately began with the General Secretary of the WCC, Dr. Blake. In a letter to Dr. Blake, Mr. John Rees, who was acting on behalf of the South African church leaders, issued the invitation "to come to South Africa in order that we may discuss with you the reasons and theology behind the grants which you have given to certain organisations operating in Southern Africa and, further, to offer your delegation the opportunity to learn first hand the feelings of the member churches in South Africa about the decision."[33]

It was deemed wise that correspondence between the various parties be shared in order that there be no room for misunderstanding at any point. Thus, correspondence from the planning committee in South Africa to the General Secretary of the World Council was also submitted to the Prime Minister. And copies of Mr. Vorster's letters to the South African committee were forwarded to Dr. Blake.[34] This meant that considerable care had to be taken in clarifying and stating the issues, a difficult task.

Perhaps the consultation was doomed from the start. One of the church leaders who had visited Mr. Vorster to obtain his permission for the meeting, had spoken of a "confrontation" between the churches and the WCC. And this is what the Prime Minister insisted should be the case. He wanted the South African churches to confront the WCC on the grants they had made "to terrorists in Southern Africa" on the basis of the reactions of the member churches "in terms of their respective resolutions against this abhorrent decision."[35] The WCC, on the other hand, while it obviously found this unacceptable, also regarded the wording of the original invitation as too vague. The members of the WCC wanted a more detailed agenda in order to prevent any misconstruing of their reasons for visiting South Africa. They were coming to explain, not to backtrack on their position. They proposed that the Program to Combat Racism and the Special Fund be discussed in terms of the history and the whole life and work of the WCC.[36] This was certainly acceptable to the South African leaders. How else could the grants be understood and debated? But the more detailed the prepared agenda, the more difficult it was to ensure that the consultation would take place at all. They knew that any departure from the agenda as stated in the original request would mean an end to the consultation as far as the Prime Minister was concerned. As it was, his wording of the agenda was already very different from that of the South African churches.

In the end, the consultation floundered, not on the agenda as such, though that was certainly the major issue, but on additional conditions laid down by the Prime Minister in a letter to the convener of the South African delegation, Dr. Alex Boraine, in May. Mr. Vorster stated that he was "not prepared to allow the visiting delegates to go further than the International Hotel at Jan Smuts Airport and to stay longer than the actual duration of the confrontation."[37] This was totally unacceptable to the WCC; it was also unacceptable to the South African church leaders. It meant the end of the consultation before it had even begun.[38]

It is instructive to look back and reflect on this abortive attempt in the light of the Cottesloe Consultation held ten years before. First of all, the reason for Cottesloe was the deteriorating race situation in South Africa demonstrated by Sharpeville. After Sharpeville, many black political leaders left South Africa, and the eventual result of this exile was the growth of external forces seeking the overthrow of white South Africa. Cottesloe attempted to find just ways of resolving racial conflict and so prevent the escalation of violence. Ten years later, the situation had changed dramatically. A black armed struggle was gathering momentum throughout southern Africa, chiefly against the Portuguese in Mozambique and Angola, and the white UDI government in Rhodesia, but inevitably aimed at South Africa as well. Secondly, whereas in 1960 the WCC leaders still believed that the DRC and the other churches could play a major role in changing the direction of South Africa, by 1970 they had begun to despair regarding the churches. For them, the liberation movements were legitimate expressions of political revolt, and while their methods might be questioned, the rightness of their cause was not. This did not mean that the WCC had completely written off the churches in South Africa as agents of social change, nor that they had espoused violence as the means to achieve that change, but that they did not foresee change coming except through pressure from beyond the country. Moreover, the black liberation armies included many members of South African churches, and these required humanitarian aid. Thirdly, whereas the real stumbling block to Cottesloe had been the attitude and demands of Archbishop de Blank, ten years later neither he nor the DRC was in the picture. The real tussle lay directly between the WCC and the Prime Minister, with the other churches caught in the middle. Dr. Verwoerd had only come into action after Cottesloe, when he stepped in to prevent its resolutions from being accepted by the DRC synods. Mr. Vorster acted from the outset, and eventually made the proposed consultation impossible. Perhaps he wanted to avoid another Cottesloe. In the end, the South African churches had very little power to do anything about the impasse. But in a final letter to the Prime Minister in June, Dr. Boraine stated the feelings of the churches: "I must point out that our understanding of our meeting with the World Council of Churches is not a meeting between people in opposite camps but Christian leaders who belong to the world-wide family of Christ, who share the concern for the problem of racism but who differ on the methods whereby this problem can be faced and overcome."[39]

The years between 1960 and 1971, with Cottesloe at the beginning and the proposed PCR Consultation at the end, were critical for the church in South Africa as well as for South Africa as a whole. This was scarcely understood by white South Africans, since from the second half of the decade, there was tremendous economic growth in the country, and the diplomatic activities of South Africa seemed to be paying off in other parts of Africa. But dramatic changes were taking place nonetheless—changes within the black community in South Africa that would eventually surface in the black consciousness movement; changes in the black struggle for power in southern Africa which eventually led to the withdrawal of Portugal from her colonies and the advent of Marxist states; and changes in world opinion, reflected in the decision of the WCC to support liberation movements. The WCC was certainly ahead of Western countries, but the chart of the future was being plotted. These dramatic changes were acutely felt in the member churches of the WCC in South Africa. As the issues were debated, usually with great emotion, if not always with comparable clarity, the churches rapidly became aware of how urgent and critical everything was becoming for both themselves and the country. Synods were a kind of barometer, forecasting coming storms. Earlier winds of change would be insignificant in comparison to the approaching hurricane.

The full impact of the WCC grants upon the life of the churches in South Africa is still difficult to determine. The grants did not end in 1970. They were continued and increased every year until the present time. Thus, the debate about the WCC was kept alive in the churches and in public. Perhaps it is possible to make some tentative observations about the impact of all this on the churches themselves.

First of all, the WCC action tested the fellowship and

commitment of the churches. In one synod in 1970, during a heated moment in the debate on membership in the WCC, a white pastor spoke out against continued membership on the grounds that his son was at that time in the army defending the borders of South Africa against attacks by terrorists funded and supported by the WCC. In response, a black pastor spoke for continued membership because his nephew was fighting on the other side of the border as a member of the liberation army. It is difficult to imagine a greater test of fellowship within one church than this radically different and highly emotive pair of responses to the same issue. It was nothing short of a miracle that the churches did not fall apart at the seams. At times it seemed as if they would. Fellowship, if not consensus, has somehow been maintained. Nevertheless, the white members of the churches were divided down the middle, and this division has continued since then and has seriously affected other aspects of the life and witness of the churches. Only the future will tell if this somewhat fragile fellowship will remain unbroken.

Secondly, for black Christians, without whose participation some of the churches might have withdrawn from the WCC, the issue was not primarily membership in the world body. Membership was important because it meant contact with Christians throughout the world. But membership meant more than that. It meant continued commitment by their churches in the struggle against racism in South Africa. If the WCC action did anything, it raised this question for the churches: How real was their commitment to this struggle?

Thirdly, and arising out of this question, the WCC action, whatever it was intended to achieve, awakened the South African churches to the fact that time for change was running out. The liberation movements in southern Africa were not only achieving some success, but were gaining influential international support. The real issue was not so much what the WCC was doing, but what the churches in South Africa were doing to prevent disaster. God was not calling the churches to emulate the WCC, but to renew their commitment to him, and to be more faithful to his purposes. In other words, the WCC action could be regarded as a call to repentance and action on the part of the South African churches. Whatever else the WCC might have achieved, this was certainly of significance in the long run. From now on, a new note of determination could be detected in the churches. But events were not going to make that determination any easier to translate into action.

The Conscientious Objection Debate

THE ANNUAL NATIONAL CONFERENCE of the SACC was held in 1974 at St. Peter's Catholic Seminary in the black area of Hammanskraal, north of Pretoria. Hammanskraal was a name unfamiliar to most South African church people at the time. But for those who were in any way involved in the churches' attempt to relate to the events that were happening in southern Africa, Hammanskraal soon became known as the place where the SACC first made its far-reaching proposals on conscientious objection, and so launched a debate as intense and demanding as those associated with the *Message* and the Program to Combat Racism.

The historical context of the debate is important, as is the fact that it took place at Hammanskraal. The seminary at Hammanskraal provided an opportunity for the delegates to share a common life in a way that had never been the case before at a national conference of the SACC. This sense of community made white delegates more aware of black concerns than might otherwise have been the case. But Hammanskraal was also a center known for polarization between black and white. A number of other conferences, not of the council, had come to grief here on this issue, and the seminary itself had been the scene of black revolt against the white authorities in the Roman Catholic Church. More important than the place, however, was the time. The national conference was held shortly after the war in Mozambique had concluded, with Frelimo in power. Thus, many younger blacks in South Africa were full of expectation, anticipating the beginning of the end of apartheid. The conference was held during the period in which the Angolan Civil War was most intense. South African troops were increasingly involved in the fighting there, a fact unknown to the majority of the country's population. It was also held at a time when guerrilla warfare was escalating both in Rhodesia and Namibia. South Africa was arming herself as she never had before, certainly not since the end of the Second World War. Military training and service was being intensified, and the defense budget was growing beyond all recognition.

In this tense situation the SACC National Conference met at Hammanskraal. Whites were aware that in spite of many resolutions and programs, little had been achieved to resolve the urgent problems arising out of apartheid, and the escalation of violence was now a major concern. Black delegates were aware both of the rising mood of discontent among their fellows and of the sense of expectation in the air. They were aware of black polarization, symbolized by Hammanskraal itself, and felt the need for the SACC to take a stand on the issue of nonviolence that would indicate serious commitment to a Christian solution to the escalation of events that might soon engage southern Africa in a holocaust. There was the feeling that while the position adopted by the churches on the grants to liberation movements was correct, insofar as violence was rejected as a solution, the churches had not really come to grips with the growing militarism of South Africa. Yet, both issues hung together. This provides the background to the challenge to council members which required a response as costly for whites as resolutions had normally been for blacks. The response came in the form of resolutions on conscientious objection.

The CO debate at Hammanskraal was sparked by a series of statements and resolutions prepared by a white Presbyterian theologian, the Rev. Douglas Bax. Mr. Bax had long reflected on the question of conscientious objection. He had contributed to the report of the Study Project on Christianity and Society (Spro-cas), *Apartheid and the Church*, where the question of conscientious objection was tentatively raised in relation to the church struggle in South Africa. But the statement he presented to the council was not the product of detailed study; it was certainly not the result of some commission's work. It was an attempt to confess Christ as Lord in a way that related directly to the situation at large, and to the growing anguish of black fellow Christians.[40] It was a serious response to the declared position of the churches that violence could not be supported in defense of the status quo. Mr. Bax's proposals, seconded by Dr. Beyers Naudé, started a debate which, like the *Message* and the Program to Combat Racism grants, not only made headlines but evoked the wrath of the government.

The SACC Resolution on Conscientious Objection is a very revealing document.[41] In spite of its hurried preparation, it opened up major issues facing the churches, and so requires careful attention. In the Preamble to the resolution, the whole question of peace in South Africa is rooted in justice, and justice is seen in relation to the will of God to "set at liberty those who are oppressed" (Luke 4:18). The Preamble maintains that "the Republic of South Africa is at present a fundamentally unjust and discriminatory society," and thus must be regarded as responsible for the threat to peace. Since "the military forces of our country are being prepared to defend this unjust and discriminatory society," the question must be asked: Can it be right for Christians to participate in the military?

The Preamble develops a second theme in its argument. The Christian is called to "obey God rather than men," especially "in those areas where the government fails to fulfil its calling to be 'God's servant for good' rather than for evil and oppression" (Acts 5:29; Romans 13:4). The Christian dare not regard military service as an unquestioned duty simply because it is demanded by the state. Indeed, Christian tradition, both Catholic and Reformed, "has regarded the taking up of arms as justifiable, if at all, only in order to fight a 'just war,'" and this would exclude the "defence of a basically unjust and discriminatory society." A third thrust in the argument of the Preamble raises the question of Christian integrity and consistency in opposing the use of violence. If

the violence of "terrorists or freedom fighters" is to be condemned, can Christians defend institutionalized violence?
Moreover, if one says that Afrikaners were justified in the
use of violence in their struggle against British imperialism,
or that the British were justified in the use of violence to
further their aims, "it is hypocritical to deny that the same
applies to the black people in their struggle today."

The Preamble, after much heated debate, was accepted,
clause by clause, by a majority at the conference. There then
followed a series of resolutions, all of which were adopted by
the council meeting. One of the resolutions asked the
churches of the SACC to consider whether or not the South
African situation required Christian discipleship to be expressed in the form of conscientious objection to military
service. Another raised questions about military chaplains,
and the churches were asked to "reconsider the basis on
which they are appointed and to investigate the state of
pastoral care available to the communicants at present in
exile or under arms beyond our borders and to seek ways
and means of ensuring that such pastoral care may be properly exercised."

It is not difficult to imagine the impact all this had in the
country within the days following the meetings at Hammanskraal. The opponents of the SACC pointed out that the
churches who now spoke about conscientious objection were
the same as those who supported the WCC grants to "terrorists." The fact that the CO statement explicitly indicated
that violence was deplored as a means to solve problems,
and clearly did not therefore justify the black use of violence, was lost from sight. Most people did not really want to
know the full position of the churches, which was submerged
beneath a plethora of press publicity and propaganda. Government reaction was as strong as it was inevitable. The
Minister of Defense, Mr. P. W. Botha, intimated that he
would introduce the Defense Further Amendment Bill in
Parliament. This new bill provided for a fine of up to 10,000
rand or ten years imprisonment, or both, for anyone attempting to persuade any person to avoid military service.
Existing legislation, Mr. Botha said, was inadequate to take

action against persons or organizations guilty of this "reprehensible conduct."[42] This meant that not only was conscientious objection unacceptable to the state, but any positive discussion of it was also illegal. As John Rawls has said, "Conscientious refusal based upon the principles of justice between peoples as they apply to particular conflicts ... is an affront to the government's pretensions, and when it becomes widespread, the continuation of an unjust war may prove impossible."[43]

The bill aroused strong opposition from a variety of quarters, including the opposition parties in Parliament, the member churches of the SACC, and some Dutch Reformed theologians. For a few days, Parliament itself indulged in heated theological debate, as the views of Paul, Tertullian, Aquinas, Kuyper, and Karl Barth were tossed to and fro. Dr. Alex Boraine, a former president of the Methodist Church and now a Progressive party member of Parliament, led the attack sympathetic to the SACC Resolution. He made it clear that if the bill was passed, many would have no alternative but to break the law.[44] Similar statements were forthcoming from other church leaders, including Archbishop Dennis Hurley, and the newly elected Archbishop of Cape Town, the former General Secretary of the SACC, Bill Burnett. By this time, Archbishop Burnett was deeply committed to the "charismatic renewal" then growing apace in his church. In his enthronement sermon before a massive congregation in St. George's Cathedral in August, 1974, a congregation that included the state President and military chiefs, Burnett called for a new Pentecost and expressed the hope that the SACC Resolution, which he supported, would help the church to "grasp the significance of the fact that some Black South Africans, many of whom are Christians, are outside our country seeking to change our power structure by force.... "[45] The connection between charismatic renewal and nonviolence had found a powerful advocate. It is not surprising, then, that the synods of the churches that year also came out in general support of the Hammanskraal Statement and Resolution, as it was by then known. This was not done without heated debate. But the churches were clear in their rejection of any cheap call to patriotism behind which a multitude of unchristian attitudes and commitments were hidden. Eventually the bill was passed by Parliament, but it was slightly modified, possibly because of DRC influence, to read:

> Any person who uses any language or does any act or thing with intent to recommend, to encourage, aid, incite, instigate, suggest or to otherwise cause any other person . . . to refuse or fail to render any such service to which such other person . . . is liable or may become liable in terms of this Act, shall be guilty of an offence and liable on conviction to a fine not exceeding five thousand rand or to imprisonment for a period not exceeding six years or to both such fine and such imprisonment.[46]

These were strong sentences indeed, sufficient to deter most who might have had a desire to influence others.

The conscientious objection debate needs to be put into perspective. First of all, it should be understood that there is virtually no pacifist tradition in South Africa. There were Quakers at the Cape in the early 1800s, and the Society of Friends has a number of meetinghouses today, but the number is very small. The only other religious body that has opposed participation in the military is the Jehovah's Witnesses, who have strongly resisted at considerable cost. But theirs is a particular situation, which has resulted in special treatment by the state. There are also members of the Fellowship of Reconciliation, but they too are very few. Thus, the Hammanskraal Statement was not the product of peace churches; in fact, it was not a strictly pacifist statement. Fundamental to its logic is the "just war" theory, a theory dependent upon situational analysis, and one which no thoroughgoing pacifist would use to defend or promote his position.

The debate at Hammanskraal and in the ensuing months revealed that the churches, to say nothing of the public, were ill-prepared for it. They had categorically rejected violence as a means either to prevent or to promote change, but they had not worked through the implications of the former. Now they were forced to do precisely this. The wonder is that they were able to deal with it as well as they did. Whatever else may be said about the debate, there is no doubt, especially in the light of subsequent developments, that it awoke the churches to an issue they had never really faced, but one which has become tremendously important in southern Africa today. It would certainly be surprising if, as a result, churches with little traditional commitment to a pacifist position came to regard this as the only possible Christian option in today's world. But this is the logic of the stand they have tentatively taken.

Secondly, conscientious objection is a highly emotive issue. It raises the whole question of patriotism in the sharpest possible way, and its pacifism is embarrassing for many opponents of apartheid who fought in the war against Hitler. Indeed, the SACC Statement went far beyond anything that the Confessing Church in Germany even thought of doing during the Hitler regime. The question was raised by Dietrich Bonhoeffer, but was deemed too embarrassing for the Confessing Church to handle. This was one reason why he left Germany in 1939 for the United States. When he returned shortly after, his position had also shifted. Thus, it is understandable that many in the churches, some who had fought against Hitler in the Second World War, found the Hammanskraal Resolution exceedingly difficult to accept. It is not difficult to imagine, then, how the bulk of the white population felt.

Thirdly, the Hammanskraal Statement advocated a "situational pacifism." As Douglas Bax subsequently indicated: "The Hammanskraal resolution does not proceed from a perfectionist, pacifist point of view but from the point of view that seems to take seriously the ethical approach which is called selective pacifism."[47] The position adopted depends on how unjust a particular situation is regarded. But this is a very difficult position to adopt with any consistency. Granted that South Africa is an unjust society, can this not be said about most other countries as well? If it is a matter of degree, by what criteria do we determine that a society has become sufficiently unjust to make conscientious objection a Christian obligation? And who, in these days of a divided church, is to decide when this is the case?

Fourthly, not only had the churches done little thinking on the question of conscientious objection prior to Hammanskraal, they had also given virtually no attention to the actual legislation on military service currently existing in the country and affecting the lives of many young people. This made it very difficult for them to respond to the Defense Further Amendment Bill when this was published in the Houses of Parliament. Fortunately, the situation has since improved, and considerable reflection and some research is enabling the churches to deal with the issues today. The perceptive analysis by Dr. James Moulder in a brief to the Episcopal Synod of the Church of the Province is worth noting.[48] According to Dr. Moulder, South African law "allows a conscientious objector to be a *conscientious noncombatant;* that is, it allows him to be exempted from combat training in the South African Defense Force. But it does not allow him to be a *conscientious non-militarist:* that is, it does not allow him to be exempted from every kind of military service whatsoever." In this respect, South African law is virtually the same as that which pertains in most Western countries, although the penalty of three years imprisonment for conscientious objection is more severe than in most other countries. It is Moulder's contention that the authorities have been relatively liberal in their interpretation of the law with regard to those who wish to be conscientious non-combatants. Religious reasons for not bearing arms are generally accepted. But there is no alternative to military service in a noncombatant role, unless there are medical or similar reasons involved.

The Hammanskraal Statement did not ask the churches to adopt a pacifist position but to consider whether or not in the South African situation conscientious objection and military chaplaincies should not be rethought. The results have been reasonably positive. The churches have supported the SACC Resolution by asking the state to reconsider the position of the conscientious objector. The state has not complied with this request; in fact, it has increased the penalties for both advocating and adopting the position. But the churches are united in maintaining that conscientious objection is a valid Christian option. Among the many church resolutions which might be quoted, the Catholic bishops' statement of February, 1977, reads:

> We defend the right of every individual to follow his own conscience, the right therefore to conscientious objection both on the grounds of universal pacifism and on the grounds that he seriously believes the war to be unjust. In this, as in every other matter, the individual is obliged to make a moral judgment in terms of the facts at his disposal after trying to ascertain these facts to the best of his ability. While we recognise that the conscientious objector will have to suffer the consequences of his own decision and the penalties imposed by the State, we uphold his right to do this and we urge the State to make provision for alternative forms of non-military national service as is done in other countries in the world.[49]

This statement expresses well the mind of the other churches belonging to the council.

The churches have also taken a fresh and serious look at the military chaplaincy. The debates in the synods during 1976 and 1977 were as heated on this matter as any on the Program to Combat Racism. Apart from the question of providing pastoral care for members of the churches, the question of patriotism loomed large. On the whole, black members have been against and white members for continued chaplaincies, but the issue has not been primarily the rightness of having chaplains in the military. Rather, it has been the one-sided nature of such ministry. The chaplaincy's identification with the South African army makes it virtually impossible for it to minister to opposing forces. The consensus of the non-Dutch Reformed churches is that military chaplains should be appointed, but that, as the Episcopal Synod said, "The Church must minister pastorally both to men in the SADF [South African Defense Force] and to those opposing them."[50] In the words of a resolution of the Assembly of the United Congregational Church, "The Church must ensure that those on both sides of the operational front lines ... receive the ministry of Christ."[51] These concerns of the churches have thus far received a sympathetic hearing from the Chaplain General of the South African Defense Force.[52] The churches believe that the command of Jesus to love both neighbor and enemy, which is not conducive to blind patriotic obedience, remains the command of the Lord of the church for Christians in South Africa today.

In this chapter several important themes and issues have emerged that require theological reflection. The problem of church and state has become more acute than before, as seen in the banning of the Christian Institute, the reaction of the government to the SACC and its member churches following the publication of the *Message,* and its response to the WCC Program to Combat Racism and to the Hammanskraal Statement on Conscientious Objection. As we have seen, the Prime Minister was personally involved on a number of occasions. The question of the church's involvement in social change was also raised, especially by Spro-cas and related programs. Related to this are further questions concerning the economic order of society, problems of labor, human rights, and a host of similar thorny issues. All of these directly affect the lives of people, and people are the concern of the church. Moreover, today South Africans find themselves in a situation of growing violent confrontation both within and outside the country. The Program to Combat Racism and the question of conscientious objection have forced the churches to a new and urgent consideration of violence and nonviolence.

Another theme, less explicitly dealt with in this chapter, but present throughout, is the renewal of black protest and struggle within the churches, within the country, and through external anti-apartheid organizations. Related to this is the gradual change in white consciousness as the whole situation in southern Africa undergoes remarkable and swift change. It is to these latter issues of black protest and white awareness that we must now turn, before reflecting more fully on the questions of social change and the political responsibility of the church in our final chapter.

4

Black Renaissance,
Protest, and Challenge

Black Consciousness and Theology

BLACK PROTEST in South Africa died down in the wake of
Sharpeville, with the banning of the African National Congress and the Pan African Congress, due largely to the growing strength of state internal security measures. Many
within the black community, especially of the generation
that had borne the brunt of the early years of apartheid and
struggle, despaired of meaningful change. Albert Lutuli was
banned, Robert Sobukwe and Nelson Mandela, together
with other leaders, were imprisoned on Robben Island, and
many others went overseas into exile or into the shadowy
world of the political underground in South Africa itself.

By the mid-sixties, however, there were some black
community leaders who were reluctantly and cautiously
prepared to consider the only option that now seemed open
to them—working through the system of separate development. Some avowed apartheid critics, such as Chief Gatsha
Buthelezi of Kwazulu, finally accepted that they had no
other alternative but to take at least part of what was being
offered to them by the government. Often they did this with
the declared intention of exploiting the system as much as

possible for the sake of their people, and ultimately as a means of destroying the very policy of apartheid itself. They were unequivocal about the fact that their working through the system was not intended as a compromise with apartheid. As most of these homeland leaders were devout members of their respective churches, this espousal of separate development, however critical, implied that at some point in the future, church opposition to government policy would be affected. Present developments indicate that this is so, but it is still too early to ascertain how the churches will handle this problem, made more intense by the rise of black consciousness and its relationship to the churches.

About the same time as the reluctant acceptance of separate development was gaining ground within some black quarters, another movement was beginning to emerge mainly among younger urban blacks who categorically rejected the role of the black homeland leaders. Ironically, this new generation was largely the product of separate development, unlike their parents, unlike the members of the African National Congress and the Pan African Congress, and unlike the homeland leaders. The recently founded black ethnic universities of Zululand, the North, Durban-Westville, and the Western Cape, together with Fort Hare, were producing a new generation of leaders reared in terms of government policy. One result of this separate education was that these new leaders had little meaningful contact with white people. As a result, they were suspicious of all whites—Nationalists, because of apartheid, liberals, because they appeared only theoretically concerned about the black struggle. Thus, this rising generation of blacks became increasingly committed to the politics of polarization as the first necessary step in destroying the fabric of apartheid: "Black man, you're on your own!"

If they felt on their own in South Africa, however, they did not feel out of touch with what was happening in the rest of the world, especially in Africa and North America. The idea of negritude, so powerfully expressed by such African leaders as Leopold Senghor, joined the black cry for political freedom with the song of personal discovery. In Africa, the sixties saw the culmination of decolonization and independence throughout most of the continent. Where colonial authorities were reluctant to hand over power, black liberation movements and guerrilla armies were formed to win independence by force. By the end of the decade, these movements were gaining in momentum, world-wide support, and effectiveness, and were beginning to make headway in southern Africa itself. In the United States, the sixties witnessed the civil rights struggle. While this was not a fight against colonial oppression, it was a confrontation with white racism that finally paid off. Like the struggle for *uhuru* in Africa, it was also part of the growing consciousness among black people everywhere that their rights had been trampled on for too long, and that there was nothing inferior about their own culture and identity.

Black South Africans did not have to be told by outsiders that their own rights and dignity had been crushed by racism, nor that their culture was thought to be second-class to that of whites. But they had to be made more aware of what their identity meant, and of their potential for changing the situation in which they lived. Black consciousness aimed at doing precisely this.

Its youthful leaders grew increasingly aware of what had happened within their own community since Sharpeville, and were determined that they were not going either to opt out of the struggle or to espouse separate development. Moreover, they were very much the product of a rapidly changing urban environment. Whereas many of their elders were born in the rural areas, with all that that meant in terms of cultural and kinship ties, this younger generation by and large was born and brought up in townships such as Soweto, Umlazi, New Brighton, and Langa. Cultural roots remained important, but the process of detribalization had made its impact. The binding factor in this new situation was not tribal identity but black awareness of the dehumanizing power of apartheid. Separate development might promise something in the distant, rural homelands, but it held out little hope for urban blacks. Thus, black consciousness, formulated and guided by student leaders such as Steve Biko, sought to raise the level of awareness within the black community—awareness of their situation and identity as blacks, and of their potential to change their lot.

Within a remarkably short time, the black consciousness movement injected a potent dynamism into South African social and political life. It provided a bridge across ethnic divisions within the black community, binding in one all African, Coloured, and Indian students who rejected separate development, and who were striving for alternative ways of combating apartheid. And while it started off mainly as a youth movement, it soon gained adherents across the generation gap. But this success inevitably meant that the movement had to face the full impact of government action, and eventually the elimination of much of its leadership. However, this did not happen until after black consciousness had already made a tremendous impact upon both South African society in general, as well as the churches, and upon the black community in particular.

The churches, especially those associated with the SACC, could not avoid being affected by this black renaissance. Eventually even the DRC, and especially its black "daughter" churches, did not escape its impact. In the first place, many of the black students and their leaders, like the homeland leaders, were members of these churches. Some were even seminarians. In the second place, the awakening of black consciousness and the struggle for political rights were rooted in Christian convictions. Blacks were taking seriously the gospel they had heard preached concerning God's love and grace for all, irrespective of race or color, and concerning his purposes of justice. Black consciousness was a spiritual reawakening which drew its resources from Christianity, but also discovered new meaning in African culture, which, for many, was closer to Christianity than European culture. Speaking about this, Manas Buthelezi, a Lutheran theologian, declared:

> In a very real and special sense this decade marks the beginning of a 'Black Renaissance'. Never before now have black people been so successful in retrieving the image of their blackness from the dung-heap of colour prejudice and a maze of stat-

utes that make it difficult for the black man to be proud of his colour. Never before now have black people derived inspiration and strength, not in possessing military might, wealth or constitutional power—for all these are denied them—but in delving into the immeasurable resources of the liberating gospel and exploiting that which God has implanted in their souls.[1]

A third reason for church involvement in black consciousness was the existence of black theology, which gained considerable prominence through the University Christian Movement (UCM) in the late sixties.

Before discussing the significance of black theology it is necessary to clarify the terms black consciousness, black power, and black theology. Dr. Allan Boesak has helpfully summed up their meaning as follows:

> *Black Consciousness* may be described as the awareness of black people that their humanity is constituted by their blackness. It means that black people are no longer ashamed that they are black, that they have a black history and a black culture distinct from the history and culture of white people. It means that blacks are determined to be judged no longer by, and to adhere no longer to white values. It is an attitude, a way of life. Viewed thus, Black Consciousness is an integral part of Black Power. But *Black Power* is also a clear critique of and a force for fundamental change in systems and patterns in society which oppress or which give rise to the oppression of black people. *Black Theology* is the reflection of black Christians on the situation in which they live and on their struggle for liberation.[2]

There is, then, an integral relationship between black consciousness, power, and theology. Yet, they can and must be distinguished. Black theologians vary in the way they handle this relationship, but it is no different from the traditional problem of Christ and culture. Their respective positions reflect the different ways this problem has been resolved by Christians throughout the centuries.

The earliest articulation of black theology under that title was primarily the work of American theologian James Cone.[3] By the end of the sixties, Cone's original expositions of the subject were widely known to black theological students in South Africa, stimulating their own search for an authentic theology and Christianity related to their personal experience. The Federal Theological Seminary of the Anglican, Congregational, Methodist, and Presbyterian Churches, situated then in Alice near the University of Fort Hare, as well as the Lutheran seminary in Mapumulo, Natal, and the Catholic seminary at Hammanskraal, were all places where black theology was debated, and sometimes taught.

Though influenced by James Cone and others, black students of theology were not content to import theologies from elsewhere. They sought to develop a theology which spoke directly to their own condition. In this they found special help and support from the UCM and its General Secretary, Dr. Basil Moore, a white Methodist minister. A special Black Theology Project was soon established in the UCM, and this became the major focus of the movement.

The UCM was formed by the English-speaking churches in 1966, shortly after the Student Christian Association changed its constitution and divided into separate ethnic organizations. At the same time, the SCA adopted a conservative evangelical statement of belief which excluded some members of the churches from holding office. For these reasons, especially the first, the English-speaking churches decided to launch their own student movement in the universities.

The story of the UCM is full of controversy. Within a short time, it had adopted a radical theological position at once removed from conservative evangelicalism and its supporting churches. Apart from some of the leaders, not many students went along with this avant-garde theology, or with some of its expressions in liturgy and lifestyle. Certainly the supporting churches felt uneasy about much of it. There was more support for the UCM in its attempt to bridge the racial gap between students, for this, after all, was the major reason for rejecting the reorganization of the SCA. But the radical approach adopted soon brought the UCM to the harassing attention of the government, and eventually led to its being investigated by the Schlebusch/Le Grange Commission of Inquiry in 1972. By then, however, the movement had already disbanded.

By the end of the sixties, the UCM was largely a black students' movement. Most white students had withdrawn from active participation because of the emphasis placed upon black consciousness and black theology within the movement. The mood among black students was very much one of polarization. The National Union of South African Students, a liberal multiracial organization, split down the middle in 1969 when black students under the leadership of people such as Steve Biko moved out to form SASO, the South African Students' Organization. Biko's personal pilgrimage was typical of many black students. His role as a leader began in the black Student Christian Movement at the University of Natal's medical school. A committed Christian, Biko grew disillusioned with both the churches and liberalism as agents of change, but he was deeply influenced by the Christian tradition and the development of black theology. Indeed, it was at a UCM Conference that Biko and others first conceived of the need to form SASO, of which he then became president. One of the ironies in this black withdrawal and consolidation was that this went completely counter to the original vision of UCM as envisaged by the churches; it was, in fact, spawned by the racial policies of the government. Separate ethnic universities promoted polarization. A further irony, from our later perspective, is that since that time the SCA has increasingly encouraged multiracial programs and become more committed to social witness.

During 1971 the UCM conducted, in various parts of the country, a series of seminars on black theology, which resulted in the publication of the first South African book on the subject, *Essays in Black Theology*.[4] The seminars succeeded in bringing black theology to the attention of the public and the churches. One reason for this was that the distinguished Bishop of Zululand, Alphaeus Zulu, was arrested during one of the seminars on a technical pass-law offense. Another reason was the banning of *Essays in Black Theology*, as well as the subsequent banning of leaders within the UCM and the Black Theology Project, including Basil Moore and the director of the project, Sabelo Ntwasa. But no matter how many people and publications were banned—and essays on the subject soon proliferated—nothing could prevent the development of black theology.[5] Seldom has a new theological movement achieved such publicity. From then on, it simply could not be pushed under church carpets, escape the vigilance of the authorities, or fail to influence the black community.

Whatever its immediate cause, in an important sense black theology in South Africa began with the revolt of black Christians at the turn of the century, a revolt which found institutional expression in the African independent churches. Black theology is rooted in the on-going search by black Christians for authentic expressions of Christianity in Africa. For this reason, it is wrong to suggest that there is a fundamental difference between what is now called African Christian theology and black theology.[6] The latter is one expression of the former. As such, it is in continuity with it, while also breaking fresh ground in the search for Christian witness and thought. This new development has been demanded by changes in the existential experience of blacks in South Africa. It is inseparable from black consciousness.

The integral connection between African and black theologies in South Africa distinguishes them from much African theology in other parts of the continent, and from most American black theology. Black theology as a theology of liberation is not presently of particular relevance in decolonized Africa. There the search is for an indigenous theology relevant to African culture. African theologies of indigenization, on the other hand, have not been of great importance for black theology in America, because there the problem has been regarded as the need for liberation from white domination. In South Africa both concerns come together. Black theology, like the implicit theology of the African independent churches, is a theology of indigenization, but it is decidedly more than that. It is primarily a theology of contextualization. Indigenization describes the attempt to ensure that Christianity becomes rooted in African culture. Culture here refers to language, music, and lifestyle. Contextualization, however, is more embracing. A contextual theology has to wrestle with the socio-political and economic

situation. It is this which provides the context for the life
and mission of the church. In black theology in South Africa
these two streams come together—the concern for cultural
indigenization and the struggle for liberation from socio-
political bondage.

An interesting and helpful illustration of this relationship between indigenization and contextualization in black
theology is seen in the concept of communalism. In traditional African society, personal identity has always been
societal, with strong emphasis on the kinship system. Kinship ties played an important role in the emergence of the
African independent churches, for they supported such ties,
or else, in detribalized situations, provided the sense of belonging so fundamental to African society. Black theology
likewise sees the importance of the kinship system and relates it to the biblical concept of "corporate personality."
This concept was made explicit in a paper given at one of the
black theology seminars in 1971, when Bonganjalo Goba
compared the biblical and the African ideas:

> What we discover in the concept as it manifests itself in Israel
> and Africa is the unique idea of solidarity, a social conscious-
> ness that rejects and transcends individualism. Apart from
> this, one discovers a unique sense of a dynamic community, a
> caring concern that seeks to embrace all, a love that suffers
> selflessly for others.[7]

Under the growing impact of colonization, urbanization, and
racial discrimination, African communalism and solidarity
have suffered severely in South Africa. It was Goba's concern and contention that black theology would help to re-
store this fundamental biblical and African idea within contemporary society. This is very important for understanding
black theology, for black solidarity is of its essence. It rejects
any attempt to divide the black community along ethnic or
denominational lines, and hence rejects separate development.

What, then, is black theology as understood by black
theologians in South Africa? Manas Buthelezi answers: It
"comes out of an attempt to characterise by means of a word
or phrase the reflection upon the reality of God and his Word

which grows out of that experience of life in which the category of blackness has some existential decisiveness."[8] The use of the word "black" to qualify theology is not intended as racialism in reverse, nor even to suggest a new theology. "Because the word *black*," writes Elliot Mgojo, "has been given such a negative connotation there is a further assumption that Black Theology cannot be good theology. Interestingly enough, our interrogators do not question the legitimacy of British, German, American and Afrikaner theologies as valid expressions of Christian theology although they are identified with specific *cultures* and national entities."[9] Black theology is "an attempt by black Christians to grasp and think through the central claims of the Christian faith in the light of black experience."[10]

In order to understand this emphasis on "blackness," white people have to realize how much black people have been dehumanized because of their color. Color has become the crucial quality for determining the identity of people. Although the term "non-white" has gone out of vogue, when black theology originated, "non-white" was still the main way of describing black people. Hence blacks felt the need to stress "blackness." Manas Buthelezi put it perceptively when he said:

> The fact that Africans, Indians and Coloureds have been collectively referred to as "non-whites" in official terminology suggests that they have the identity of non-persons who exist only as negative shadows of whites. In a theological sense this means that they were created in the image of the white man and not of God. I am aware of the fact that many people never think of the theological significance of calling us non-whites. The practical consequence of this "non-white theology" has been the belief that "non-whites" can be satisfied with the "shadows" of things the white men take for granted when it comes to their needs. Hence "non-whites" have not had a meaningful share in the substance of the power and wealth of the land and they were treated to the shadow of the substance. There was therefore a need for the substitution of a "non-white" theology with a "black theology" or a theology of the image of God in order to put the question of human identity in a proper theological perspective.[11]

This emphasis on "black" has often been misunderstood and misrepresented by critics of black theology. Although some black theologians, especially in North America, have made "blackness" into some kind of basic criterion for Christian faith and action, this is certainly not true of black theology in South Africa. Allan Boesak has made this quite clear in his criticism of James Cone. For Boesak, as for most others, "black" has to do with the existential situation, not with the criterion of theology: "The black situation is the situation within which reflection and action takes place, but it is the Word of God which illuminates the reflection and guides the action."[12] It is vital to understand this, for otherwise it is impossible to appreciate the evangelical conviction and motivation of black theologians in South Africa.

Similarly, it is important to clarify the connection between black theology and liberation theology, since most black theologians expressly make this connection. Liberation theology is an umbrella term. There is no definitive theology of liberation; indeed, there are significant differences between the various theologians who regard themselves as liberation theologians. These differences are evident especially in ecclesiology, that is, the study of the nature and task of the church, and on the issue of the relationship between Christian faith and ideology, notably Marxism. Little wonder, then, that liberation theology means different things to different people. To equate black theology with it without qualification is misleading. Black theologians in South Africa, for example, unlike some Latin Americans, have never advocated any ideological alliance with Marxism.

Thus, it is difficult to generalize. Black theology in South Africa is not identical with Latin American liberation theology. By its very contextual nature it cannot be. It is therefore wrong automatically to level the same criticisms at black theology as may be levelled at Latin American theologies of liberation. Yet, black theology is *a* theology of liberation. There is a clear connection. "For us," writes Ephraim Mosothoane, "liberation as a theological theme represents a central element in today's theological contextualisation."[13] Desmond Tutu expresses his understanding of black theology as a liberation theology in this way:

> I count Black Theology in the category of liberation theologies. I would hope that my White fellow Christian theologians would recognise the bona fides of Black and therefore liberation theology, since I don't want us to break fellowship or cease our dialogue. I desire this earnestly. But I want to say this with great deliberation and circumspection. I will not wait for White approbation before I engage in Black or liberation theology, nor will I desist from being so engaged while I try to convince my White fellow Christian about the validity of Black or liberation theology, for I believe that the Black or liberation theology exponent is engaged in too serious an enterprise to afford that kind of luxury. He is engaged in gut-level issues, in issues of life and death. This sounds melodramatic, but, you see, in the face of an oppressive White racism, it is not a merely academic issue for my Black people when they ask "God, on whose side are you?" "God, are you Black or White?" "Is it possible to be Black and Christian at the same time?" These are urgent questions, and I must apply whatever theological sensitivity and ability I have trying to provide some answers to them under the Gospel. Indeed I will subject my efforts to the criticism of fellow Christians and will attempt to pay heed to their strictures; but I will not be held back because they withhold their approval. For one thing, it is an evangelical task that is laid on me to ensure that the Black consciousness movement should succeed, and I will not be deterred by governmental disapproval or action. Because, for me, it is a crucial matter that Black consciousness succeeds as a theological and evangelical factor because I believe fervently that no reconciliation is possible in South Africa, except reconciliation between real persons. Black consciousness merely seeks to awaken the Black person to a realisation of his worth as a child of God, with the privileges and responsibilities that are the concomitants of that exalted status.[14]

Black theology is a theology of liberation both in its basic methodology and its content. While, in the words of Manas Buthelezi, black theology is "nothing but a methodological technique of theologizing,"[15] this technique inevitably affects what theology says, that is, its content. Theology as Buthelezi and others understand it, cannot be separated from what God is presently doing in history, and therefore from the task of the church in the world today. Black theology is not a theoretical exercise trying to get at philosophical truths. It is reflection on "doing the truth," that is, on "praxis," in obedience to the gospel amid the realities of contemporary suffering, racism, oppression, and everything else that denies the lordship of Christ.

Like all dynamic theologies that attempt to relate the Word of God to the human situation, black theology has both a negative, critical thrust and a positive, constructive dimension. It is a theology of protest against apartheid, but it is also one of liberating reconstruction.

In the first place, then, the gospel provides the black theologian with the tools for critique. It dissects the dehumanizing power of apartheid, and brings a word of judgment upon the structures which embody this power. It challenges white domination in the church, liberal elitism, cheap reconciliation, economic injustice, and pseudo-multiracialism. In short, it protests against the destruction of the Christian faith because of racism, especially as this manifests itself in social structures. Black theologians in South Africa are deeply conscious of the fact that Christianity is on trial in the black community because it has too often been experienced as a white person's religion and a means of black subjugation. Christianity has to be liberated from every form of racial bondage if it is to speak meaningfully to blacks of today and tomorrow.

Manas Buthelezi spelled this out with great effect at the South African Congress on Mission and Evangelism in 1973. Speaking on the subject of evangelism in the South African context, he proposed the following six theses:

1. The future of the Christian faith in this country will largely depend on how the Gospel proves itself relevant to the existential problems of the Black man. This is so not only because the blacks form the majority in the South African population, but also because Christendom in this country is predominantly black. Almost all the churches have more blacks than whites in national membership. This means that the whites currently wield ecclesiastical power out of proportion with their numerical strength.

2. The whites in as far as they have incarnated their spiritual genius in the South African economic and political institutions have sabotaged and eroded the power of Christian love. While professing to be traditional custodians and last bulwarks in Africa of all that goes under the name of Christian values, the Whites have unilaterally and systematically rejected the black man as some one to whom they can relate with any degree of personal intimacy in daily life and normal ecclesiastical situation. They have virtually rejected the black man as a brother. Love can never be said to exist where normal fellowship is banned. Christian love is one of the most misunderstood Christian concepts in South Africa. This has created credibility problems not only for white men as messengers of the Gospel, but also for the Gospel itself. The days for the white man to tell the black man about the love of God are rapidly decreasing as the flood of daily events increases the credibility gap.

3. For the sake of the survival of the Christian faith it is urgently necessary that the black man must step in to save the situation. He should now cease playing the passive role of the white man's victim. It is now time for the black man to evangelize and humanize the white man. The realization of this will not depend on the white man's approval, but solely on the black man's love for the white man. From the black man's side this will mean the retrieval of Christian love from the limitations of the white man's economic and political institutions.

4. For this to be a reality it is imperative for the black man to reflect upon the Gospel out of his experience as a black man in order to discover its power as a liberating factor for him as well as for the white man. The black man needs to be liberated from the white man's rejection so that the white man's rejection may cease to be a decisive factor in the process of the black man's discovery of his human worth and potential. He needs to see his own blackness as a gift of God instead of the biological scourge which the white man's institutions have made it to be. The white man will be liberated from the urge to reject the black man in that his rejection will be rendered irrelevant and inconsequential.

5. The black theologian must therefore discover a theological framework within which he can understand the will and love of God in Jesus Christ outside the limitations of the white man's institutions. He is the only one best equipped to interpret the Gospel out of the depths of the groanings and aspirations of his fellow black people.

6. The future of evangelism in South Africa is therefore tied to the quest for a theology that grows out of the black man's ex-

perience. It will be from this theological vantage point that the black man will contribute his own understanding of Christian love and its implications in evangelism.[16]

These theses probe deeply into the sickness of society and the way in which the dominant white Christian culture too often becomes captive to the system. They declare that the bondage of black people is concomitant with the bondage of white people to a social, political, and economic system contrary to the gospel. The theses stress that blacks, who make up the bulk of the churches, have heard the gospel of Christ's liberating power. Therefore, the theses call on blacks to claim their freedom in Christ, both for their own sakes and for the sake of the future of the gospel in South Africa. This, in turn, will enable whites to hear again the good news of their own liberation. Of course, black theologians are aware that liberation has to do with more than socio-political bondage. It is "fundamentally liberation from sin to which we are all (oppressed and oppressors alike) in bondage; it means a readiness to forgive, and a refusal to be consumed by hate, a refusal to conform to worldly standards; it means reminding the oppressed that we do have a common humanity which has, as Paul declares, made us all fall short of the Glory of God; and that this means we should not forget that the oppressed of today become the oppressors of tomorrow."[17]

Protest against injustice and racism is only the first word of black theology, and though it is the most dominant emphasis at present, it is really only the clearing of the ground for the positive message of liberation and renewal. In the second place, then, black theology speaks of black freedom and the recovery of black dignity and solidarity, primarily within the Christian community, but also within the black community as a whole. Like other liberation theologians, the exponents of black theology regard the exodus as the paradigmatic event in God's dealings with the world, an event which finds its culmination and fulfillment in the gospel of the resurrection of Jesus Christ from the dead. According to these events, it is clearly God's purpose to set people free from bondage, and to make "all things new." While this purpose cannot be realized in any ultimate sense in this life and present history, it is not unrelated to the here and now. The ministry and message of Jesus make it abundantly clear that the gospel intends life to be lived to the full. Jesus came to make people whole in every facet of their lives, as individuals and in society.

Boesak refers to the persistent temptation to spiritualize Christianity. Reflecting on Jesus' sermon in the synagogue at Nazareth, he remarks on the fact that most Western commentators have so spiritualized what Jesus said, that they have destroyed what he meant:

> The spiritualization we have indicated not only compartmentalizes life, but also leads to a distortion of the gospel message which then serves to sanction unjust structures and relations. It forces Jesus and his message into a western, white mould, degrades him to a servant of mere self-interest, identifies him with oppression. It makes the gospel an instrument of injustice instead of the expectation of the poor.[18]

Drawing on the Old Testament concept of jubilee as an interpretative clue for the ministry of Jesus, Boesak says: "There is not a single aspect of the life of Israel that is not confronted with the demand for liberation. This is what Black Theology calls the 'wholeness of life' and 'total liberation'. This is the scope within which the gospel should be understood, proclaimed and lived."[19]

Critics of black theology have been quick to label it as a heresy, "another gospel." Certainly, as we shall indicate, black theology is by no means beyond criticism, but we must pause before we use the label "heresy" too readily. That some theologies so distort the gospel that they become destructive of Christian faith is beyond doubt, but, as Manas Buthelezi has reminded us, the New Testament itself distinguishes between "salutary and destructive" heresies. Addressing a major theological conference of the Church Unity Commission in South Africa, Buthelezi referred to the fact that "heresy," strictly speaking, means "to choose," that is, to take a position. In this sense, since all theology takes sides and is inevitably inadequate to its subject, it is all one-sided in some respect, and therefore open to the charge of heresy. The question is whether or not a particular theology points towards or away from Jesus Christ. Buthelezi remarks:

> For our purpose, this means that mutual acceptance involves taking seriously each other's heresies and incorporating them as legitimate subjects for our ecumenical discussion. This is to say, in other words, that we should use as points of departure not only the 16th century insights but also what is being articulated today, e.g. the insights of black theology or liberation theology. Then when our children sing the hymn "Faith of our Fathers living Still", they will also think of the contribution of South African blacks.[20]

The fact is that at this historical moment, for many black Christians, "Black Theology is not only 'part of' the gospel, or 'consistent with' the gospel, it *is* the gospel of Jesus Christ."[21] In other words, there is no sense here of destroying Christian faith, but of restoring it. For the black theologian, the false gospel is that which dehumanizes people because of their race. The true gospel judges this distortion of Christianity and sets people free to be the "children of God."

Perhaps the most important point on which black theologians in South Africa appear to differ is on how to relate their theology to political issues in the situation.[22] Boesak, as we saw, maintained an integral relationship between black theology, black consciousness, and black power. For him they are inseparable entities. Others are more cautious. Without denying the political implications of black theology, Elliot Mgojo says he does not want it to become "a mere instrument of propaganda for certain political ends."[23] But Boesak would agree with that too, for he, like the others, is as aware of the dangers of ideological captivity from the black side as he is of the dangers from the white. Buthelezi puts it sharply:

> To interpret the quest for a Black Theology purely in terms of the awakening of black nationalism or the consolidation of Black Power forces us to trifle with one of the most fundamental issues in modern Christianity. We know that this not uncommon appraisal of the phenomenon of the quest for a Black Theology is often expressed in pejorative phrases calculated to call in question the theological integrity of the quest itself.[24]

Buthelezi is clearly *not* saying that Christian faith is unconcerned about politics. As we have already seen, black theology arises out of black reflection on the biblical message from within the socio-political context. It involves no dualistic spiritualization of the gospel. But for black theology it is the Christian faith that determines how to relate to the socio-political situation, not the situation which determines the faith.

Ironically, black theology is, in principle, not that much different from Calvinism as expressed by many DRC theologians. In fact, for Boesak, as a Reformed theologian, black theology is Reformed theology arising out of the context of black Christianity. As black theologians indicate, Calvinism has played precisely the same role in the historical struggles of the Afrikaner as black theology is playing in that of the black community. "It is the same message of the Bible," writes Manas Buthelezi, "which inspired the spirit of the Afrikaner ... which is motivating us to sing the song of Black Theology."[25] There would be something wrong with black Christianity if it did not relate to the needs and hopes of black people. But the crucial question for black theology is one that was raised by Professor Keet for the Afrikaner, and now by theologians such as Boesak for blacks: Is it politics and culture which determines theology and practice, or is it the other way around? Is the Word of God the norm, or is culture and ideology?

Reflecting on the similarity between Afrikaner religion and black theology, Dutch Reformed theologian David Bosch asks: "Theology must be contextual, that is true, but may it ever be exclusive? We have to ask in all seriousness whether the category 'people' or 'nation' may be the object of the church's concern for liberation. 'People' as cultural and ethnic entity is *not* a theological category and wherever it is made into such a category (as an 'ordinance of creation' or 'God-given distinctive entity') it cannot but lead to mutual exclusiveness which endangers the life of the church as the new community."[26] The focus of redemption in the Scriptures is the people of God. Can we then make use of the Christian gospel as a tool in the liberation of an ethnic group? Dr. Bosch's position has been attacked by both Afrikaner and black theologians, the former in defense of separate development, the latter in advocating the role of Christianity in the cultural and political struggles of the black community. But Bosch's warning needs to be taken seriously. The real danger in any alliance between faith and ideology, Christ and culture, is that the gospel becomes exclusive in a false sense, and the nature of the church as the body of Christ becomes radically distorted. This does not mean that "the people" or culture is unimportant, but that they are relative and not determinative for the Christian faith. It is at this point that Allan Boesak expresses a basic disagreement with James Cone. Unlike some forms of Latin American liberation theology, both Boesak and Cone regard the covenant relationship between God and his people as essential to the biblical message of liberation, but whereas Cone virtually confines the covenant community to blacks, Boesak expressly does not. He rejects any notion of a black Christian nationalism.[27]

As we have now shown, black theology in South Africa is neither beyond criticism, nor is it without inner tensions. Its leading exponents are not uncritical of their efforts,[28] but they are convinced that black theology is a valid and necessary expression of the Christian faith in South Africa today. They are also increasingly aware, along with others, that their understanding of the gospel has implications beyond the black community itself. Before commenting on that, however, it is well to remember that black theology in South Africa is not an academic exercise. It is a direct challenge to the system of apartheid and separate development. As such, it involves a costly commitment on the part of those involved in it. Dr. Buthelezi has said that "What is significant about it is that its appearance has aroused anything from positive interest to alarm even outside the theological arena, especially among politicians. This proves beyond doubt its timely relevance. . . . "[29] One symbol of this relevance and its cost is the story of the Federal Theological Seminary in Alice, which was expropriated by the Government in 1974.

The Federal Theological Seminary (FEDSEM) was established in 1961 by the English-speaking churches for the training of their black candidates for ordination. While the churches were against segregated seminaries in principle, South African law gave them little option if such a seminary was to be residential. FEDSEM was built on a large tract of land donated by the Church of Scotland adjacent to the black University of Fort Hare in Alice. During its thirteen years in Alice, FEDSEM not only developed a good tradition in theological education, it also helped to stimulate black theological thinking related to the South African scene. An inevitable result was that students at Fort Hare found in FEDSEM a window on the world concerned about helping the black community fight racism. In 1974, however, the government decided to expropriate the land and buildings of the seminary for use by the university. In doing so, they not only went back on their word, but also aroused the anger and disgust of those who knew the story behind the headlines. An editorial in *South African Outlook* described the action of the state as follows:

> In expropriating the Seminary the Government is breaking its word; it is taking by force, nay violence, land which has belonged to the black community since long before white men came to this country; it is marching with hobnailed boots over the history of a people; it is highjacking the Church.[30]

There was little the churches could do to prevent this from taking place. Today, the seminary continues to exist in rented buildings in Pietermaritzburg, Natal, though it will shortly move onto its own campus nearby. Despite government compensation for the land and property in Alice, the churches have been penalized for providing the black community with spiritual leaders opposed to the system. But the churches have held fast to their convictions. In 1976 the Congregational and Presbyterian colleges at FEDSEM united to form the Albert Luthuli College, thereby honoring one who believed that the Christian faith is central to the black struggle for political rights.

It is our conviction that black theology is an authentic attempt to understand the gospel of Jesus Christ in South Africa, and to spell out its implications for witness and mission. No one, not even its opponents, can doubt its significance for the future of the gospel in our land. It is a tragedy, then, that many white Christians have too often overreacted, and seen it as a threat, rather than as a genuine attempt to express the Christian faith. This has meant that its creative possibilities have too often turned to protest, and its prophetic insights been rejected. It is important to realize that we are witnessing a result of the great missionary enterprise which, for all its faults, brought the gospel to South Africa in the first place. Like all theologies, it must not be allowed to turn in on itself or lose the ability of self-critique in the light of the Word of God, but it needs the freedom to express and fulfill itself for the sake of the church and society.

For a white South African Christian, black theology can and should have a significance which few have yet recognized. Whites have generally been critical of and closed to the possibility that God is speaking to his church through black prophets. Before we deal with this, however, we will need to consider the impact of Soweto upon white South Africa, for the word of the black theologian cannot be separated from the anguished cry of the black community.

Soweto: Symbol of Black Protest

UNTIL THE MIDDLE of 1976 the black township of Soweto, on the southwestern border of Johannesburg, was largely unknown outside of South Africa. In June that year, black students took to the streets in protest against government educational policies that required the use of Afrikaans in the teaching of high school subjects. Soon the original reason for the protest was largely forgotten, for by then Soweto was in turmoil and South Africa was confronted with a situation of graver significance than even Sharpeville. Within a very short time, young black students, as well as Coloureds and Indians, throughout the country joined in solidarity with their Soweto counterparts, especially in the sprawling townships of the eastern and western Cape. Soweto became

a symbol of protest against apartheid, a new symbol generated by young blacks who were no longer prepared to accept
the situation in which they found themselves.

Government action in Soweto and throughout the country was immediate and Draconian. Riot police were sent into
every troubled area. Soon there were reports of scores of
students killed or badly injured by police action. Hundreds
were arrested and detained. The action of the police became
the focal point for new waves of protest, and by this stage the
reticence of the older generations to join in with the students
had changed to support and participation. The ugly escalation of violence and counterviolence grew apace as the tactics of the authorities met with continued resistance and
rejection. The concerted attempts by black leaders to bring
order into the chaos were hamstrung time and again by
insensitivity on the part of government authorities and provocative police action as well as by continued boycotts of
schools and burnings of community buildings. Arrests and
detentions without trial added fuel to the fires. Though
there were periods of relative calm, sporadic outbursts of
protest indicated that the tension and conflict had by no
means been resolved. This state of uncertainty and violence
plagued the black townships of Johannesburg and elsewhere
for more than a year. A hiatus came with the death in September, 1977, of student leader Steve Biko, the arrests of
many black community leaders, and the bannings of October 19, 1977.

Soweto is such recent history that it is difficult to assess
its significance. As yet, the official government inquiry into
the event has not been published.[31] But few people, if any,
will deny that Soweto is a powerful symbol in the contemporary history of South Africa. As such, it is important for
understanding the struggle of the church.

First of all, Soweto has become an international symbol.
By the time of Biko's death, Soweto was already a household
word throughout much of Europe and North America. The
death of Biko gained prominence largely because of the
awakening of intense interest in South Africa and in young
blacks in the aftermath of Soweto. For the outsider, Soweto

stood for the total rejection of apartheid by blacks. It suggested that revolutionary change was only a matter of time. It reinforced all that the anti-apartheid movements in the Western world had been claiming through the years in their attempt to expose South Africa. Indeed, on the admission of government spokesmen, Soweto has done far more to damage the reputation of white South Africa than anything else in its history. It also has done far more to awaken sympathy and support for black South Africa than any political rhetoric has managed in the councils of the nations.

Secondly, Soweto is a symbol of a new generation of politicized blacks who are in revolt against the system of apartheid. Over the past few years, there have been other signs of black protest. The large-scale strikes by workers in Natal and confrontations on the mining compounds near Johannesburg from late 1972 onwards, are obviously of great significance. But they have not had the same impact on South African consciousness as Soweto, nor have they stirred the sympathetic imagination of others throughout the world. Soweto began as a children's crusade. Black students were protesting against their educational curriculum and system. But all of a sudden, the demonstration flared up into a situation of total confrontation on a massive scale. Observers in Soweto spoke of the bewildered spontaneity of the eruption. Everyone seemed surprised. But even more remarkable was the persistence and endurance of the protesters against immense police odds. Indeed, it is a remarkable thing that young people still at school virtually took on the might of the police force by themselves, and persisted in spite of heavy casualties. Hundreds were killed.

How are we to explain this? It is a dubious analysis to suggest that Soweto was the result of careful planning by the African National Congress or the Black People's Convention, or some other black political organization. Such bodies may have played a role during and afterwards, but it seems unlikely that they were the instigators of the protest. Soweto, it appears, was not the result of some organization's planning, but was part of an interconnected web of circumstances and events. And central to this was the rise and impact of black consciousness within and upon the black community. Soweto could not have happened if the message of black dignity and protest, a message which had its greatest impact upon young black students, had not been preached and heard during the years before it took place. Black school teachers have subsequently remarked on the fact that most of their pupils, even in junior school, were highly politicized. And if some were not politically aware before Soweto, they were soon deeply affected by it. This is a new phenomenon in the South African situation, and it is of tremendous consequence for the future. To use a Latin American term, the younger generation of blacks have been "conscienticized."

Thirdly, Soweto symbolizes the failure of separate development, especially in the urban areas. In an interview early in 1977, Bishop Manas Buthelezi, a resident of Soweto, made it clear that the Soweto protests went far beyond education. He stated:

> Separate Development is not acceptable to the black community. The recent happenings in Soweto were evidence of that. We would like to have a share in the decision-making process of the country. Even concerning separation; if we came together and then agreed that the solution is that we should separate, then separate development would have a moral basis. But now only one section says we must separate and dictates how we should separate. As a Christian I also find some problems with this.[32]

Fourthly, Soweto is a symbol of the violence that lurks so near the surface of our society. Many white South Africans have been living with an illusion in this regard. They have surveyed the major trouble spots of the world, Northern Ireland, the Middle East, Southeast Asia, and the long hot summers of black protests in the United States and elsewhere, and have concluded that there is an absence of violence in our own country. The facts are quite different, as both the government and those working for change clearly recognize. If this were not the case, there would have been no need for the vast array of security legislation and the immense strengthening of the police force and its powers.

The average white person had confused law and order with genuine peace, and so was caught by surprise when violence erupted in Soweto in 1976.

This myopic condition of many whites today is not surprising, given the movement towards isolation, the growth of censorship, and an unwillingness to face reality. It is true, of course, that the nationalist government has been able to maintain order during its thirty-year period in office, but order does not mean the absence of violence. Over the years, people have been banned, detained, imprisoned without trial, and have died, all for the sake of maintaining the present order. Unfortunately, too few whites are aware or even willing to become aware of this reality. Soweto was the overflowing of a volcano. What most whites have refused to acknowledge is the suppressed frustration and fury that lies beneath the surface in the black community. Soweto burst that illusion, at least for those willing to hear the anguished cry, and it indicated as never before the lateness of the hour.

Finally, Soweto is a powerful symbol of black protest against the church itself when it identifies with white power and white domination. Before exploring this challenge to white Christianity, however, let us consider how the churches themselves reacted to Soweto.

Shortly after the initial protests began in Soweto, the moderature of the General Synod of the DRC expressed itself as follows:

> To a great number of innocent people, White and Black, who suffered these losses, the Church expresses its sincere sympathy, and trusts that local church councils and other bodies charged with the task, will make the necessary support and emergency aid available. Further, the Church calls its members to a worthy plan of action in which the example of the Lord can be followed, and the Christian demand of love of God in one's neighbour can be practised. The younger churches are assured of our Church's sympathy and prayer in these times of tension.[33]

The leaders of the DRC also indicated that they would make representations to the government on the issues affecting Soweto and other townships. But there was little if any attempt to express an opinion on the underlying causes of Soweto, or on such matters as police action. This was not the case with the reaction of such churches as the Roman Catholic or those belonging to the South African Council of Churches.

Church leaders meeting in the Greater Durban Area on June 21, 1977, expressed their convictions by attempting to provide a "true interpretation of the riots":

> We urge all our members to listen to the anguished plea of Black people which has so often gone unanswered and has now resulted in violence. Though we deplore violence as a means of effecting change or of preventing change, we have little difficulty in understanding why such an explosion of rage has taken place. We realise, however, that many of our White Christians will not understand, and that they see in the riots an unjustified outburst. While we recognise that in any situation of violence irresponsible elements will be involved, we earnestly urge our members to take note of the deep groundswell of bitterness and resentment that exists among Black people throughout our country, and that can so easily be fanned into violence. If attention is not paid to well-known causes of that discontent, no amount of security legislation, repression, deportations, detentions or bannings will give this country genuine and lasting peace.[34]

On the subject of police responsibility, the church leaders said: "That there is profound hostility to the police in the black community may not be widely known among whites, but in all the legal harassment and suppression it experiences, the black community sees the police as agents of white power...."

It is unnecessary to quote from all the statements and resolutions uttered and adopted by the churches on the subject. Virtually all those who have been critical of apartheid over the years expressed sentiments similar to those of the Durban church leaders.[35] We shall refer to just two documents which seem to sum up the feelings of the churches. First of all, the following statement was issued by the General Secretariat of the South African Catholic Bishops' Conference in September, 1976, following the arrest of two black Catholic priests, Father S'mangaliso Mkhatshwa and Father

Clement Mokoko. After protesting their arrest, the statement went on to say:

> In expressing sympathy and solidarity with them, we express the same with dozens of others so detained under excessively harsh security laws against which we protested last year and also previously.... We consider the present wave of unrest sweeping the country to be at most the inevitable result of unjust and oppressive laws against which we with other churches have continually witnessed for almost three decades. We renew our protest against these laws in the strongest possible terms and urge that they be repealed forthwith. At the same time we request that it be recognised that the phenomenon of Black Consciousness correctly understood is an inevitable demand by the Black Community for recognition of their human dignity and legitimate aspirations. We appeal to the Government to relieve the present tension not by repressive acts but by rapid and practical moves towards full citizenship and shared responsibility.[36]

Secondly, we refer to the pastoral letter of the president of the Methodist Church, the Rev. Abel Hendricks, written in October, 1976:

> South Africa stands on the threshold of war and peace. The last three months have seen the outpouring of years of Black frustration, suppression and anger that has burst into manifestations of protests, strikes and peaceful marches, but also violence, death and destruction. The White *status quo* has in turn allowed their fear, confusion and ignorance of Black suffering and aspirations to manifest itself in violence, brutality and the detention of those crying out for liberation.... Time is running out and the Church of God must raise her voice for justice so that there may be peace. If we fail here, we will not only be disobeying the call of the Lord, to cry aloud and lift up our voices like a trumpet in declaring to our people their transgression (Isaiah 58:1), but we will be judged by history to be simply irrelevant....[37]

Clearly, the churches in opposition to apartheid saw the cause of the Soweto protests as apartheid itself. They regarded the escalation of violence as generated in varying degrees by the tactics of the police and the enforcement of security legislation.

Those churches which responded to Soweto in the way we

have just described have also been positive about the role of black consciousness itself. This does not necessarily mean that black consciousness has been approved without qualification, but neither does it mean that it has been rejected by the churches as contrary to Christian faith. On the contrary, in spite of government action against its proponents within and outside the churches, notably on October 19, 1977, an editorial in *Kairos,* the monthly paper of the South African Council of Churches, could state:

> Many Christians see Black Consciousness as being directly in line with the Biblical doctrine of creation—that all men are created in the image of God. This doctrine and concept has received particularly strong emphasis among Black South African Christians—something clearly attributable to their reaction to apartheid, which, even in its most sophisticated "separate freedom" guise, is still humiliating to Blacks.

Polarization, the editorial maintained, is not caused by black consciousness, but is the result of apartheid. It went on to say, "Indeed, it has been said by Afrikaner academics that in many ways Black Consciousness resembles the emergence of Afrikaner nationalism as a reaction to the humiliations imposed by British imperialism," and it concluded:

> Yet, in choosing the path of confrontation and seeking to bind Black Consciousness, the authorities will be shown in time to have been merely trying to wish away reality. Out of Christian convictions we and others will continue to accept Black Consciousness as naturally as we breathe. No State can prevail against a mass spiritual movement in the long run.[38]

Whatever the dangers of black consciousness, and whatever its significance for the black community, let us turn to the challenge it presents to white Christians in South Africa. In particular, the challenge focuses on two things. On the one hand, it raises the questions: How Christian have white Christians been in South Africa? Is it not they, perhaps, who need to be liberated? Has their Christianity become captive to their own interests, culture, and ideologies? On the other hand, it raises the question: What kind of society do white Christians want? In other words, it forces whites to face the implications of Christian faith for their own existence, and therefore for the structures of social life, human rights, and economic justice.

Another Perspective on White Christianity

LONG BEFORE the rise of liberation or black theology, or Marxist treatments of colonial history, black South Africans had the feeling that, whatever its benefits, the Christianity of the white settlers was concomitant with their sense of superiority and linked to their socio-economic dominance. The early opinions of leaders in the African independent churches provide evidence for that. And this feeling has been strengthened over the years. It was eventually given penetrating expression from a Christian perspective in Bishop Manas Buthelezi's "Six Theses on Evangelism," which we quoted earlier. Let us sum up our discussion thus far in this chapter by reflecting on South African history again, but this time attempting to see the development of Christianity and the church from the perspective of many black South Africans today.

The Dutch settlers regarded the indigenous peoples as culturally inferior heathen destined by God to be the "hewers of wood and the drawers of water" for their superior masters. The settlers prospered; the indigenous peoples and imported slaves suffered. The Christian faith seemed to provide the rationale necessary to justify the situation. As the white settler community pushed into the interior, notably at the time of the Great Trek, Christianity was used to justify and explain what happened.

Whatever the Christian virtues of most of the Trekkers, they were by no means missionary-minded, driven by a desire to evangelize the "heathen" in the interior. Indeed, Daniel Lindley, the American Board missionary in Natal, whom the Trekkers invited to be their pastor, wrote the following to his board in Boston in July, 1839, justifying his acceptance of the call:

> I do sincerely believe that the cheapest, speediest, easiest way
> to convert the heathen here is to convert the *white ones* first.
> More, the whites must be provided for, or we labour in vain to
> make Christians of the blacks. These two classes will come so
> fully and constantly in contact with each other, that the influ-
> ence of the whites, if evil, will be tremendous—will be irresist-
> ible, without a miracle to prevent. To their own vices the
> aborigines will add those of the white man, and thus make
> themselves two-fold more the children of hell than they were
> before.[39]

The Great Trek arose out of a desire for freedom from
British domination and out of the effects of the emancipation of the slaves, an emancipation regarded as detrimental
to Christian faith. The vision of the Trekkers was the establishment of a Calvinist republic in which neither white alien
nor black native would be eligible for a meaningful role in
the social and political life of the community.

A great deal has been written about the role of the
nineteenth-century European missionaries in South Africa.
They have been variously depicted as the defenders of the
blacks and the critics of the colonists. More recently it has
become fashionable to decry them as handmaidens of colonial power. The truth is far more complex than either of
these polar views will allow.[40] Yet, it seems clear that many
were at fault in at least two respects. First of all, they
were far too insensitive to African culture, and secondly,
they allowed themselves to be used by the agents of European
colonial expansion. The result of cultural insensitivity was
that the gospel contributed to the undermining of the foundations of African culture. The resultant identity crisis, has-
tened by urbanization and industrialization, was traumatic
for the African community. Once again, the rise of independent churches was a sign of missionary failure. The result of
being part of colonial expansion, wittingly or not, aroused
suspicions that the church had ulterior motives. This suspi-
cion erupted with a vengeance throughout Africa during the
1960s, and led some to reject Christianity in favor of Islam
or Marxism. Thus, in spite of the laudable intentions of the
missionaries, and their courageous deeds of compassion and

service as well as their many achievements in education and evangelism, many blacks today regard white Christianity, if not Christianity itself, as a form of European domination.

British rule at the Cape and in Natal, and the imperial push north en route to Cairo, were also bound up with the idea of extending Christian civilization into "darkest Africa." But the diamond and gold rush, and the ensuing wars between the British and the Boer republics, were hardly edifying for the "heathen." There was nothing Christian or civilized about the concentration camps or the grasping for economic gain and power. Just as two world wars between so-called Christian nations raised serious questions about Christianity in the Third World, so the clash between British and Afrikaner Christians demonstrated how religious faith was easily set aside and sacrificed on the altars of political and economic interest. The cause of God's kingdom and the integrity of the church are always the casualties in this kind of conflict.

And now, to cap it all, Christianity has become identified by many blacks with apartheid. In protest against government policy and action in the name of Christianity, a small group of black ministers staged a march in Johannesburg in 1977. They were arrested and charged in the Magistrates Court with breaking the law. The following is the statement they made in court:

> The Honourable Minister of Police and Prisons, Mr. Jimmy Kruger, has stated that people who do not accept the concept and policy of APARTHEID can say so without fear of being PROSECUTED, harassed and intimidated. It is on the strength of his words and of the truth of the Gospel of Jesus that we stage this PROTEST MARCH as testimony of our non-acceptance of APARTHEID and its attendant evil effects. This march registers our TOTAL AND ABSOLUTE REJECTION of the Bantustan Apartheid Policy. We want to say that this policy is responsible for a great deal of unhappiness in our country:
>
>> Detentions without trial, Banning orders, the unjust enforcement of Bantu Education, mass removals, job reservation, muzzling of the Black Press, a disproportionate and disastrous military budget, etc....

In the face of these injustices perpetrated by the White Christian Government, we have great difficulty as Ministers of Religion in explaining the Gospel to our Black people.

The White people came here and told us they were bringing a Gospel of brotherhood. But they will neither live in the same areas as us, nor sit in the same coach in a train.

They told us that they believed "you must love your brother as yourself", but they will allow us none of the things they wish for themselves, no equal opportunity in work, no say in Government, no free movement.

They told us their Gospel was one of sharing, yet they have taken more than three quarters of the whole land for a small minority, and force us to work so that they always gain ten times as much as us.

They told us that Christian life was based on the family, yet there are a million of our men working with them not allowed to have their families where they work, driving our people to sin.

They told us Christianity brought the light of civilised culture, yet they oblige our children to a form of Education that is narrowed and impedes their access to the education and culture of the world.

They told us the Grace of Christ made the human person priority No. 1, yet in a country full of wealth they leave hundreds of thousands out of work and with no unemployment benefit, their children starving.

They told us it was a Gospel of kindness, yet they push us so far from our work that parents are fourteen to sixteen hours away from home and do not see their children awake between Monday and Saturday.

They told us that Christ had broken down all barriers between peoples, yet their Christian Government is forcing us who have worked together for a hundred years and more to become separate nations.

They told us "truth would set us free", yet when we try to speak the truth of all this as we see it, our spokesmen are detained or banned, our free associations crushed, quotation of our leaders forbidden.

The result of this is that our voices sound hollow when we preach this Gospel in Church. We implore the White Christian Government to examine its Conscience and heed the voice of the Gospel.[41]

Shortly after the riots began in Soweto, a series of random interviews with black students conducted by a black newsman confirmed what many had half-suspected: "Most blacks regard the Church in South Africa as an irrelevant institution if not an extension of the status quo."[42] This may be an exaggeration, but it is true of many young blacks nonetheless. Religion is scornfully rejected as a drug which induces apathy towards apartheid. When a black Dutch Reformed minister was asked why church buildings were gutted by the rioters, he replied: "Because the Black people identify the D.R. Church with the political dispensation in our country."[43] In a way strongly reminiscent of the classic Marxist critique of religion, a young black is reported as saying: "The white man's god has been used to tame the black people."[44] Even if this is only a partly true, emotive response, it is surely a damning indictment of the Christian presence and witness in South Africa for more than 300 years. It dramatically portrays that the path chosen by many younger blacks is becoming radically different from that of whites, and even from that chosen by their Christian parents. They have chosen a secular terrain for their struggle, and, if sociologist Archie Mafeje is correct, "because they have rejected the status quo and have no wish or way of going back to the African past, they are destined to produce the necessary revolutionary paradigms, even for the unliberated African Christians."[45]

This black protest against the racial bondage of Christianity is not directed only against the advocates and defenders of government policy. For many blacks, the English-speaking and Catholic churches are also regarded as part of the problem rather than the solution. For them, Christianity itself needs to be liberated before it can become meaningful for their situation, liberated, that is, from bondage to white interests in church and society.

Thus, the relationship between younger blacks and Christianity has rapidly become problematic for the churches, especially in the urban townships. It is true, of course, that black Christian student organizations and church groups still flourish. Indeed, even the more radical students of Soweto and elsewhere have a love/hate relationship with the church, rather than one of total rejection. This ambivalence was very true of Steve Biko himself. Throughout the disturbances in 1976 and 1977, black protesters sought the counsel of their pastors and looked for refuge within the precincts of the churches. They were aware that time and again it has been the gospel itself that has inspired blacks to break out of bondage and to struggle and endure with courage and hope. However, as we have said, it is becoming evident that some blacks have moved away from Christianity and found in Marxism an attractive alternative. Without a doubt this movement has been powerfully stimulated by events in southern Africa during the past few years, especially the Frelimo victory in Mozambique. This means that the church in its struggle against racism has to contend not only with injustice but also with the growing power of a hostile ideology.

This rejection of the church by some younger blacks includes a rejection of the African independent churches as well. Indeed, the mainline churches have often been regarded as more relevant to the black struggle than the independent churches. In his original study of the latter, particularly in his treatment of "Zionist healers," Sundkler made the observation that these churches are "a very definite threat to the progress of the African."[46] The same theme is reiterated by Mafeje: "They are unable to confront structure with structure but instead take refuge in self-induced hallucinations."[47] The African independent churches have been as apolitical as any movement could be. In a comparative study of such churches among the Kikuyu, who were largely responsible for winning independence from the British in Kenya, and of others among the Zulu in Natal, Robert Janosik came to the conclusion that although the situations regarding white domination were very similar, the Kenyan sects were deeply involved in the political struggle, while the Zulu sects, both "Zionist" and "Ethiopian," were politically indifferent: "A few anomic exceptions notwithstanding, the message of the Zulu sects and churchmen has been one of political deference and quiescence."[48] We would question Janosik's conclusion about the similarities of the situation, but he is largely correct in his assessment of the political role of the independent churches in South Africa, at least until very recently.

The radical black protest against Christianity which we have described has come as an intense shock to most whites who are aware of it and willing to listen. Moreover, it has confronted the church, which has had things its own way ever since European colonization began in southern Africa, with a dynamic ideological alternative within the black community, a challenge which views the so-called relevance and integrity of the church with disdain and even contempt. For the more ideologically astute, this rejection is not simply pragmatic; rather, the church is regarded as a failure in the struggle for human rights because it is based on false claims. Thus, the gospel itself is seen as a stumbling block on the way to true liberation.

It is against this background that we must see the significance of black theology. Black theologians are fully aware of the fact that younger blacks are turning their backs in increasing numbers on Christianity and the church. They are very conscious of the challenge of Marxism within the South African context, but unlike some liberation theologians, they do not want to form some kind of alliance with Marxism. On the contrary, their concern is to rescue the gospel from ideological captivity to white interests, and thereby show its relevance to both black aspirations and white fears and expectations. Black Christians are convinced that the power of the gospel can effect their liberation as well as the liberation of their white fellow men and women, but they are also convinced that the church has to be liberated from ideological bondage and self-interest if this is to happen.

Towards White Evangelical Liberation

A SIGNIFICANT DEVELOPMENT in theological reflection today is the fact that the challenge of "Third World" liberation theologies is gradually being heard by "First World" Christians—the privileged and relatively affluent. This is not only true among those most sympathetic to liberation theology, but also among some who are very critical. Jürgen Moltmann's call for a liberation theology for oppressors might have been anticipated.[49] Yet, when a similar call comes from conservative evangelicals, the consensus is almost overwhelming in its potential impact. In a recent symposium entitled *Evangelicals and Liberation,* Clark Pinnock spelled this out: "The 'theology of liberation' is in reality God's instrument for the refinement of our own commitment to the gospel, and has been leading many to reflect on the need for the liberation of North American Christians."[50] This understanding of the challenge, which is not the same as espousing liberation theology, is gradually being grasped by white Christians in South Africa, both evangelicals and others. Black theology is a powerful challenge to white Christianity, and a catalyst for Christian renewal and change in society. In other words, black theologians do not simply have a word for blacks, they also have a message for whites.

Bishop Alphaeus Zulu has often expressed the dilemma of the black South African Christian in his relationship to the white person. In his T. B. Davie Memorial Lecture at the University of Cape Town in 1972, he put it like this:

> Some black people find strength from appreciation of the humanity of the white man. They refuse consciously and deliberately to retaliate by shutting their eyes and calling a white man a beast because he regards them as such. They consider it a duty and privilege to strive to help open the eyes of their fellow men to values presently closed to them. Such people will endure, at least for a time, criticism and disparagement from their fellows on account of their continuing against odds to expect brotherly relationships to be forged across the colour barrier.[50]

But he warned:

> At the same time it would be a grave mistake to presume to think that such attitudes will survive callous white discrimination indefinitely. And even if the patience of such persons should be strangely endless, it may be necessary for them to act

with severity in the way that God himself deals with the humanity he loves. . . .[51]

That was four years before Soweto. A year after Soweto, speaking at the South African Renewal Conference in Johannesburg, Bishop Zulu returned to this theme. He told the vast audience that many blacks no longer felt it possible to be reconciled with the whites, that blacks now spoke openly about whites as their oppressors, and that this made the position of black Christians working for reconciliation extremely difficult.[52]

Yet, in spite of Soweto and other events which have hardened black attitudes, it is almost incredible how much concern there is among black Christians for their white fellow citizens. Reporting on the Annual National Conference of the South African Council of Churches in 1977, Dr. Wolfram Kistner wrote:

> Towards the end of the Conference the question was raised whether it could be expected for black people to love their oppressors in the present situation. It was pointed out that this question was often asked by young people in the black community. The way in which a considerable number of black delegates responded to this question was a surprise. In a very pronounced manner they expressed their commitment to unconditional love in a time of crisis. This to them was an integral part of the Christian faith and of the Christian message. In some cases such statements assumed the form of a very personal compassion.[53]

Kistner's account is substantiated by that of black journalist Obed Musi, who reported on the openness of black delegates to whites. He quotes Constance Koza, Director of Inter-Church Aid for the SACC, as opposing a motion condemning detentions, bannings, and the like, of blacks. A black leader herself, Mrs. Koza declared, "It's not blacks alone who have been suffering. Whites too were involved. So I'd rather see the wording in the motion changed to read just 'people' who have been banished, banned or detained. . . ." Musi comments: "And there was not a single voice of dissent. Rather the movers of the motion looked sheepishly at their rough drafts and later gleefully accepted the change in wording."[54]

It would be wrong to read this as a sign that black attitudes towards whites are without rancor, bitterness, or hatred, or that polarization has ended. In the light of circumstances, it would be difficult to imagine that this could be so. What we have, however, are black Christians who have become liberated as persons, black Christians who no longer feel inferior, black Christians who know that, in spite of everything, their God-given dignity cannot be destroyed again. They are therefore free to take the risk of loving whites in a way that is as far removed from sentimentality as is the love of the cross. And rising out of this love is a deep and profound concern for white liberation. As Manas Buthelezi put it in his "Theses": "It is now time for the black man to evangelise and humanise the white man. The realisation of this will not depend on the white man's approval, but solely on the black man's love for the white man." In a similar vein, Bishop Desmond Tutu, General Secretary of the SACC, declared:

> We are involved in the black liberation struggle because we are also deeply concerned for white liberation. The white man will never be free until the black man is wholly free, because the white man invests enormous resources to try to gain a fragile security and peace, resources that should have been used more creatively elsewhere. The white man must suffer too because he is bedevilled by anxiety and fear and God wants to set him free, to be free *from* all that dehumanises us together, to set us free for our service of one another in a more just and open society in South Africa.[55]

So, too, Boesak insists that black theology should include whites. "Blacks," he writes, "know only too well the terrible estrangement of white people; they know only too well how sorely whites need to be liberated—even if whites themselves don't."[56]

Thus, we have come full circle from where we were at the beginning of our story. For now, all of a sudden, the black Christian has become the missionary to the whites. Allan Boesak sums up the challenge:

> In breaking away from the old, oppressive structures of our society, seeking new possibilities, creating room for the realiza-

tion of our God-given authenticity, black theology seeks the true purpose of life for blacks as well as whites. We want to share our dreams and hopes for a new future with whites, a future where it must not be necessary to make a Christian theology an ideology or a part of a cultural imperialism.... One is only human because of others, with others, for others. This is what we mean. It is authentic, it is worthwhile, it is in the most profound sense of the word gospel truth.[57]

The past few years of black renewal and protest have radically challenged white self-understanding and raised some fundamental questions for white Christians. In spite of general antipathy towards black consciousness, whites have been profoundly affected by it. Whereas before, whites called the tune and blacks played their expected role, now blacks are refusing to play a "non-white" role, with the result that whites are being forced to face reality in a new way. What they do with reality is another matter. White liberation means responding to reality in terms of the message and meaning of Jesus Christ; white bondage means the continued denial of reality and a rejection of the good news that Christ sets people free for one another. But in order to understand this bondage better, we need to reflect more deeply on some aspects of white existence, bearing in mind that "the weaknesses of human nature are displayed more clearly in a time of storm than in the smooth course of more peaceful periods."[58]

Racism is a universal phenomenon, shaped and reinforced by historical and contemporary crises and events. Whatever its roots, and they are certainly complex in South Africa, it is part of the mechanism whites use in the struggle for survival. Although most white South Africans would react negatively to the kind of racist language popularly used in public by politicians and others even ten years ago, J. G. Strydom's belief that "South Africa cannot remain a white man's country ... if we lose our colour feeling" is still widely shared.[59] When you are not numerically threatened by another racial group, you do not normally feel the need for such an attitude or defense—certainly not to the same extent. Racism in North America would look rather different if the proportions of blacks and whites were reversed while the latter still retained political and economic power. Racism in South Africa is the problem of a white minority uncertain about its future.

White South Africa has been a privileged community, increasingly affluent amid black poverty, powerfully in command of the land, labor, and wealth of the country. As the Spro-cas Economics Commission report *Power, Privilege and Poverty* expressed it, "South African society assumes a set of economic objectives which may be manipulated to ensure the socio-economic privileges of the white group but which are insensitive to the needs of the black group."[60] Affluence is, of course, relative. There are some poor whites and a few wealthy blacks—but the opportunities open to the former are largely closed to the latter. Housing, education, travel—the list is almost endless where white power ensures white privilege. And yet, this kind of advantage might be called a fatal privilege, for it increases fear of change and anxiety about the future. The Spro-cas report reminds us that "the economically secure are suspicious of the aspirations of the insecure, and become repressive and resistant to change, especially where poverty is seen to be related to social and economic impotence. On the other hand, the economically insecure (supposing them to be not sunken in total apathy) have nothing to lose by militancy and intransigency in their growing demands."[61]

As a result, it seems that few white South Africans are without fear for the future. As far back as 1945, Jan H. Hofmeyr, then Deputy Prime Minister of South Africa, pointed to this powerful phenomenon. In his Hoernlé lecture that year, he quoted Hoernlé's own words: "The price which the white caste pays for its domination is fear—fear for the continuance of its own domination, fear for its future."[62] It can be argued that this fear is irrational. It cannot be argued that it is unreal. The majority of white South Africans have no other homeland, and they fear deeply for their future here. Furthermore, they fear "the unexpected consequences of letting go of control to another group."[63] This is especially true when groups are ethnically and culturally very different, as is the case in South Africa. This fear is not always expressed in words; often the very contrary is what is verbalized. It may not even be acknowledged. But it demonstrates its presence in a variety of ways. H. Richard Niebuhr sensed this in the United States during the civil rights struggle, and assumed the same about South Africa, as the following quotation reveals:

> In the destructive interactions of castes or racial groups in the United States and in South Africa and elsewhere in the world we must take into account that beyond all loyalty to law and beyond all idealism there is operative in the minds of the defensive group a deep fear of coming destruction. The future holds for it no promise, no great opportunities, but only loss and descent, if not into the grave then 'ad infernos'. Its actions are those that seem to it to be fitting, i.e. to fit into a situation and into a history whose past is full of guilt, acknowledged or not, and whose future is full of death in one of its forms.[64]

In *Farewell to Innocence* Allan Boesak employs Rollo May's category of pseudo-innocence to tell how he as a black person remained innocent for most of his early life of the bondage of racism that determined his daily existence. His book is, in one sense, a description of his own pilgrimage beyond that innocence.[65] But it is also a challenge to the pseudo-innocence of whites who have rationalized their power and privileges in such a way that they can no longer discern the reality that now faces them. Indeed, it is easier to live with fear and an unjust situation if you refuse to acknowledge them or the factors which cause them. Very many white people, for example, do not want to know what is happening in the black townships, what blacks are really thinking and experiencing, how many people are in detention without trial, what new legislation implies for civil rights, and the rest. Such disturbing facts are pushed down into the unconscious. But, of course, the effect of this constant sublimation is not less anxiety, but more, and the greater the anxiety the greater becomes the possibility of irrational behavior, especially in times of crisis.

Part of this pseudo-innocence is a lack of a sense of guilt for what has happened to black people as a result of whites' attitudes, actions, and policies throughout the centuries. In the name of maintaining security whites are constantly informed that they have nothing for which to feel guilty. Such a refusal to acknowledge what history plainly describes does not mean an absence of guilt, only an absence of admission and acceptance of it. This has disastrous consequences for whites' coming to terms with reality. In fact, what could be one of the most potent forces for healing society's wounds, has become one more burden which prevents social wholeness and reconciliation. Of course, there is a vast difference between the acknowledgment of real guilt and that cringing confession of sins that seems to gain special satisfaction in one's failure. The latter is pathological; it is a way of escape from reality and responsibility, rather than a way to creative change. To acknowledge real guilt is not a sign of weakness, it is a sign of maturity. It is also one of life's great therapies. Archbishop Bill Burnett rightly said in his open letter to Mr. Vorster in September, 1976: "Unless White Christians in particular admit the wrongs they have done to Black people and take action to redress them, there can be no possibility of healing in our Land."[66]

It is tragic that Christianity among white South Africans is often misused to escape the realities of our situation. This leads us to another phenomenon of white existence, pseudo-pietism. Theologians have often been unjustly derogatory about pietism. Contrary to what is so often thought, the great Pietist leaders of the eighteenth and nineteenth centuries were in the forefront of social witness in their day. They believed that such social action arose directly out of Christian regeneration, and if it did not, there was something fundamentally wrong with that conversion. Pseudo-pietism is the debasement of this tradition. It is a misuse of religion in such a way that Marx's dictum about religion being the opiate of the masses becomes painfully obvious. It is a form of escapism. It is religiosity hiding inadequacy, justifying social irresponsibility, and giving ungodly deeds a sanctimonious aura. Some people, remarked Dietrich Bonhoeffer, "who seek to escape from taking a stand publicly find a place of refuge in private virtuousness." But this, he said, is "an act of self-deception."[67] And that is what much white Christianity has too often become: a kind of self-deception. Religion can become a smokescreen for unrighteousness. The witness of the great Hebrew prophets makes this clear.

Many whites who have been working for positive and just social change have come to the point where they no longer believe that evolutionary transformation is possible. Violence seems to be the only alternative. They dislike what is, and they dislike what they anticipate. They feel like Charles Darnay in the *Tale of Two Cities,* who expostulated to his harsh land-owning uncle in pre-revolutionary France that he was bound to a system that was frightful to him, a system in which he was powerless, yet a system for which he was responsible.[68] Whites, too, have a sense of living in a world that seems by definition to be against them, simply because they are white South Africans; they have what might be called a feeling of being in a "lose-lose" situation. In brief, what they feel is despair, a mood of hopelessness and helplessness, intensified by a sense of isolation from the rest of the world.

Despair usually leads to cynicism.[69] There is the cynicism of power, just as there is the cynicism of powerlessness. Whites suffer from both. Those who oppose apartheid wonder what their vote can mean in a situation that seems impossible to change through the ballot box. Programs designed to reduce racial tension, change attitudes, and foster trust between black and white have for too long been curtailed by the authorities, who fear them as a threat to state security. When you have tried for so long, and succeeded so little, you become cynical about new initiatives and possibilities. This leads to fatalism. Responsibility for the future is surrendered into the hands of the powerful and before the encroachment of the inevitable. History is allowed to become a dark, menacing force that must overtake us, irrespective of what we do. It is seen as something that will either erupt into some apocalyptic nightmare or a more rigid form of what we already have. Fatalism erodes conviction and courage. It eats away the will to accept responsibility and to work towards a more just society. When such fatalism is combined with fear, the result is usually flight. Flight can take two forms. The one is inward—flight from reality into pseudo-innocence and pseudo-piety; the other is outward—emigration. But for the majority of whites, emigration is not possible. For them, the future must be here. There can be "no further trek," for there is no land beyond this.

It would be very misleading if at this point in our phenomenology of contemporary white existence we did not refer to, or underestimated, the growing determination of white South Africans to stay in the country and work for the resolution of its problems. While this is partly a "backs-to-the-wall" determination, it is far more than that. South Africa is a relatively powerful country, especially economically and militarily speaking, with considerable resources for meeting the challenges that are increasingly coming to it. Certainly white South Africans will not surrender what they have achieved without considerable struggle, a struggle that could plunge southern Africa into a disastrous war. But there is more to this sense of determination than simply a commitment to stay and fight if that becomes necessary. South Africa is rich in resources of another kind, and especially since Soweto these resources have become more and more apparent. There are many white South Africans within business, politics, education, the church, and other crucial fields who are determined to work out as speedily as possible evolutionary solutions to the problems facing the country. While their efforts might not satisfy those who wish to see more radical action, it would be false to underestimate or simply to reject the commitment and the achievements of such leaders. Whether or not they will succeed in their efforts, however, will depend on many factors. Not least among these is the mood of black South Africans in this post-Soweto era.

The awakening of black consciousness, expressed in black theology and symbolized by Soweto, has thus been a massive shock to the white South African system. While it has enabled blacks to rediscover and affirm their identity as human beings, it has forced whites into a state of cultural crisis. It would be wrong to suggest that all whites are aware that this is happening, but it is certainly part of the awareness of those whites, Afrikaans and English, who are reflecting on their situation and not just reaching for a gun or retreating into their shell. This becomes evident when whites begin to affirm that they belong to Africa rather than to Europe, and refer to themselves as white Africans. In such a situation, the old demarcation "European-Non-European," which was inscribed on all apartheid installations, falls apart. Up till now, whites have belonged, as Nadine Gordimer has put it, "to an imported cult that they have not had the will to transform." This "lack of will to transform their imported culture," she continues, "has been—under so many different names—the carapace of white supremacism."[70] The question whites face is thus rather traumatic: How are they to resolve their identity crisis and respond to the black challenge of today in such a way that the result is reconciliation rather than destruction, a growing together rather than a splitting apart into polarized oblivion? It is sobering to recall the words of a Cape Town clergyman written in 1900, words which in one sense are dated but which still speak to our time:

> To neglect the black man, or keep him down as a mere servile dependent of the white man, spells ruin to our South African community. A huge black democracy will some day assert itself, as all democracies are bound to do; and if it has been neglected or unfairly treated it will assert itself in a way terrible to think of, and then the black terror will be to our children what the red terror has been to France.[71]

If the first step to liberation is an awareness of the situation in which one finds oneself, then the next step is a way of redemption that relates to that situation. For the Christian, such redemption is embodied in the message of the kingdom of God, a message which not only provides a perspective on history and its crises, but which also enables people to respond courageously and hopefully to the realities confronting them.

5

The Kingdom of God
in South Africa

The Kingdom in History

SOME FORTY YEARS AGO, H. Richard Niebuhr showed how the
theme of God's rule in and over history dominated the
theological understanding of North American Protestantism from its beginnings until our era. It was this discovery which led him to write about *The Kingdom of God in
America*.[1] Niebuhr discerned in the representative writers,
preachers, and thinkers of each period an overwhelming
sense of the sovereign presence and purpose of God beneath
and beyond the flux of history. At the same time, he saw
that the kingdom of God was understood by them in a variety of different but complementary ways, ways appropriate to the needs of their day, as pilgrims and pioneers
sought to establish and build the kingdom of the United
States. Thus, for Niebuhr, the theme of the kingdom of God
provided a powerful symbol for interpreting and evaluating
the North American experience.

The Puritans of New England stressed the sovereignty of
God over history. The providence of God ruled supreme. But
God did not only reign over universal history, his dominion

impinged directly upon the life of the settler community itself. The kingdom of God meant theocratic government. The commonwealths of New England were intended to be replicas of the commonwealth of heaven. That this proved impossible to achieve is well known, and the frightening story of the Salem witch hunts shows how the attempt could provoke the opposite of what the kingdom is all about.

The evangelicals of the Great Awakening in the eighteenth century also stressed the sovereignty of God over history. But for them, the emphasis lay more specifically on his sovereign grace at work in the hearts of men and women, awakening conscience and creating new life in the soul. The redemption of society required, as a prerequisite, the renewal of the affections, and this was only possible through faith in the redeeming love of Christ and his subsequent kingly reign in the heart. The kingdom of God had to be internalized before it could be socialized.

In the twentieth century the emphasis changed to the so-called social gospel. Walter Rauschenbusch and others developed a theology and encouraged a Christian witness which sought the extension of the kingdom into every corner of social life. Rauschenbusch did not deny the importance of personal regeneration, but declared that the "individualistic gospel ... has not given us an adequate understanding of the sinfulness of the social order. ... It has not evoked faith in the will and power of God to redeem permanent institutions of human society from their inherited guilt of oppression and extortion."[2] The social gospel expressed something of the biblical hope for the kingdom of God on earth here and now, as well as at the end of time. While the movement itself failed to provide a message that could change people as well as institutions, it showed that the social gospel is implicit in the biblical message of the kingdom of God.[3]

The Puritans, the evangelicals, and the proponents of the social gospel all agreed that the kingdom of God meant the sovereignty of God over history, both now and in the future. They also agreed that the sovereign grace of God at work in human lives was essential to the gospel. And all in their own way sought to bear witness to the demands of the kingdom for their own society. The difference between them was one of emphasis. Providence, the redeeming work of Christ, and the renewal of the social order, all found a place, but the stress inevitably fell on one dimension rather than all.

In a more recent North American theology of history, *Reaping the Whirlwind,* Langdon Gilkey also interprets the kingdom of God in history in terms of these same three dimensions: the sovereign providence of God as the foundation of history, the redemptive and healing grace of God in Jesus Christ for the person and the community, and the socio-political implications for the present of God's ultimate purpose for the future of the world.[4] Like H. Richard Niebuhr before him, he concludes that these three aspects are inseparable components of the meaning and message of the kingdom of God, both in the biblical tradition and in interpreting history and the task of the church today. For both Niebuhr and Gilkey, there is a coherence to the kingdom when these various dimensions are held together. When they are separated from each other, the church ends up with a distorted understanding of history, as well as its message and mission.

Since the pioneering biblical research of Albert Schweitzer and Johannes Weiss at the turn of this century, the theme of the kingdom of God has dominated theology. Eschatology and apocalyptic have been rediscovered as fundamental to the biblical message for our time, and certainly central to any proper understanding of the mission and the teaching of Jesus.[5] Right across the confessional and denominational spectrum, from Catholic to conservative evangelical, and certainly within many contemporary European and Latin American political and liberation theologies, the kingdom of God has become, in the words of André Dumas, "the deepest factor which is held in common."[6] Moreover, there is a remarkable agreement on what the kingdom means in Scripture, and considerable consensus on what it implies for today. Few scholars, if any, would disagree with George Ladd's assertion that "the Kingdom is the reign of God, not merely in the human heart but dynamically active in the person of Jesus and in human history."

And, further, that it is both "present and future, inward and outward, spiritual and apocalyptic."[7] In other words, the message of the kingdom of God, centered in the person and proclamation of Jesus himself, relates to our personal and social existence and history today in its totality, as well as to our future.

This rediscovery of biblical eschatology enables us to bring together in a dynamic new synthesis the dimensions of the kingdom of God as understood at various times in the thought and experience of the church. The past, the contemporary situation, and the future find their meaning in the kingdom. As such, the kingdom provides the criterion by which we must evaluate what is happening in history, and the focus for the life and mission of the church. "The central concern of the Church," writes Wolfhart Pannenberg, "and the primary point of reference for understanding the Church, must be the Kingdom of God. That is, the Kingdom must be the central concern of the Church if the Church is to remain faithful to the message of Jesus."[8] If this be so, then it is of crucial significance for us in our reflections on the struggle of the church in South African history.

The theme of God's providence, which is never absent from devout reflections on South African history, is never more pertinent than at times of historical crisis like our own. It reminds us of purposes that are sure and certain, even if beyond our understanding. The theme of God's sovereign grace in Christ crucified, the king who reigns from the cross, reveals the depths of human evil and human pain and proclaims the ultimate triumph of God's purpose. Here we have the touchstone whereby we may know how God's judging and saving will works in history, the criterion for evaluating human ways and means, directions and goals. The message of grace and forgiveness in Christ is also the word of promise that the present can be transformed, past mistakes transcended, and human life changed through repentance, faith, and obedience. Binding all this together is the certainty of God's future for the world, a future that has already broken into the present in Christ.

God's eschatological purpose is to transform this world

and so make all things new through his Spirit. The promised kingdom judges our clinging to the past, or our attachment to the present status quo, and, in Gilkey's words, "lures us into the future," making us dissatisfied with anything less than God's righteousness, justice, and peace in the world. The message of the kingdom makes us restless with things as they are. It confronts us with the need to decide for or against God's will here and now. It is the goad for mission in the world. It stimulates hope for the fulfillment of God's purpose for the universe. While it challenges and destroys the utopias people plan and seek to build, it nevertheless awakens within us a profound desire for the coming of God's kingdom on earth "as in heaven." And, as Dietrich Bonhoeffer points out, "the more exclusively we acknowledge and confess Christ as Lord, the more freely the wide range of his dominion will be disclosed to us."[9] The church is not the kingdom; indeed, it is only the church as it journeys in faith, hope, and love towards the coming of God's rule along "the way taken by a sovereign God through the reign of Jesus Christ."[10]

As the struggle of the church in North America was a struggle for the kingdom of God, so, too, the struggle of the church in South Africa is for the kingdom of God in another segment of world history. Indeed, as we look back over the history of South Africa, and the theologies that have shaped and interpreted that history, the cruciality of the kingdom emerges strongly and resembles in an almost uncanny way the story of the kingdom of God in America.

We have already seen how akin the Afrikaner tradition is to that of the New England Puritans, though, as Charles West has indicated, the parallel must not be pushed too far.[11] Like the Calvinism that shaped the New World, the Calvinism of the "Puritans in Africa" provided the spiritual backbone and drive that opened up the interior of southern Africa for the white tribe. It also ensured that belief in the sovereignty of God would become a part of our historical heritage and national consciousness. A vital component of this sense of divine purpose is the deep-rooted desire of Afrikaner Nationalism to establish and maintain a theocratic utopia of order where every tribe and person has his rightful place in the economy of God and the republic. Thus, the hand of the Almighty is discerned in the unfolding of Afrikaner history in a way that corresponds and mirrors that of Israel in the Old Testament.

Of course, while Afrikaner conviction has most significantly etched the message of providence onto our interpretation of history, it is not only Afrikaner Nationalism that is so anchored in this belief, or so influenced by the typology of Israel, the exodus, and the promised land. The exodus motif of Afrikaner "liberation theology" in the struggle for identity and power is also central to black theology today. Both believe firmly in the hand that guides history.

The analogy with North America can be taken further. The great evangelical missionary movement that spread like fire through the world in the nineteenth century, profoundly influencing South African history, had its roots in the Wesleyan Revival in Britain and the Great Awakening in New England. Andrew Murray, Jr. stands as a symbol of this evangelical tradition in South Africa, a tradition of piety that has greatly affected the life not only of the churches but also of the nation to this day. The Student Christian Association, with its motto, "Make Jesus King," developed out of this movement at the end of the nineteenth century and brought together in one fellowship of worship and service Christians of all races and cultures. The lordship of Christ and his saving work in individuals engendered a common commitment to the creation of a more Christian society. Some of South Africa's greatest sons and daughters of the twentieth century, including B. B. Keet, Jan Hofmeyr, and Alan Paton, are the products of this tradition.[12] And you do not have to look far beneath the surface of black Christianity itself to discover a very similar spirituality. Thus, in South Africa too, the rule of Christ in the heart is part of the history of the kingdom, affecting Christians of all kinds. And its degeneration into pseudo-piety should not detract from the fact that, for many, the saving grace of Christ meant the awakening of social conscience and the beginning of sharing in the struggle for justice.[13]

What of the third dimension of the kingdom, the renewal of the social order? In America we find the social gospel; is there an equivalent in South Africa? The neo-Calvinism of Kuyper may appear to be a strange bedfellow with the social gospel of Rauschenbusch, and yet in at least one respect it is not. Both were concerned that the kingdom of God should affect every aspect of social life. And, of course, this was also true of Anglican Christian socialism as expounded by F. D. Maurice and William Temple, and of the Nonconformist conscience that influenced the social struggles of Methodists and Congregationalists. Each of these groups is different, but all agree that God's authority and rule has to be acknowledged and obeyed in every dimension of life, and that this has direct implications for the mission of the church to the world. On this at least, there is consensus between the drafters of the *Koinonia Declaration* and the *Message to the People of South Africa,* and between the Gereformeerde theologians of Potchefstroom and the Catholic Bishops' Synod.

Let us now reflect more critically on these three dimensions of the kingdom of God in the historical experience of South Africa. Their separation from each other, and from their basis in the message and mission of Jesus himself, has happened so often in Christian history that it would not be surprising to find the same in this case as well.

Our first observation is that the doctrine of providence has been distorted by ideologies, especially Afrikaner Nationalism. This does not exempt British imperialism or African nationalism from a similar critique, but it has been Afrikanerdom that has most powerfully shaped South African society. This distortion of the biblical belief in providence has four aspects. First of all, national history is given a quasi-sacred character. It functions as another norm beside the kingdom of God for evaluating history and for determining future plans. In all past and present events—the Great Trek, the Wars of Independence, the National party victory in 1948, the establishment of the republic in 1961, or South Africa's role in war-torn southern Africa today—God is declared to be *our* God. With him on our side, victory is assured, our cause will be vindicated and our enemies vanquished. We are given an assurance upon which we may build for the future. Secondly, the Afrikaner nation (*volk*) has become a special people, a holy people, a church. Afrikanerdom has a peculiar relationship to the Almighty; it has assumed the mantle of Israel in southern Africa; it has a particular vocation among the nations. Thirdly, the policies of Afrikaner Nationalism have become transfused with a sense of divine calling and mission, if not to the whole world, then at least to this subcontinent. This means that separate development has become, for many, more than a pragmatic attempt to solve a complex political problem; it is regarded as part of the divine purpose.[14] Opposition to it is, per se, unchristian. And fourthly, because providence has led us to this point, the present order must have been ordained by God. Separate development may evolve, but it cannot be allowed to change radically without denying the very order of creation.

In such a distorted view of providence the orders of creation stand in the way of the purposes of redemption. Thus, we can see that belief in providence can become, as G. C. Berkouwer remarks, "a piously disguised form of self-justification."[15] In the New Testament, providence has been transformed by the incarnation, God's radical breaking into history to fulfill his purposes of redemption. Thus, these purposes are not read in creation alone, they are discerned in Jesus Christ, his death and resurrection, and the fulfillment of all things in him. The Almighty who is worshipped is the Father of our Lord Jesus Christ. Thus, our history, our nation, and our politics do not automatically have God's blessing because they exist, or because we believe in him, but only if they conform to his will in Christ. Karl Barth has reminded us that the separation of providence from Christology always leads to a false belief in our own history, so that even Hitler could claim the patronage of the Almighty. Barth has also shown that such a view of providence proves inadequate to the crises of history; it is either too optimistic or too fatalistic. It cannot face reality.[16]

Our second observation is that the doctrine of redemption has been individualized by pseudo-pietism. The evangelical tradition rightly stresses the need for personal repentance, conversion, faith, and obedience, in relation to the death and resurrection of Jesus Christ and the work of the Holy Spirit. Nothing we write is meant to deny this in any way. On the contrary, we affirm it as strongly as possible. But faith in Christ can be distorted by separating it from social and historical existence. In other words, genuine piety can give rise to a pseudo-pietism which turns the believer and the church away from the world and results in a form of deism and a *deus ex machina* understanding of providence. The kingdom thus becomes purely transcendental and spiritual, and personal faith, which is so central to discipleship, becomes distorted.

The good news about the kingdom is not Platonic, and neither is it some kind of psychotherapy. Genuine piety is not a way of escape from the world, but is a response to what God has done and is doing in history. In other words, faith is eschatological. It is a response in obedience to the new age that has dawned in Christ; it is a sharing in what God is presently doing in the world; it is an anticipation of God's ultimate purpose for the world.

In the New Testament, the good news of the kingdom is always proclaimed to people in terms of their life-situation.[17] It is good news to the poor, liberty to the captives, sight to the blind; it is also a challenge to the rich, comfort to the fearful, and a way of rebirth for those unable to break out of their old way of life and enter the kingdom of God. In the New Testament, sin and salvation have to do with the real world, the world of everyday existence, human power and pain, and the historical events that determine people's lives. If the good news of the kingdom did not relate to our existential and historical situation, it would not be good news. If it does not speak to the black South African both as a person and as someone affected by apartheid—the two cannot be separated—then it is bad news. If it does not address the white South African at the point of his or her present predicament, then it is not the gospel of Jesus Christ. The message of redemption is the message of God's sovereign grace in Christ transforming real lives in a real world in which both personality and sociality are irrevocably intertwined.

The so-called social gospel is biblically correct insofar as it proclaims that the message of the kingdom relates directly to corporate sin and the possibility of social change in the direction of God's justice. Pseudo-pietism denies this. It reduces eschatology to what happens at the end of time to the individual. What was meant to be the basis for challenging an unjust status quo becomes the means whereby it is sanctioned and preserved. Rewards are offered in the hereafter for those who suffer in silence at the hands of the powerful. But, as George Ladd points out, "eschatology is not an end in itself, standing in detachment upon the horizons of time. Eschatology finds its significance primarily in relationship to history, for both are concerned chiefly with the will of God for his people. The prophets usually took their stand in the midst of an actual historical situation and addressed themselves to it. They proclaimed God's will for the ultimate future, that in its light they might proclaim God's will for his people here and now."[18] Pseudo-pietism, with its escape-from-reality techniques, abounds in our churches, but it is a blatant contradiction of the message of the prophets and of Jesus himself.

Our third observation is that the social message of the kingdom has been weakened and distorted by secularism. This has been especially true of white English-speaking South Africans, and it is reflected to some extent by the English-speaking churches. There has always been a close connection between British religious Nonconformity and the liberal tradition. Indeed, the Liberal party in Britain had its origins within the Baptist, Congregational, and Methodist Churches. But the danger has always been that the liberal tradition might be severed from its roots in the Judaeo-Christian prophetic understanding of man and the world, and degenerate into individualistic secularism. At the turn of the century, P. T. Forsyth, a British Congregational theologian who bridged the evangelical and liberal traditions, warned his Nonconformist colleagues: "We are at least preparing for ourselves a disappointment in every effort to christianize Society, so long as we pursue it on lines that are merely socialist, humane, or based on that natural and unconscious Christianity which is too often the liberal note."[19]

This kind of secular liberalism errs in believing that the kingdom will come through education and social programs. Liberation theology is more realistic, holding that the kingdom will come through revolutionary action. But both do not take seriously enough the fact that unjust social structures are not simply the product of history, but are the result of human sin, and thus no amount of education or political revolution can ensure the birth of utopia. To say this is not to reject education or political action, but to affirm that justification by grace alone "creates the ethical disturbance that turns the world upside down."[20] Or, as Langdon Gilkey puts it, "the ultimate resolution lies in the relation of man's inwardness to God, in faith, obedience and love, rather than directly in historical and political action."[21]

The danger of the social gospel when it is divorced from the evangelical message of Christ, is that it leads either to an individualism that has little sense of corporate responsibility, and a cynical view of history that has no hope or vision for the future, or to an overly optimistic view that is incapable of dealing with historical crises and the struggle against evil. As such, it is inadequate to the situation South Africa now faces. Somehow the church has to deal with a crisis of faith and morality at the very heart of society, and engage the "principalities and powers" at work in institutions and structures. Only the moral power of the gospel of redemption itself is adequate for this task. Langdon Gilkey gives us a timely reminder:

> It is on the inward level that the nemesis of sin arises—and so arise history's catastrophes. Thus it is on that level alone that the ultimate issues of history can be resolved, healed, and history given grounds for hope. This new level, this new being of human reality in history, this new beginning of God's end time, forms no separate history. The inner life of men and women, where both creativity and sin gestate, is part and parcel of their objective history.[22]

Ours is not the simplistic notion that if individuals change, social ills will automatically be righted. Rather, it is the belief that the message of the kingdom cannot be separated into personal and social realms—it is one message and it affects the totality of our lives as persons in community within the historical situation of our time and place.

H. Richard Niebuhr's analysis of North American history in terms of the kingdom was very much an analysis from the perspective of white Anglo-Saxon Protestant America. It would have to be radically revised in some respects if written today. In particular, it would have to reflect the experience of native Americans as they witnessed the progress of the kingdom across the continent, and the experience of black Americans as they struggled for civil rights and liberties. Langdon Gilkey is naturally more up-to-date. A theology of history today is meaningless unless it responds to the cry for liberation and grapples with the theme of the kingdom as this is explored in political and liberation theologies.

Our consideration of black theology, black consciousness, and black protest in the previous chapter was an attempt to look at the South African reality through "black eyes." It was an attempt to see things "from below" as Bonhoeffer put it, "from the perspective of those who suffer."[23] Now, in order to reflect on the issues arising from this "view from below," we will consider another theology of the kingdom of God in history, that of Latin American liberation theology with its close affinity to black theology. As Niebuhr enabled us to see things from the point of view of Protestant shapers of history in North America, let us attempt to see things from the perspective of Christian revolt in Latin America. For this purpose we shall consider Methodist theologian José Míguez Bonino's *Revolutionary Theology Comes of Age,* because of the clarity with which he raises the issues.

"Christianity," writes Míguez Bonino, "entered Latin America under two historic movements: conquest and colonization in the sixteenth century and modernization and neo-colonialism in the nineteenth."[24] The Spanish conquistadors understood their task as planting the Christian kingdom of Spain in a new environment on top of the existing Indian culture. "Obedience to the great king of Spain and submission to the King of heaven were demanded as one single act."[25] But the promised utopia was never realized. Instead, the kingdom of Spain and its colonial landlords flourished, but the kingdom of God was reduced to the rule of the church in subservience to the state. The indigenous population in turn suffered severe economic, political, cultural, and spiritual deprivation. In the words of Míguez Bonino, "the Christian faith, co-opted into the total Spanish national-religious project, played the role of legitimizing and sacralizing the social and economic structure implanted in America. It served as an ideology to cover and justify existing conditions."[26]

Protestant Christianity began to penetrate Latin America towards the end of the nineteenth century with the arrival of Protestant immigrants, Anglo-Saxon missionaries from North America and Europe, and later it flourished with the rapid growth of Pentecostalism. Míguez Bonino does not elaborate on this Protestant incursion into Catholic territory, except to make one important point: "Protestantism, in terms of its historical origin, of its introduction to Latin America, and of its ethos, came into our world as the religious accompaniment of free enterprise, liberal, capitalist democracy."[27] It helped undermine "the medieval, prescientific, feudal, aristocratic world" which existed in Latin America, and gave religious sanction and impetus to liberal ideas and modernizing projects. However, Míguez Bonino contends that this Protestant development was the religious sanctioning of another kind of unjust society, a new form of colonialism, economic dependency. Protestants have only recently begun to discover that their churches have become "the ideological allies of foreign and national forces that keep the countries in dependence and the people in slavery and need."[28]

Throughout the history of the church in Latin America there have been those who have attempted to serve the people in terms of the gospel of the kingdom rather than for the sake of political, ecclesiastical, or economic power and

gain. Míguez Bonino refers to the "small but never inter-
rupted stream of prophetic protest in Latin American Christianity," and suggests that those Christians who are seriously struggling for liberation today are heirs to that heritage. And this is where liberation theology as such begins. It
is a response to revolutionary Christian action or praxis; it
is a theological reflection on radical deeds undertaken by
Christians who have rejected both the status quo and the
liberal/reformist approach to social change. The latter, say
liberation theologians, by concentrating on development
aid, fails to deal with the real problem. Instead of bringing
about radical social change, it perpetuates dependence on
foreign capital under the guise of promoting real change.

In the radicalizing process, concerned Christians, both
Catholic and Protestant, bishops, pastors, and laypersons,
have discovered what Míguez Bonino refers to as the "un-
substitutable relevance of Marxism" in the Latin American
situation, and the need for a strategic alliance with it.[29] A
positive relationship with Marxism is necessary, he claims,
because it alone provides an adequate analysis of the situation and a strategy for changing it. Such an alliance is possible because Christianity shares with Marxism a common
concern for alienated man and a similar understanding of
people's immediate needs in society, and because both are
convinced that truth has to do with more than ideas. Yet,
the alliance is not philosophical but methodological. Active
involvement in changing the situation requires more than
theology. It requires an engagement of reality through
ideological commitment and praxis. Thus, the alliance between Christians and Marxists concerns an active relationship with reality, namely, its transformation.

Without identifying the kingdom of God with socio-
political action and achievements in historical situations,
Míguez Bonino sees a positive connection between them. He
writes:

> God builds his Kingdom from and within human history in its
> entirety; his action is a constant call and challenge to man.
> Man's response is realized in the concrete arena of history with
> its economic, political, ideological options. Faith is not a dif-

ferent history but a dynamic, a motivation, and in its eschatological horizon, a transforming invitation.[30]

In other words, in order to obey God's call it is "necessary 'to name the Kingdom' in the language of everyday history." Míguez Bonino is surely correct in this insistence that the kingdom of God should relate directly to our historical situation. There can be nothing Platonic about the kingdom if it is to be biblical. But is he correct in his understanding that for the church to bear witness to this kingdom in history, it has to be allied with some appropriate ideology?

The Kingdom, Ideology, and the Church

CHRISTIANITY never exists in some pristine, unhistorical form. It is always embedded within particular cultures and mediated through them. The mere fact of language is sufficient evidence of this. It cannot be otherwise, for Christians, whether in the first century in Palestine, the sixteenth century in Spain, the seventeenth century at the Cape, or today in Soweto or Pretoria, are part of a culture, even if they happen to be critical of it. But culture is also a problem. In his classic study, *Christ and Culture,* H. Richard Niebuhr called it an "enduring problem"[31] and provided examples of the many attempts to resolve it.

Roland Bainton went to the heart of the matter when he wrote: "If there is no accommodation [to culture] Christianity is unintelligible and cannot spread," but "if there is too much accommodation it will spread, but it will no longer be Christianity."[32] In our discussion of the church in South Africa we have seen both the need for and the danger of this relationship between Christian faith and culture. The church exists under God for people. It cannot exist for people if it refuses to speak their language or relate to their existential situation, their fears, and their aspirations. The churches of the West have learned, to their great sorrow, that the missionary uprooting of indigenous cultures was no prolegomenon to evangelism. It was a disaster; hence the protest of the African independent churches. At the same time, the church does not exist to serve culture; it exists for people, and its primary loyalty is to Jesus Christ and his kingdom. The tragic saga of the culture-Christianity of Nazi Germany is more than adequate warning of the dangers that attend the wedding of Christian faith and culture. But the problem is not only evident in such obvious examples as this. The confusion of European civilization with Christianity has pervaded the West for centuries to such an extent that, for many, they are synonymous. Far too often, Christian mission and "evangelizing the natives" have been regarded as the same. The bearers of white, European culture have presumed that their culture is Christian and free from other ideological commitments. This is not so.

It is Míguez Bonino's contention that not only is the church inevitably bound to culture, it cannot be ideologically neutral. Together with other liberation theologians, he maintains that the Latin American church has been committed over the years, consciously or by default, to right-wing regimes and support of neo-colonial economic structures that have kept the majority of people in poverty. But Míguez Bonino does not decry ideological commitment *in principle*. He insists that this particular alliance is fundamentally wrong because it means using Christianity to support injustice. In order to serve the needs of the oppressed and to break out of this captivity, he maintains, the church must align itself with Marxism, for this is the only option in the Latin American situation that has similar penultimate goals to those of Christian faith. Indeed, for him, Christianity cannot serve the interests of the kingdom of God unless it does make this kind of strategic commitment. Míguez Bonino complains that some European theologians such as Jürgen Moltmann and Johannes Metz, in spite of their anti-ideological stance, remain captive to a liberal ideology, and that their supposedly anti-ideological attitude actually prevents Christians from becoming involved in the transformation and liberation of society.[33]

Though we disagree with Míguez Bonino's position on a

"strategic alliance with Marxism," the problem of ideology and ideological commitment is not easily resolved. Of course, much depends on one's definition of terms; therefore, it is important that we begin by seeking clarity about the meaning of ideology. In doing so, we will soon discover that the word is used in two very different ways. First of all, there is what Clifford Geertz calls the non-evaluative understanding of ideology as a cultural system, which is inevitable and important for our social well-being. It is, he writes, "some vision of public purpose anchored in a compelling image of social reality."[34] It is with this kind of understanding of ideology that Robert Bellah affirms the need for and the importance of civil religion in society.[35] Similarly, Juan Luis Segundo, perhaps the most radical of the Latin American theologians, speaks of ideology as "the system of goals and means that serves as the necessary backdrop for any human opinion or line of action."[36] Ideology, then, as a non-evaluative entity necessary for society, is obviously something to which we cannot take exception.

Secondly, there is the pejorative sense of the word. Gustavo Gutiérrez, another Latin American theologian of liberation, writes:

> Ideology does not offer adequate and scientific knowledge of reality; rather, it masks it. Ideology does not rise above the empirical, irrational level. Therefore it spontaneously fulfils a function of preservation of the established order. Therefore ideology tends to dogmatize all that has not succeeded in separating itself from it or has fallen under its influence. Political action, science, and faith do not escape this danger.[37]

This is the way in which Marx used the term against Christianity; but it is also the way in which Christians have used it against such contemporary ideologies as Communism, Fascism, and Nazism. From a Christian perspective, these are seen as a form of idolatry or paganism.[38] Here, ideology means more than just a system of ideas and values; it means a system of ideas "which takes on a totalitarian structure linked with a corresponding state of mind," and which conceals "the political, economic and social interests of the group holding those views."[39] In this sense, as Bonhoeffer says, "ideologies vent their fury on man and then leave him as a bad dream leaves a waking dreamer."[40]

If ideology is taken in the first sense, that is, as a system essential to the existence of any culture, then it seems obvious that Christianity cannot avoid some kind of alliance with it, if it is to exist for people. However, if ideology is understood in the second sense, then clearly it is in opposition to Christian faith, and destructive of both the identity and integrity of the church. Míguez Bonino uses ideology in both senses. For him, an alliance with Marxism is necessary if the church is going to be relevant to the needs of the people in Latin America. But it is an uneasy alliance. He writes: "When the cause of Jesus Christ (and consequently the Church in any missionary understanding of it) is totally and without rest equated with the cause of social and political revolution, either the Church and Jesus Christ are made redundant or the political and social revolution is clothed in a sacred or semi-sacred gown."[41]

This brings us to the heart of the problem facing the church in South Africa. In order for the Afrikaner to break free from the bondage of British imperialism, Afrikanerdom developed a cultural system adequate to the task. In doing so, it was supported by the Dutch Reformed Church and the other Afrikaans churches. But gradually this system took on an ideological character in the pejorative sense of the word. Apartheid was born. The legitimate aspirations of a people became destructive of the equally legitimate claims of others, and the whole process was given religious justification. Today, the attempt by the DRC and others to extricate separate development from apartheid is an endeavor to rid a cultural system (i.e., pluralism) of its ideological character in the bad sense.[42] We have already expressed our reservations about this possibility, insofar as separate development perpetuates the basic apartheid philosophy.

Similarly, in order for the black South African to break free from the chains of apartheid, blacks have developed African nationalism and black consciousness. In doing so, the black community has inevitably gained support from black Christians and their churches. But the problem is precisely that faced by the DRC—how to exist for the people without becoming captive to the ideological system they have espoused, or, to put it in another way, how to keep the ideology human and so prevent it from becoming demonic.

The Christian response to ideologies, and therefore its attitude towards ideological commitment, must be worked out on the basis of a careful and critical evaluation of the particular ideology in question. For example, in responding to the challenge of Marxism, the Christian will have to distinguish between the Marxist analysis of a situation and the program of action proposed. But throughout, the biblical proclamation of the kingdom of God revealed in Jesus Christ remains the basis for evaluation. This proclamation implies certain things about history, human nature, values, and society that radically challenge other ideological presuppositions. In other words, the Christian critique must go beneath the surface, and not simply question, accept, or reject the ideology at a superficial level. The questions addressed to separate development in chapter two (what does it promise [goal], and how and at what cost will it be achieved [means] go far deeper than may be apparent at first. Separate development, like Marxism, does not only offer an analysis of the situation, nor does it simply propose a solution to the problem; it operates on certain assumptions about man and society. Because of this, the Christian critique has to probe the claims of ideologies at different, though inter-related, levels. As this is a highly complex issue, we can do no more at this point than suggest, somewhat simplistically, the basic thrust of a critique that attempts to be faithful to the kingdom of God.

The kingdom of God promises a "new earth" where justice and righteousness shall flourish. It promises God's *shalom,* God's gift of a renewed creation and a fulfilled humanity. But neither this goal nor penultimate expressions of it here and now can be achieved by means that run contrary to the end in view. One cannot dehumanize in order to humanize. And that is the kingdom critique of ideologies, and the criterion by which commitments must be determined and evaluated. Paradoxical as it may seem, putting "first the Kingdom of God and his righteousness" results in a proper humanism, while deifying human systems destroys people. God must be allowed to be God if man is to be man. It is our conviction that concern for people runs throughout the biblical message, finding its culmination in Jesus himself. Jesus relativized all human institutions, codes, and programs so that the love of God for men and women could become the operative absolute in human and social life. Karl Barth called this God's humanism.[43] And, contrary to much popular opinion, the view of John Calvin is similar to that of Barth, as André Bieler shows in *The Social Humanism of Calvin*. "Ideology," writes Bieler, "has the power to raise up a sacred enthusiasm, to set human groups one against another, and to lead them finally into destruction. In such a situation we can well see what Calvin can still offer to the world. Calvin's universal humanism can save us from corruption and destruction."[44] The key question for all ideologies is whether or not they try to play God, for if they do, they will surely destroy man, and the Christian has no other duty but to pull down such idols from their self-appointed thrones.

The Christian rejection of Marxism is not a rejection of a just social and economic order. How can the Christian not desire and work for that—more so, indeed, than the Marxist? No, the objection to Marxism is that the way chosen to achieve that end—revolution and violence—is destructive of the end itself. Furthermore, the Marxist solution must be inadequate because it only relates to man as a social being, the worker, the oppressed, not as a whole person.[45] This is the very reason for the neo-Marxist revolt against Communism. Marxism ends up dehumanizing man in the very process of seeking his liberation. "A Christian can, therefore, ask," with Míguez Bonino, "whether the Marxist search for a concrete and effective expression in history of solidary love does not lead to something much deeper and total. And, therefore, whether man's alienation does not require a deeper and more radical remedy."[46] We believe that that more radical remedy is the gospel of the kingdom, but that it needs to be set free from those forces that destroy its liberating power.

If we do not advocate a "strategic alliance with Marxism," how then are we to respond to its challenge? It is commonplace today to say that Marxism would not have seen the light of day if Christians had been true to the gospel of the kingdom in nineteenth-century Europe. Marx's critique of religion was not just based on science and philosophy; it was a reaction to the empirical condition of the church. That condition was one of captivity to the power structures of the world. The 'god' proclaimed and worshipped was too often not the God who rules in Jesus Christ, but an alien 'god' who sanctioned the unjust status quo of European society. The atheism which then swept over working class people was not primarily a rejection of God, but a repudiation of the 'god' in which the church apparently believed. The subsequent judgment on the church was severe. It is by no means complete. The Marxist critique was devastating, not of the God revealed in Jesus Christ, but of the idols of Christian Europe. Helmut Gollwitzer has written that "Marxist accusations are a catalogue of actual Christian degenerations."[47] In other words, the rise and growth of Marxism is a sign of the failure of the church.

It is necessary to consider whether or not Marxism and related liberation movements in southern Africa today are not instruments of divine judgment on our so-called Christian civilization. An outrageous idea? Not at all. It is perfectly in accord with the word of the prophets in the Old Testament.[48] Of course, being instruments of judgment does not make them instruments of salvation, except perhaps insofar as they force us back to discover the God of the Bible and the gospel of the kingdom. The year after Frelimo came to power in Mozambique, the superintendent of the Methodist Church there wrote in his report to the South African Conference of his church:

> ... the Church as an organization will undergo radical change if in fact it is not entirely dismantled. But we also know, that that dismantling will not destroy the Spirit of Christ, who will still move and work in the lives of those who respond to him,

and give him their total allegiance. The Church of Christ will continue to exist, but the form in which it will exist will be determined by our obedience to what the Holy Spirit is saying to us in a new situation.

And, then, after analyzing the historical significance of his situation, he asked: "Can we as a Church in South Africa get the message of Mozambique?"[49]

The church's proper response to this critical, unmasking challenge from alien sources dare not be self-righteous rejection. But it must not be naïve acceptance either. Rather, the challenge should be received as "an invitation for self-criticism, repentance and rebirth."[50] A church which is faithful to the kingdom of God is the true iconoclast in the world, the unmasker of human pretense and will-to-power, the demythologizer of ideological myths, and the defender of humanity. But a church which fails to be faithful causes people to turn away and look elsewhere. The tragedy is that the alternatives are themselves inadequate, and in the long run cannot satisfy the total needs of man and society. Marxism is a valid protest, but it is not the answer. The answer lies in the gospel of Jesus Christ; and yet, without the renewal of the church it is impossible for this message to be proclaimed and to make its transforming impact upon society.

"The time has come for judgment to begin," wrote Peter in his first letter, "and God's own people are the first to be judged" (4:17). Again and again, the true prophets of Israel addressed their most urgent warnings to the people of God themselves. Thus, Peter, writing in the midst of intense persecution and suffering, tells his Christian friends that what is happening is a process of judgment. The judgment of the world is beginning, and it must begin with the church in order for the church to fulfill its true function in the final drama of redemption. Could it be that the church in South Africa is being judged, not to be cast aside but to be renewed for ministry in a new and critical epoch? Is this one way in which the Holy Spirit works? The Holy Spirit, so John's Gospel tells us, unmasks human sin and pretense.[51] In humbly responding to the judgment of the Spirit in history, the church begins to be renewed. The alternative? Perhaps a fate similar to that which overtook the church in northern Africa in the seventh century, as it crumbled under the impact of Islam.

Renewal requires more than confession of and repentance for guilt. But it does not require less. Writing in his *Ethics,* Bonhoeffer reflects on the guilt of the church in Germany, even the Confessing Church, and declares:

> The free confession of guilt is not something which can be done or left undone at will. It is the emergence of the form of Jesus Christ in the Church. Either the Church must willingly undergo this transformation, or else she must cease to be the Church of Christ.[52]

The church is called to act as a deputy on behalf of the nation. It is unlikely that a nation will confess to its guilt; but the church under the cross must, and must do so vicariously on behalf of all. This is part not only of its renewal, but of its witness to the kingdom. Certainly, the nation will not and cannot confess its guilt until the church has confessed its complicity in that guilt. On the question of repentance, Bonhoeffer writes from prison that *metanoia* is "not in the first place thinking about one's needs, problems, sins and fears, but allowing oneself to be caught up into the way of Jesus Christ, into the messianic event," that is, "into the messianic sufferings of God in Jesus Christ."[53] Repentance is not only words, it is service of the world under the sign of the cross. But what is the nature of that service? Or, to put it in another way, how does the kingdom take form in history, and what is the role of the church?

The Politics of the Kingdom

No ISSUE evokes more heated and frustrating debate than the question of politics and religion. But the fact that the debate is perennial indicates its continual relevance. The story of the church in South Africa demonstrates that religion is directly and intimately related to the socio-political history of the country. One may ask whether or not the church should have been involved in politics in the ways it has been and still is, but nothing can alter the fact that in South Africa, politics and the church have been, and remain, bound together in one historical drama, one persistent struggle.

The *polis* is the city, that is, the arena of human social transactions affecting the common life of the community in all its dimensions. A moment's reflection will show that nothing is excluded from the *polis*, and therefore nothing is exempt from politics—the art of keeping society functioning properly. Everything from family life to education, from daily bread to economic policies, is included. Cabinet portfolios touch on every aspect of existence, and some aspects are at their mercy. The church itself does not escape, nor can it, for it too falls within the *polis*. And insofar as the church is a vitally interested partner in the life of people, there must inevitably be some kind of relationship between church and state. This means that the church is involved in politics, whether it wants to be or not. The important consideration is the nature of that relationship.

In his *Politics of Jesus* John Howard Yoder has cogently argued that an ethic of the kingdom is not irrelevant to the world of politics, but impinges directly on it. "Theologians," he writes, "have long been asking how Jerusalem can relate to Athens, here the claim is that Bethlehem has something to say about Rome—or Masada."[54] By this, Yoder does not mean that the ethics of the kingdom can be fully understood or implemented by the world or the state, but that the Christian community, when faithful to the kingdom, injects into the life of the world another alternative to those normally recognized or accepted. The church has a unique contribution to make to the struggle for justice and peace. To detract from this uniqueness is to make the church redundant and to allow political philosophies and ideologies free rein, unchallenged by prophetic critique. There is a distinct politics of the kingdom, a politics very different from the triumphalist approach of the medieval church or the secularized approach of much contemporary Christianity. In order for such politics to be a reality, however, the church has to retain its freedom from ideological captivity, and at the same time become concretely involved in social issues and critically engage the ideologies that claim the allegiance of people and societies.

The task of relating the message of the kingdom of God to the political process is fraught with problems. Indeed, we do well to acknowledge John Gladwin's warning that "the Kingdom theme can be a dangerous place from which to begin in thinking through a Christian view on the exercise of power in the present age. It has a tendency towards political idealism and utopianism."[55] That temptation we must face, however, but not at the expense of commitment to the kingdom. In Berger's timely phrases, we must not be simply "apocalyptic utopians" nor "hard-nosed realists."[56] What we need is a healthy dose of both vision and realism, for that will more adequately reflect the judgment and the promise of the kingdom.

Since the Constantinian era began in the fourth century, making the Christian religion the faith of the Roman Empire, there has been a very close relationship between the church and the state in those countries that have traditionally constituted Christendom. Even with the demise of the power of the church as a major political institution, the idea of Christendom has persisted. This has not necessarily meant the existence of an official state church. There is no such church in South Africa, but the idea of Christendom is very much alive, as seen in the notion of a Christian civilization that pervades so much official and popular thinking. The essence of Constantinianism is that the church upholds the authority of the state, blessing and sanctifying its policies when necessary, and in return the state protects the freedom of the church to fulfill its religious functions. Under the guise of separating religion and politics into two distinct realms under God, the two-kingdoms theory achieves a remarkable synthesis of mutual self-interest. The religious realm is protected and the political order legitimated. Prophecy ceases, or else is used to serve the interests of those in power and to justify their crusades. In turn, the church may receive some limited voice in the shaping of public policy, but the degree of such participation will vary according to the relationship the church has to those in power. This kind of relationship, however, irrespective of its extent, has so often resulted in the church supporting unjust causes that it has given rise to the popular cry: "Keep the church out of politics!" The complementary cry is for the church to become more "spiritual."

A diametrically opposed model has been that of the revolutionary involvement of the church in the political arena, and the willingness to use violence, if necessary, to bring about social change. There are examples of this model throughout history, especially since the Reformation shattered the unity of Christendom. Sectarian movements such as that of Thomas Müntzer in Germany have taken up arms in the name of Christ, "the Lord of hosts," to bring in the kingdom and establish utopia. More often than not, however, the religious vision that sparked the revolt is forgotten, and Christian faith is once again used to legitimate political interest, whether or not this conforms to the message of Christ. In any case, such involvement in radical social action is generally what is meant today when the comfortable of the earth deplore "the intrusion of religion into politics." Perhaps when they were the underdogs, they did not have the same scruples.

There are those who shun both models, and consciously attempt to extricate themselves from this world and its political machinations. With their citizenship planted in heaven, they regard themselves as being above the strife and turmoil described in the daily newspapers and depicted on television. Religion is a private matter between man and Maker; the church is the community of saints separated from the world of unbelief and ungodliness. Whether this approach has been embodied in monastery or gospel tabernacle, the rationale and the result have been the same. Yet this radical separation of the spiritual and the secular does not succeed in getting the saints out of the political scene, though they may reject any responsibility for it. They remain dependent on the state, bound by its rules (unless they break them and become sectarian revolutionaries or rebels) and benefitting from its daily administration. They remain a political factor as long as they remain in the *polis*. To avoid that, they would have to leave the world. When people say that we must get religion out of politics, they do not normally expect things to go this far. For them, this would be far too religious and not responsible enough.

In one sense, our description of these three models has been simplistic. Yet there are sufficient examples of each in the history of the church and in South Africa to justify the way in which we have depicted them. In fact, they are represented within the New Testament itself, corresponding more or less to the positions adopted by the Sadducees, the Zealots, and the Essenes at Qumran. Moreover, there have been those who have identified the position of Jesus with each of them. But the politics of Jesus is different; it is unique. The following words of Jesus, though often misunderstood, provide the clue: "My kingdom does not belong to this world; if my kingdom belonged to this world, my followers would fight to keep me from being handed over to the Jewish authorities" (John 18:36). Many presume that this means that the rule and realm of Jesus have nothing to do with the social realities of this world. But Jesus is not saying that at all. He is saying that his kingdom does not derive its authority from this world, but from God. In the sense in which we have defined politics, Jesus' reign is no less political than the other options we have mentioned, but it is a new and distinct type of politics, the politics of the cross—politics in the service of human redemption and reconciliation.

Jesus was certainly tempted to pursue other ways of achieving his goal; that is clear from the temptation narratives. But he refused every other option but the one that led to his death. Jesus did not escape into the desert and hide with the monks at Qumran; he bore a faithful witness to his kingdom to the end, and he did so in a way that was consonant with that kingdom. It was an unholy alliance between religion and the state, helped by the apocalyptic zeal of the Zealot Judas, that brought Jesus to the cross. In his death on the cross, he overcame and judged every attempt at human self-justification, every venture to divinize politics, and every endeavor to use God. Jesus was dehumanized at the cross; but in raising him from the dead, God sealed the fate of all dehumanizing powers, and ensured human salvation.[57] Thus, Moltmann can rightly speak of the "political consequences of the Cross." He writes:

> For believers, Christ crucified was made the righteousness of God, and for them political authority was deprived of its religious sanction. Christ, crucified in powerlessness and shame, has become their highest authority. Consequently, they no longer believe in religio-political authority, for the anxiety and fear that demanded it has been eliminated. Modern political theology considers the mortal conflict of Jesus with the public powers of his day to be central. Such conflict played no part in the old political theology that developed a "state metaphysics". The only question is how this conflict of Jesus with the public powers can today be expressed in individual Christian and ecclesial public life.[58]

Moltmann's concluding question leads us to reconsider the nature of the church in terms of the politics of Jesus. The consequences of Jesus' mode of expressing and establishing his authority are spelled out for the Christian community by Paul in his letter to the Romans: "Do not be conformed to this world, but be transformed by the renewal of your mind, that you may prove what is the will of God" (12:2). Once again, this is not an admonition to retreat from the world, but an injunction to be present in a particular way. The "world" referred to is not the context in which we live, but the way of life and the style of authority that characterize those who deny that in Christ the "new age" has dawned. In other words, Paul is telling the church not to become captive to the ways and means of the world, but to pursue God's will (i.e., his kingdom) in Christ's way.

This nonconformist style of ecclesial life inevitably involves a struggle against those powers that refuse to accept the fact that God's kingdom has been established in Christ. Hence Paul frequently refers to the conflict that is waged against "principalities and powers" of this world.[59] While these "principalities and powers" may have other meanings as well, they do refer to what we have pejoratively called ideologies.[60] Ideologies are more than "flesh and blood," they are destructive, dehumanizing forces that grip the minds and imaginations of men and women. According to Paul, and this relates well to our own discussion of ideologies in both senses of the word, evil works through those very structures which God has given to regulate human life in community. We cannot live without these structures; God has created them for our good. And yet, we cannot simply live with them either, for they are fallen, harmful, and enslaving. They are subject to the power of sin. This does not mean that the Christian is called to be an anarchist, for in spite of their sinfulness, he still recognizes the need for structures. Yet, neither can he be a defender of the status quo. The structures are in constant need of transformation. Thus, the Christian and the church live in a state of tension when serving the kingdom of God. They are caught in the cross fire from reactionary and revolutionary. They become, like Jesus, provocative to both sides. This means, in the end, that the church cannot avoid suffering. Thus, it is essential that the church resist what Yoder calls the temptation of the Sadducees—"the assumption that the forces which really determine the march of history are in the hands of the leaders of the armies and the markets, in such measure that if Christians are to contribute to the renewal of society they will need, like everyone else—in fact in competition with everyone else—to become in their turn the lords of the state and the economy, so as to use power toward the ends they consider desirable."[61]

But just as the church is not called to rule the world, neither is the church called to redeem the world. The church is not the kingdom, nor is it the Christ; its responsibility is to bear witness to, not to replace, them. Bonhoeffer put it well when he wrote from prison: "We are certainly not Christ; we are not called to redeem the world by our own deeds and suffering, and we need not try to assume such an impossible burden. We are not lords, but instruments in the hand of the Lord of history."[62] It is of the utmost importance for the church in South Africa to realize its proper limitations if it is to fulfill its proper tasks.

In serving the interests of the kingdom through a ministry of suffering love, the church is called to identify with the powerless. The New Testament shows how much the kingdom of God is "biased" in favor of the poor, the oppressed, the downtrodden, the weak, the casualties of society. Abraham Kuyper himself reminds us that Jesus and his apostles "invariably took sides *against* those who were powerful and living in luxury, and *for* the suffering and oppressed."[63] From a Christian point of view, the powerful, wealthy, and strong are quite obviously able to look after their own worldly interests. That is why they are in a position of power. The church, in serving the kingdom, is given a special responsibility for those who are unable to look after their basic rights and interests as human beings, personally and corporately. This is the God-given "bias" of the church. It is built into its mission. It is of the essence of biblical religion.[64]

But this bias does not mean that the church is unconcerned about those in power. It has a special ministry to them as well, both because they are human beings, and because they control the lives of others and shape the course of events. In other words, it has a ministry to those who are in bondage to privilege. There is little chance that those with power will share it with others if they fear for the future, or that those with more than enough will accept the risk of less than sufficient if this is what justice demands. And yet it is precisely this fear attendant upon clinging to privilege that poses the greatest threat both for them and for the powerless. Thus, the politics of the kingdom includes an evangelical mission, a converting task, of enabling men and women to discover in the gospel of the kingdom a way beyond fear, a way to accept justice and to see that it is done to others.

This brings us to the witness of the church to the state, a theme that has recurred often in these pages. The New Testament portrays the state with "two faces." On the one hand, civil authority is affirmed as good, given by God, and necessary for order in society. On the other hand, civil authority is depicted as fallen, in the grip of "principalities and powers," and seeking to be more than a servant of God and the people. Yoder has shown the remarkable consistency of the New Testament on the question of church and state. On his reckoning, there is no contradiction between Romans 13 and Revelation 13. In both, the witness of the nonconforming Christian community remains the same. "No State can be so low on the scale of relative justice that the duty of the Christian is no longer to be subject; no State can rise so high on that scale that Christians are not called to some sort of suffering because of their refusal to agree with its self-glorification."[65] Jesus and the early Christians submitted to the just claims of the state and counseled others to do the same. But they also rejected and opposed any claims made by the state for absolute obedience. When the state claims such allegiance, it becomes an ideological substitute for God. It cannot be obeyed if its demands deny God's authority and kingdom. As John Calvin put it in his *Institutes of the Christian Religion,* "In that obedience which we have shown to be due the authority of rulers, we are always to make this exception, indeed, to observe it as primary, that such obedience is never to lead us away from obedience to him to whose will the desires of all kings ought to be subject...."[66] Thus, as a last resort, civil disobedience becomes justified, as the DRC itself affirmed earlier this century during the Afrikaner rebellion in 1914 when South Africa entered World War I. The DRC declared, along with the other Afrikaner churches, that "no one may revolt against lawful authority other than for carefully considered and well-grounded reasons based on the word of God and a conscience enlightened by the Word of God."[67]

We may summarize the witness of the church to the state as follows. First of all, the church has to support the state in its task of maintaining order. But it has to remind the state that justice is the only basis for true order, and that the state exists for the good of *all* people under its authority. This means that the only people who should fear the state are those who break the moral laws and promote injustice. Those who do good, who love and serve their fellows, care for the poor, seek the welfare of the downtrodden and the liberty of the oppressed, should have no reason to fear the authority of the state.

Secondly, the church continually has to remind the state of its boundaries.[68] Indeed, perhaps the greatest service the church can render the state is to prevent politics from becoming religion, to prevent state policies from becoming idolatrous. Herbert W. Richardson makes this point as follows:

> Politics does not solve the ultimate questions of life, will not bring salvation, cannot make men happy. Its goal is more modest, but no less essential. Politics allows persons and groups that have different aspirations to live together in relative peace and to co-operate in limited ways for the sake of specific finite benefits. Whenever politics seeks to be more than this, it must inevitably become far less.[69]

Thirdly, the church must not expect too much of the state. The state is not the kingdom of God, nor is it run by saints. The state is fallen. G. B. Caird concludes his study on *Principalities and Powers* by reminding us, "To expect that evil will be defeated by any of these powers, by the action of the State, by the self discipline of the conscience, or by the processes of nature, is to ask Satan to cast out Satan. The powers can be robbed of their tyrannical influence and brought into their proper subjection to God only in the Cross."[70] Thus, the church should encourage those in power to take steps in the right direction, no matter how small they may be. This does not mean that the church should be politically naïve. Some steps may only appear correct. They may in fact reinforce injustice. Therefore, the church has to keep awake, recognizing the ambiguities of politics, the dilemmas of power, and especially the pretenses of politicians. Nonetheless, as Moltmann puts it, "a concrete step is worth more than the most beautiful idea of possibilities."[71]

Fourthly, the church dare not expect too little of the state. The church is not a political party and does not have a blueprint for society, but it does have a vested interest in justice and the furtherance of peace. As such, it is deeply concerned that the direction of state policies is "towards the

Kingdom of God and not away from it."[72] The demands of the kingdom are such that they ensure the inadequacy of every step taken by the state, and so keep the church restless in calling upon the state to go further than it hitherto has gone in the interests of justice. The church is the advocate of the powerless, and as such she cannot rest until justice is done.

Fifthly, the church cannot expect of the state what it cannot achieve in its own life. The witness of the church to the state is severely compromised when its own behavior contradicts the message it proclaims, when resolutions are denied in practice, when words lack conviction and commitment. The church has no right to be heard when it speaks without competence, or when it says nothing worth saying.

Finally, in speaking the word of judgment to the state, in opposing some of its policies, or even in fundamentally rejecting its programs and so coming into a relation of conflict, the church has to resist the temptation to regard those in authority as the enemy. Evil remains the enemy, not people, even though evil works through people and their institutions.[73] And this does not change, no matter what face the state may wear. Even amid Nazi tyranny, Bonhoeffer could write that "the recommendation for a withdrawal of the Church from the world and from relations which she still maintains with the State under the impact of an apocalyptic age is ... nothing but a somewhat melancholy interpretation of the times in terms of the philosophy of history."[74]

The Hope of the Kingdom

MANY SOUTH AFRICANS are presently going through the "slough of despond." This is particularly true, as we have seen, of white South Africans. Events in southern Africa do not inspire the confidence of whites in the future. Little wonder, then, that hope is at a premium. Those familiar with Bonhoeffer's *Letters and Papers from Prison* will recall how, in the final years of his life in Hitler's Germany, he struggled to keep hope alive, to believe in God's providence in spite of personal setbacks and the war situation in general. Again and again he criticized the cynics who "think that the meaning of present events is chaos, disorder and catastrophe," those who have no concern for the future but are "consumed by the present moment."[75] How is it possible to hope in contemporary South Africa? For what are we to hope? What can we do to realize our hopes? In the last analysis, is the struggle of the church the struggle to keep hope alive?

Hope is fundamental to the message of the kingdom of God. The gospel holds out the promise of eternal life to believers, a life that death itself cannot destroy. It speaks of the "sure and certain hope of resurrection to life eternal." The gospel also proclaims that God's will eventually will be done "on earth as in heaven"; it promises "a new heaven and a new earth." A message of personal and social hope is inextricably and mysteriously bound together in the promise of the final coming of the messianic kingdom for which "the whole creation groans in travail." The promise is the promise of *shalom*—God's peace, in which his justice and righteousness rule supreme, in which human pain and suffering are no more; in which all things, people, and nations have found their fulfillment. "The Gospel," wrote Johannes Verkuyl, "contains much more than the promise of earthly *shalom*. The message of the Kingdom is concerned with victory over demons, with eternal life, with a new world."[76]

But the message of the kingdom, as Verkuyl also pointed out, is not just about the ultimate arrival of *shalom*. It is about the penultimate signs of that eventuality. Jesus' proclamation was that the kingdom had come. The new age had dawned. The promise to "our forefathers" had been fulfilled. Thus, the doubting John the Baptist is told that "the blind receive their sight, the lame walk, lepers are cleansed, and the deaf hear, the dead are raised up, the poor have good news preached to them."[77] Jesus offered a foretaste of the future. Indeed, he went further. He instructed his messianic community to go and do likewise throughout the length and breadth of the land. The joy and healing of the kingdom can be experienced now. The good news is for this life as well as that beyond, and it is no less personal than it is social, no less social than personal. The peace of God for which men and women yearn in their hearts, and which can be discovered through grace in this life, has its complement in the social hope of the church when it prays "send peace in our time." Both comprise the Christian hope, and both anticipate the *shalom* that will only come in its fullness with the consummation of all things in Christ.

The hope of the kingdom is the promise of peace. The hope of South Africans is that this promise should come true in some meaningful way, not just at the end of time, but in our contemporary situation. But is there any connection between our ultimate hope and our penultimate longing for peace? And if so, what is the task of the church in relating the two? What does it mean, in the words of Míguez Bonino, to "'name the Kingdom' in the language of everyday human history?"

Throughout our discussion of the kingdom of God, we have implicitly stressed that the church's witness to the kingdom of God in history does not "bring in the kingdom." Neither the theocratic government of the Puritans nor the social gospel of this century, neither the liberation struggles of the oppressed nor world evangelism, has the ability to usher in utopia. Certainly the church does not have, as Bonhoeffer put it, "the mission to overleap the world and make it into the Kingdom of God."[78] Nevertheless, there is a connection between the coming of the kingdom and the work and witness of men and women. In a letter to Míguez Bonino, Jürgen Moltmann reminds us that Bonhoeffer and Barth spoke constantly of "the stimulation and intensification of historical hopes through the eschatological hope." This does not mean that our struggles for justice and peace today have "a 'causal character' for the Kingdom of God. . . . rather the Kingdom attains a causal character for the experienced event of liberation, for all messianic activity realizes the possibilities that have been made possible through the inbreaking of messianic time (Luke 4:18ff)."[79] The initiative remains with God, for it is his kingdom and he alone brings it into being; yet he has already begun to do this, especially in Jesus' messianic ministry, which culminated not only in his death and resurrection, but also in the gift of the Holy Spirit. The book of Acts depicts the early Christian community as being caught up into this messianic ministry through the Spirit, in such a way that the church becomes crucial to the eventual coming of the kingdom. It does not cause the kingdom to come, but the Spirit uses it to prepare the way for the fulfillment of all things—hence the importance of repentance or *metanoia* in the sense we spoke of earlier.

Bonhoeffer discusses this relationship between the "ultimate and the penultimate" in his *Ethics:*

> Unlike all methods the preparation of the way sets out from the clear awareness that Christ himself must go this way: it is not our way to him but his way to us that has to be prepared through my knowledge that he himself must prepare it. Method is a way from the penultimate to the ultimate. Preparation of the way is a way from the ultimate to the penultimate. Christ is coming, of his own will, by his own strength, and out of his love; he has the power and the desire to overcome all obstacles, even the greatest; he is the preparer of his own way; it is this, and really only this, that makes us preparers of his way.[80]

The penultimate is important for the sake of the ultimate. It is fundamental to the witness of the church that it work for justice and peace now. This work is a sign pointing to that which is coming. It does not bring in the kingdom; it cannot produce utopia, but it prepares the way for the coming of the King. In this respect, the church is like John the Baptist, a herald of the coming kingdom: "Get the road ready for the Lord; make a straight path for him to travel" so that "all mankind will see God's salvation." Thus, the messianic ministry of Jesus through the Spirit causes the church to bear witness to the kingdom here and now in history, and this witness in turn prepares the way for the kingdom to come. The church acts in anticipation; it anticipates through action.

We have now seen that the hope of the kingdom and the hope of South Africa are related in the promise of and the desire for peace. The ultimate *shalom* is beyond us, but it is possible to have a foretaste of that peace "in our time." The ministry of the church is directly related to both. The Holy Spirit is given to enable the church to bear witness to the reality of the coming *shalom*. In relation to the South African situation, this thrusts the church directly into a ministry of peacemaking.

During the past ten years, much has been written about violence. The problem of violence has also become very evident as we have looked at the history of South Africa and the struggle of the church, and as we now look ahead into the future of southern Africa. Indeed, it is a problem so close to home that it is very difficult to discuss it objectively. The sociology of knowledge rightly tells us that our understanding is affected by our circumstances. Thus, violence becomes that which we find threatening to ourselves. For blacks, violence refers above all to the dehumanizing system of apartheid, police brutality, and the imprisonment of friends and family, often for petty offenses created by the system. For most white South Africans, violence means terrorism on the borders, black riots in Soweto, economic sanctions and blockades. For some, violence is an anarchist revolution; for others, it is the way power maintains itself. Given this set of contradictory perspectives, it is doubtful that we could arrive at a meaningful definition of violence shared in common by all concerned.

The insights of John Howard Yoder, however, are particularly helpful in trying to reach clarity, from the perspective of both social ethics and the kingdom of God. For Yoder, the essence of violence is that it attacks "the dignity of a person in his or her psychosomatic wholeness."[81] This basic definition is broad enough to include what is referred to as "systemic," "institutional," or "structural" violence, as well as the more overt kinds of violence. Violence, in other words, can become built into the structures of society. But if we broaden the definition in this way, maintains Yoder, certain important distinctions must be kept in mind. For one thing, we cannot simply equate all forms of structural violence. There is a qualitative distinction between violence done to a person because of poor wages, inadequate housing, and inferior education, and violence perpetrated by illegitimate force used to maintain such injustices—police brutality, torture, and the imprisonment of people without trial. It would be better to speak of the system as unjust, rather than violent, and reserve "violence" to describe those methods used for its maintenance. This distinction does not make the injustice any better, but it prevents our using the term violence in such a way that it means everything and therefore nothing.

It is also necessary to make the distinction between the legal use of force in society, by the police for example, a use which is necessary for the public good, and the violence that occurs when more force is employed than is necessary for the good of the public. As Yoder expresses it: "The realities to which phrases like 'police brutality' and 'harassment' point are definable and consist precisely in the use of more violence than is justified by the demands of law and order." "Structural violence" occurs when "the authorities who should be responsible for law and order use their mandate and their weapons to mishandle people."

For Yoder, then, violence is an appropriate term to apply to methods adopted by the liberation movements as well. He regards it as equally wrong to use violent means to prevent change as to use such means to bring it about. For in both cases, people are being violated in a fundamental sense. Those who argue that in some cases, as in the liberation movements, violence may be necessary, have to contend with Yoder's comment: "If violence is not always wrong, then structural violence is not necessarily wrong either." You cannot have it both ways.

Before hastily advocating Christian nonviolence as the way of the kingdom of God, however, we need to pause and reflect on the anguish of black Christians in southern Africa today on this very issue. Bishop Desmond Tutu spoke to this at the South African Missiological Conference in 1977. After expressing his own respect for and identification with the way of nonviolence, he raised a number of questions and issues from a black perspective:

(a) The Christian Church is not entirely pacifist;

(b) Blacks are left wondering what practical alternatives are available, given the palpable failure of non-violent forms of protest and opposition;

(c) There is a hollow sound to white arguments for the way of non-violence, given their at least tacit support for state and legal violence.

Thus, Tutu ended, "Can you tell me how I can commend non-violence to blacks who say that the resistance movements in Europe during World War II were lauded to the skies and still are, but what blacks consider to be similar resistance movements are denigrated because they are black?"[82]

Violence is a phenomenon far more complex, then, than the propagandists will allow. A great deal of confusion is caused when the word is bandied about, not only in political rhetoric but also in church statements and resolutions. The impasse in relationships between the DRC and the Gereformeerde Kerken in Holland reflects this problem, as does the whole discussion of the Program to Combat Racism and the question of conscientious objection. All sides are guilty to some extent of oversimplifying through either a too-easy reference to "structural violence" or a failure to understand it at all; of a glorification of liberation struggles "through the barrel of a gun," on the one hand, or the labelling of every struggle for freedom as "terrorist," on the other.[83]

Part of the problem of violence is the fact that what may start out as a comparatively mild attack on the dignity of a person, perhaps through the curtailment of some civil right, provokes a reaction, an understandable reaction. If this action and reaction intensifies, as it has in the history of South Africa, especially as a result of apartheid, then you get what Dom Helder Camara vividly describes as "the spiral of violence." The statement of the South African Council of Churches on conscientious objection recognized this when it declared that it is "injustice and discrimination" which "constitutes the primary institutionalized violence which has provoked the counter-violence of the terrorists or freedom fighters." Violence is a cumulative process, not just an isolated deed or event. If you like, it is part of "original sin."

The black protest against a cheap pacifism is totally justified. But, as Desmond Tutu himself acknowledges, it does not mean that the way of nonviolence is not the Christian way. It means that nonviolence must not become a way of escape from the struggle for justice and human rights. In a critique of liberation theology and the support for national liberation movements, Catholic sociologist Gordon Zahn writes:

> The issue, then, is not a choice between peace and liberation (or between peace and justice), as some believe. If we agree that without justice there can be no true or lasting peace, an equally strong case can be made that the "justice" to be gained at the cost of wholesale death and destruction through war or violent revolution is neither certain nor, as too much recent history shows, likely to be of long duration.... The old scholastic maxim has relevance here: The means usually do turn out to be the end "in the process of becoming". The brutality and torture applied today by the military juntas in Chile, Thailand, and far too many other places deserve universal condemnation. Whether the situation is improved by brutality and torture at the hands of would-be liberators—which, in turn, are used to "justify" more brutality and torture by the forces of the counterrevolution—is not at all certain. *At some point the vicious circle must be broken.*[84]

That is the vocation of the Christian church. It is the reason why it must be critical of ideological alliances, for in such relationships moral motives are inevitably submerged in a struggle for power, and "change one way or another can only take place through violence of one kind or another."[85]

The breaking of the "vicious circle" of violence is not possible without justice. This fundamental insight is deeply rooted in the biblical understanding of *shalom,* both in the Old Testament expectation and the New Testament proclamation of the kingdom. This insight has been the motivation behind all Christian opposition to apartheid and separate development. Racism is inevitably unjust, and thus it provokes violence and requires violence for its perpetuation. Through the years, the churches have been making this point, inadequately no doubt, but they have nevertheless made it. And in the process, they have discovered that any attempt to work for reconciliation which does not go to the root of the problem is cheap reconciliation. The struggle of the church is a struggle to "hunger and thirst to see right prevail" (Matthew 5:6). Hence the witness to human rights, the opposition to arbitrary state action—imprisonment without fair trial, bannings, and the like—and the opposition to torture and to everything else that does violence to people.

None of the churches we have discussed denies the importance of human rights, or the need for the church to bear witness to them. They differ in their stress and emphasis, they may also differ in their enthusiasm for the subject, but they do not disagree that human rights are integrally related to the kingdom of God. It seems that on this point, in theory at least, there can be some form of consensus, as is apparent from the response of the DRC to the *Christian Declaration on Human Rights,* issued by the World Alliance of Reformed Churches in 1976.[86] That this consensus is of vital importance for the future of the witness of the church in South Africa goes without saying. For too long, the church has been tied to sectional interests—the problems and aspirations of Afrikaners or English-speaking people, of whites or blacks. Its concern for people has been determined by the interests of its *own* people. But if the church is serious in its claim to be the community of the kingdom, then it has to break out of this ethnic straitjacket and become the church for all, especially for those who suffer. It has to be *the* agent for God-given rights—this is basic to its witness to the kingdom of God in South Africa.

In order for the church to be for all the peoples of the land, it has to rediscover its unity in Christ. It cannot do this through either cheap reconciliation or superficial ecumenism. It must recognize that the "middle wall of partition" has been torn down in Christ and that, above all else, this means that Christ has destroyed the barriers between black and white, Englishman and Afrikaner, rich and poor. The tremendous significance of this act of reconciliation has yet to be realized within the South African church; neverthetheless, it is this act which lies at the heart of the search for unity in the church today, a search through which the divisive course of South African history can be reversed and a true community created.

While the struggle of the church for justice and peace, for the securing and maintaining of human rights, and for the reconciliation of conflicting peoples is central to the struggle for the kingdom of God in South Africa today, many Christians concerned about these very things feel totally inadequate for the task of bearing witness to them. Their feeling of inadequacy is reflected in the rapid growth of the "charismatic renewal" in South Africa,[87] and the conviction of some that the situation is so hopeless that only God can do something about it. The danger of the "charismatic renewal" in these terms is that it can be a way of escape from reality and witness. This is how it too often appears. But the renewal is nonetheless a timely reminder to the church in South Africa that its resources ultimately lie beyond itself. The struggle of the church is impossible without the power of the Holy Spirit, for it is God alone who can liberate the church and equip it for its task. But God requires more than passivity. He requires obedient discipleship. Thus, the struggle of the church requires a servanthood-spirituality more demanding than most white Christians seem ready to adopt; it requires a spirituality which combines a reliance upon the power of God's Spirit with a wholehearted effort to do God's will in the world through that power. In the past, Bonhoeffer pointed to this need when he called the church in Germany to both prayer and righteous action.[88] Today, Jürgen Moltmann points to this need when he implores Christians to reject the "mindless alternative of either a vertical dimension of faith or a horizontal dimension of love" and to live a life of transcendence and solidarity:

> Transcendence is no longer the transcendence of the risen Christ, who lives in us and with us, if it does not lead to solidarity with those whom he came to free and for whose salvation he died. On the other hand, solidarity with the poor, hungry, oppressed, and imprisoned is no longer the solidarity of the Crucified One if it does not lead to the transcendence of that

freedom in which he was resurrected. The piety of transcendence and the piety of solidarity are two sides of Christian life which we must hold together. If they are separated, the new life in hope is destroyed and made hopeless.[89]

The power of the Spirit is the gift not only of faith and love, but also of hope. "May the God of hope fill you with all joy and peace in believing," wrote Paul, "so that by the power of the Holy Spirit you may abound in hope" (Romans 15:13). Here the joy of liberation, the peace of God, and the hope of the kingdom come together and provide the focus for the Christian community engaged in its struggle against "principalities and powers" through the power of the Spirit. We now see that hoping for the kingdom is nothing less than the vocation of the church. Commenting on these words of Paul to the Romans, Martin Luther wrote:

> He that depends on the true God has laid all tangible things aside and lives by naked hope. To call God "the God of hope" is therefore the same as to call him the God of hopers. He certainly is not the God but the enemy of people who despair easily and are unable to trust anyone. In short, he is the "God of hope" because he is the Giver of hope, and, even more, because only hope worships him. . . .[90]

At the height of the black protests in 1977, Alan Paton wrote in a South African newspaper column:

> I say to my fellow South Africans: if you have no hope, you should get out as soon as possible. If you have unbounded hope you should go and see a psychiatrist. If you can't give up hope, if you insist on hoping against hope, then persist with all the things you have been doing to make this a better country.[91]

In bearing witness to the providence of God over and in history, a providence radically transformed in our understanding by the cross and resurrection of Jesus Christ, the church reaches beyond itself to the future, a future which is God's gift of *shalom*. Thus, it keeps hope alive and, in so doing, counters the powers of this "passing age" and worships God alone.

Postscript:

A Response to Major Criticisms

AS FAR AS I am aware, four major criticisms have been made of *The Church Struggle,* each of which relates to critical issues facing the church in South Africa today. The first criticism concerns my social analysis and, related to this, my failure to take the Marxist critique of the church sufficiently seriously.

James Cochrane has rightly argued that my analysis of the role of the church in South African society failed to take the relationship of the church to the historical development of the economy into account. In particular, Cochrane maintained, I failed to show the extent to which the so-called English-speaking churches have been captive to capitalism.[1] Thus *The Church Struggle* not only does not deal with a serious weakness within the English-speaking churches themselves but it also reveals the extent to which my analysis has been affected by my church and cultural heritage as well as my class position as a white English-speaking South African. During the past few years I have become increasingly aware of this analytical weakness, and have begun to correct it.[2]

For several years now a debate has raged about whether race or class is the primary category for analyzing South African society. Broadly speaking, the debate has been between liberals and Marxists.[3] *The Church Struggle* assumes that race is the fundamental problem, and pays very little attention to questions of class and therefore to the economic gulf which separates rich and poor, the oppressor and the oppressed. It now seems clear to me that neither race nor class is primary, but that both categories are fundamental and interrelated. A rewriting of *The Church Struggle* would therefore require a much more thorough-going social analysis, and I would need to respond more adequately than I did to the practical as well as the theoretical challenge which Marxism presents to the church in southern Africa today. Central to such a discussion would be the relationship of the church to labor and the trade unions, a subject which is quite crucial both for the future of the church and the country as a whole.[4]

The second major criticism of *The Church Struggle,* made by Bob Clarke, centered on Chapter Two of the book. In an otherwise very positive review, Clarke wrote:

> I cannot understand how any book which purports to discuss the church struggle in South Africa, makes no reference whatsoever to Bishop Clayton's Church and Nation Report of 1944, Michael Scott, and the Church's response to the compulsory takeover of Mission Schools under the terms of the Bantu Education Act of 1953. Incredibly Bishop Reeves is not mentioned at all, nor is his deportation nor that of four other Anglican Bishops nor is Dr. Arthur Blaxall. The briefest of reference is made to Father Trevor Huddleston. . . . No mention is made of the Freedom Charter, the Treason Trial, nor the Treason Trial Defence Fund, nor of Canon John Collins. No attempt is made to assess the role and effectiveness of overseas pressure groups. He scarcely does justice to the significance of the churches' resistance to the Church Clause Legislation of 1957. . . .[5]

As I intimated at the time in a response to Clarke's criticism, I was and remain grateful for the detailed and helpful comments which he made. but in mitigation I would say that *The Church Struggle* was not intended to be an exhaustive account of the church's struggle against apartheid, let alone a history of the church in South Africa. Indeed, I am not primarily a church historian engaged in detailed research and analysis, but a theologian seeking to reflect on the social history of the church in South Africa. There are many omissions in *The*

Church Struggle which, if it were to be rewritten as a comprehensive history text-book, would have to be remedied. Much more, for example, would have to be said about both the Roman Catholic and the Lutheran churches. But the original intention of the book was to paint some broad strokes on the canvas—a more Breughel-like detailed portrayal might have increased its usefulness in some respects but it might also have clouded the issues. Certainly the canvas would have had to be enlarged beyond its present size.

The third major criticism of *The Church Struggle* came from Allan Boesak in a review in *Social Dynamics*.[6] Dr. Boesak's review was generally positive but he argued that while my "treatment of the relationships between Black theology, Black consciousness and the church is in fact better than most," I did not take the challenge of black theology as seriously as I should have in my final chapter on "The Kingdom of God in South Africa." Moreover, Boesak pointed out that I failed to deal adequately with the black Dutch Reformed churches and the role of the "coloured" community.

Once again I must not only admit the validity of these criticisms, especially of the first, but also express my gratitude for having them pointed out. In response I would say that since writing *The Church Struggle* I have been engaged in reworking my approach to theology, and the challenge of black theology has continued to be one of the major reasons and sources for doing so. During the past decade black theology in South Africa has grown in stature and significance, and there is no doubt in my own mind that it has begun to reshape the church in spite of strong resistance to it.[7]

On the question of the black Dutch Reformed churches, and particularly Dr. Boesak's own D.R. Mission Church (NG Sendingkerk), I would argue that their involvement in the church struggle against apartheid only really got underway in the second half of the 1970s. Nevertheless, it is true that its beginning was marked by the synod of the black NG Kerk in Africa in 1975 at which, inter alia, the church decided to become an observer member of the South African Council of Churches, and this historic event should have been discussed in *The Church Struggle*. Subsequently, it should be noted, the NG

Sendingkerk at its synod in 1978, and the Indian Reformed Church in 1980, took similar decisions which also expressed their rejection of the white DRC's support of government policy. That part of the story, and Dr. Boesak's own role within it, belongs to more recent times rather than to the period dealt with in *The Church Struggle*. Without doubt, however, the involvement of the black Dutch Reformed churches in the South African Council of Churches, the emergence of "the Belydende Kring" and the Alliance of Black Reformed Christians in South Africa, together with the declaration "Apartheid is a Heresy" and the exclusion of the white DRC from the World Alliance of Reformed Churches, have been crucial developments during these past few years.[8]

A variation on Dr. Boesak's criticism was that of Nicholas Wolterstorff who felt that I had downplayed the significance of the black church for the future.[9] If that is the message *The Church Struggle* conveyed, then it is clearly wrong and in need of correction. From a purely statistical point of view, the church in South Africa is a black church with some white members, rather than the other way around, as commonly perceived. According to the 1980 government census, 77 percent of all South Africans belong to some church denomination, and of these, 88 percent are black and only 12 percent white. Not only do the multi-racial or so-called English-speaking churches have a large majority of black members, but the black Dutch Reformed churches' membership is, taken together, comparable in size to the white DRC. Moreover, the largest and fastest-growing church group is the African Independent, or, more accurately, Indigenous church movement. Approximately six million blacks belong to churches within this group, almost 30 percent of the black population as a whole.[10]

But quite apart from statistics, it is clearly the case that the black membership within the churches, whether they be mainline denominations or independent, is increasingly providing the leadership in the struggle against apartheid and for a just and liberated society. When *The Church Struggle* was written, by way of illustration, Bishop Desmond Tutu had yet to become General Secretary of the South African Council of Churches, and the national leadership of the mainstream

churches was almost totally in the hands of its white membership. This situation has dramatically changed during the past
ten years. At the same time it must be noted that the most radical theological critique of apartheid yet to appear, *The Kairos
Document,* published late in 1985, which was largely the work
of black theologians, is also the most critical of the failure of
the established, traditionally white-dominated churches to fulfill their task.[11]

A fourth major criticism of *The Church Struggle* was that I
failed to deal adequately with the problem of violence, an issue
which is also raised very sharply in *The Kairos Document.* This
criticism was made by several reviewers, who rightly noted
that my own orientation was toward a Christian pacifism, particularly as articulated by the North American theologian
John Howard Yoder. During the past decade violence has spi-
ralled in South Africa and it has undoubtedly become the most
serious issue facing the church as well as the nation. There is
no doubt in my mind that it is no longer meaningful to ask
whether social change can come about without violence—the
fact is, violence has become a reality, and many would argue
with some justification that it is the only language which
speaks to those in power. What is required, then, is an accurate
analysis of the causes and nature of the violence, and an ability
to distinguish between the violence of apartheid and the re-
pression which goes with it, and the struggle of those who have
been driven to use violence in their quest for liberation.[12] This
does not necessarily justify the latter, but it avoids the facile
response of so many white Christians to what is happening. It
remains my conviction, nonetheless, that the church has a special responsibility to pursue nonviolent strategies for change.
This is the context within which, for example, the dis-
investment debate and the end conscription campaign have to
be considered. Nonviolence is not passivity, and it may well require acts of civil disobedience in faithfulness to the apostolic
injunction that we should "obey God rather than man" in bearing witness to the gospel and our confession that "Jesus Christ
is Lord."

The confession that "Jesus Christ is Lord" remains at the
center of my theological understanding. It is a confession

shared by all Christians, though many fail to discern its social and political implications. I remain convinced that the task of the church in South Africa today is to be a church which is faithful to this confession—therein lies its identity and its relevance. In this sense theology is a radical project; it is always seeking to relate the church of today and the issues and conflicts facing it to its biblical and apostolic roots. An example of this is the theological basis upon which the call was made on June 16, 1985, to pray for the end to unjust rule in South Africa.[13] As already indicated, my theological understanding has developed during the past ten years largely in response to the challenge presented by black theology, but I do not believe that this has led me away from the central affirmations of the Christian faith, nor from what I regard as the essence of the tradition, both ecumenical and Reformed, in which I stand. If anything, it has sharpened these affirmations and shown how important they are for the future of the church in South Africa, indeed, for the future of the country itself.

Appendix

1. Population of South Africa

	1976 Estimates	*2000 Forecast*
African	18,629,000	37,393,000
Asian	746,000	1,215,000
Coloured	2,434,000	4,890,000
White	4,320,000	5,910,000

Notes: (a) These figures include Transkei.

(b) The Forecast does not reflect possible immigration or emigration.

(c) The racial categories are those used in official government census tables. Although they are unacceptable in many respects, some such ethnic distinction is necessary in order to understand the socio-political situation. Many African, Asian, and Coloured people prefer to be called "Black."

(d) The designation "Coloured" refers to persons of mixed descent. It is a residual category for those not classified White, Asian, or African (cf. M. West, *Divided Community*, Cape Town, 1971).

(e) The statistics are taken from *A Survey of Race Relations in South Africa, 1977*. This survey, published annually by the South African Institute of Race Relations in Johannesburg, is essential for keeping in touch with racial affairs in the republic.

2. Church Membership

	African	Asian	Coloured	White	Total
Anglican	940,000	6,000	330,000	400,000	1,676,000
Baptist	170,000	2,900	19,000	47,000	247,000
Congregational	185,000		150,000	20,000	355,000
Dutch Reformed					
N.G.K.				1,500,000	1,500,000
N.G.K. in Afrika	900,000				900,000
N.G. Sending-kerk			500,000		500,000
Reformed Church in Africa		1,000			1,000
Gereformeerde	25,000	800	3,900	120,000	149,700
Lutheran	750,000	360	83,000	40,000	873,360
Methodist	1,500,000	2,500	115,000	360,000	1,977,000
Moravian			100,000		100,000
Ned. Hervormde				225,000	225,000
Missions	25,000		1,600		26,600
Presbyterian	330,000	300	7,500	120,000	457,800
Roman Catholic	1,330,000	1,400	200,000	305,000	1,836,400
African Independent Churches	3,500,000				3,500,000

Notes: (a) Church membership statistics are very difficult to obtain and tabulate. Denominational figures are not helpful in a comparative table because churches vary in their understanding of membership. We have therefore used the 1970 government census figures as a basis for our estimates.

(b) Many churches no longer divide their membership into racial categories. While we agree with this attitude, it is difficult to appreciate the dynamics within the churches without some understanding of their ethnic composition.

(c) Census figures are usually inflated by about one-third actual membership, and one-half active participation. These proportions vary from denomination to denomination.

(d) The Gereformeerde Kerk is divided into separate white and African synods, though there is also an umbrella General Synod. The Lutherans are divided into several different churches, one of which is predominantly white. The Presbyterians are divided into three main churches. The Presbyterian Church of Southern Africa is multi-racial, but predominantly white. Both the Bantu and the Tsonga Presbyterian Churches are black.

(e) The African independent churches are included en bloc. There are about 3,000 different groups, ranging in membership from about twenty people to about one million.

(f) We have omitted the statistics of a number of other churches, e.g., Assemblies of God, as these churches do not figure in the book.

Notes

Chapter One: **Historical Origins**

1. Cf. Monica Wilson and Leonard Thompson, eds. *The Oxford History of South Africa,* vols. 1 & 2 (Oxford, 1969 & 1971).
2. Cf. W. E. Brown, *The Catholic Church in South Africa, from its Origin to the Present Day* (London, 1960).
3. A short, basic introduction to the history of the church in South Africa is Peter Hinchliff's *The Church in South Africa* (London, 1968). See also Jane M. Sales, *The Planting of the Churches in South Africa* (Grand Rapids, 1971).
4. Bernard Kruger, *The Pear Tree Blossoms: The History of the Moravian Church in South Africa, 1737-1869* (Genadendal, 1966).
5. Charles Brownlee, *Reminiscences of Kafir Life and History,* 2nd ed. (Lovedale, 1896), p. 349.
6. The early history of the Dutch Reformed Church is told in A. Moorrees, *Die Nederduitse Gereformeerde Kerk in Suid-Afrika, 1652-1873* (Cape Town, 1937).
7. *Ibid.,* pp. 881ff.
8. *Ibid.,* pp. 863f.
9. Cf. Walter J. Hollenweger, *The Pentecostals* (London, 1972), pp. 111f.
10. Cf. J. du Plessis, *A History of Christian Missions in South Africa* (London, 1911; Cape Town, 1965), chap 28. On the history of the Coloured people, see J. S. Marais, *The Cape Coloured People, 1652-1937* (London, 1939; Johannesburg, 1968); Sheila Patterson, *Colour and Culture in South Africa: A Study of the Cape Coloured People within the Social Structure of the Union of South Africa* (London, 1953).

11. Cf. Guillaume Groen van Prinsterer, *Unbelief and Revolution,* trans. and ed. Harry van Dyke with Donald Morton (Amsterdam, 1975), first published in 1847.
12. Cf. Abraham Kuyper, *Calvinism* (Amsterdam, 1899).
13. Irving Hexham, "Dutch Calvinism and the Development of Afrikaner Calvinism," in *Southern African Research in Progress,* ed. Christopher R. Hill and Peter Warwick. Collected Papers, vol. 1, Centre for Southern African Studies (University of York, 1974), p. 14.
14. Cf. A. Moorrees, *op. cit.,* p. 595; the text of the Resolution is taken from "The Dutch Reformed Churches and the Non-Whites" Fact Paper 14, July, 1956, where the issues are also discussed.
15. Cf. J. C. Hoekendijk, *Kerk en Volk in de Duitse Zendingswetenschap* (Amsterdam, 1948), pp. 83f.
16. B. B. Keet, *Whither South Africa?* (Stellenbosch, 1956), p. 38. For a detailed study of the issues from a sympathetic viewpoint see N. J. Smith, *Die Planting van Afsonderlike Kerke vir Nie-Blanke Berolkingsgroepe deur die Nederduitse Gereformeerde Kerk in Suid-Afrika,* Annale, Universiteit van Stellenbosch, vol. 34, Serie B, no. 2, 1973.
17. Cf. H. G. Stoker and F. J. M. Potgieter, *Koers in die Krisis* (Stellenbosch, 1935).
18. Owen Chadwick, *The Victorian Church,* vol. 1 (London, 1971), p. 1.
19. Cf. Moorrees, *op. cit.,* pp. 410f.; J. du Plessis, *op. cit.,* pp. 99f. For a sympathetic account of John Philip, see W. M. Macmillan, *Bantu, Boer, and Briton: the Making of the South African Native Problem* (Oxford, 1963).
20. John M'Carter, *The Dutch Reformed Church in South Africa* (Edinburgh, 1869), p. 141.
21. Jane Sales, *Mission Stations and the Coloured Communities of the Eastern Cape, 1800–1852* (Cape Town, 1975). Klaas Stuurman was a Khoi leader allied with the Xhosas; the Black Circuit, initiated at the request of John Philip, was a travelling court which tried white farmers for the ill-treatment of their laborers.
22. Horton Davies, *Great South African Christians* (Oxford, 1951), p. 35; cf. L. A. Hewson, *An Introduction to South African Methodists* (Cape Town, 1951).
23. Francis Wilson and Dominique Perrot, eds., *Outlook on a Century: South Africa, 1870–1970* (Lovedale & Spro-cas, 1973), p. 390.
24. *Ibid.,* p. 378.
25. *Ibid.,* p. 379.
26. The story of Congregationalism in Southern Africa, including the LMS and the American Board Mission, is told in D. R.

Briggs and J. Wing, *The Harvest and the Hope* (Johannesburg, 1970).

27. Cf. Peter Hinchliff, *The Anglican Church in South Africa* (London, 1963).
28. Letter to Edward Gray, February 10, 1857, published in Charles Gray, ed., *The Life of Robert Gray,* vol. 1, p. 420.
29. Hinchliff, *Anglican Church,* pp. 91f.; see also his *John William Colenso, Bishop of Natal* (London, 1964); cf. C. Lewis and G. E. Edwards, eds., *The Historical Records of the Church of the Province of South Africa* (London, 1934).
30. Hinchliff, *The Church in South Africa,* p. 71.
31. Cf. Janet Hodgson, *Zonnebloem College, 1858-1870,* unpublished M.A. thesis (University of Cape Town, 1975).
32. Quoted by I. D. MacCrone, *Race Attitudes in South Africa* (Oxford, 1937), p. 126.
33. Cf. Harrison M. Wright, *The Burden of the Present: Liberal-Radical Controversy over South African History* (Cape Town & London, 1977). See also the debate in *Social Dynamics,* A Journal of the Social Sciences, University of Cape Town, vol. 3, no. 1 (June, 1977).
34. L. A. Hewson, "The Historical Background," in *The Christian Citizen in a Multi-racial Society,* a report of the Rosettenville Conference, 1949 (Christian Council of South Africa), p. 44.
35. Cf. A. Dreyer, *Die Kaapse Kerk en die Groot Trek* (Cape Town, 1929).
36. Cf. T. Dunbar Moodie, *The Rise of Afrikanerdom: Power, Apartheid and Afrikaner Civil Religion* (California, 1975).
37. M. Nuttall, *The Making of a Tradition, 1870-1970* (Johannesburg, 1970), pp. 11f.
38. Cf. the "Statement of the Executive of the South African Native Congress, 1903" to the Rt. Hon. Joseph Chamberlain, *From Protest to Challenge: A Documentary History of African Politics in South Africa, 1882-1964,* ed. Thomas Karis and Gwendolen M. Carter (Stanford, 1972), I, 18f.
39. A copy of the sermon is in the Bethel College Historical Library, North Newton, Kansas.
40. Karis and Carter, *op. cit.,* p. 18.
41. *Ibid.,* pp. 18-61.
42. Cf. David Welsh, *The Roots of Segregation: Native Policy in Natal, 1845-1910* (Oxford, 1971).
43. Vol. 2, p. 364.
44. *A History of Christian Missions,* p. vii.
45. Cf. F. A. van Jaarsveld, *The Afrikaners' Interpretation of South African History* (Cape Town, 1964); Moodie, *op. cit.*; W. A. de Klerk, *Puritans in Africa* (London, 1975).
46. Quoted by Moodie, *op. cit.,* p. 1.
47. *Ibid.,* pp. 52ff.

48. Quoted in the *Oxford History of South Africa,* vol. 2, p. 373.

49. Quoted in Moodie, *op. cit.,* p. 67.

50. *Ibid.,* p. 66; cf. Charles Villa-Vicencio, "South African Civil Religion: an Introduction," *Journal of Theology for Southern Africa,* no. 19 (June, 1977), pp. 8ff.

51. Hexham, *op. cit.*

52. J. C. G. Kotzé, *Principle and Practice in Race Relations* (Stellenbosch, 1962), p. 15.

53. De Klerk, *op. cit.,* p. 199.

54. Quoted by David Bosch, "The Church and the Liberation of Peoples?", *Missionalia,* vol. 5, no. 2 (August, 1977), p. 33.

55. Cf. Peter Hinchliff, "The 'English-speaking Churches' and South Africa in the Nineteenth Century," *Journal of Theology for Southern Africa,* no. 9 (December, 1974), pp. 32f.; John W. de Gruchy, "English-speaking South Africans and Civil Religion," *Journal of Theology for Southern Africa,* no. 19 (June, 1977), pp. 45ff.

56. John Bond, *They Were South Africans* (Oxford, 1956), p. 5.

57. Cf. James Leatt, "Liberalism, Ideology, and the Christian in the South African Context," *Journal of Theology for Southern Africa,* no. 22 (March, 1978), pp. 31ff.

58. H. L. Watts, "A Social and Demographic Portrait of English-speaking White South Africans," *English-speaking South Africa Today,* ed. André de Villiers (Cape Town, 1976), pp. 46f.

59. Cf. Hinchliff, *Anglican Church,* pp. 183ff.; Louis Bank, "An analytical outline of the socio-political role of the Church of the Province of South Africa, as reflected in the Resolutions of Provincial Synods from 1910-1948" (Research paper, University of Cape Town, 1976).

60. Cf. Bank, *op. cit.*

61. Cf. "What my Church Has Said," a pamphlet published by the Church of the Province, n.d., p. 1.

62. Hinchliff, *Anglican Church,* p. 231.

63. Cf. E. Strassberger, *Ecumenism in South Africa: 1936-1960* (Johannesburg, 1974), pp. 134ff.

64. *Ibid.,* pp. 157ff.

65. Wilson and Perrot, *op. cit.,* p. 375.

66. *Ibid.,* p. 377.

67. Karis and Carter, *op. cit.,* pp. 39f.

68. Cf. Leo Kuper, "African Nationalism in South Africa, 1910-1964," *The Oxford History of South Africa,* II, 434f.

69. Bengt Sundkler, *Bantu Prophets in South Africa* (Oxford, 1948).

70. Bengt Sundkler, *Zulu Zion and Some Swazi Zionists* (Oxford, 1976), pp. 308f.

71. Cf. Trevor Verryn, *A History of the Order of Ethiopia* (Johannesburg, 1972), pp. 17ff.

72. Cf. Monica Wilson and Archie Mafeje, *Langa: A Study of Social Groups in an African Township* (Oxford, 1963), pp. 91ff., 175f.; Martin West, *Bishops and Prophets in a Black City* (Cape Town, 1975).

73. Cf. A. P. Walshe, *The Rise of African Nationalism in South Africa* (London, 1970); Kuper, *op. cit.*

74. Karis and Carter, *op. cit.*, pp. 86f.

75. *Ibid.*, p. 85.

76. Kuper, *op. cit.*, p. 434.

77. Karis and Carter, *op. cit.*, pp. 218ff.

78. Statement by S. N. Mvambo on the Purpose of *Imbumba*, December, 1883, *ibid.*, p. 12. *Imbumba Yama Afrika*, founded in 1882, was a forerunner of the African National Congress.

79. Kuper, *op. cit.*, p. 435.

Chapter Two: **The Advent of Apartheid**

1. Cf. Stanley G. Pitts' "Introduction" to *The Christian Citizen in a Multi-Racial Society* (Christian Council of South Africa, 1949), p. 5.

2. T. R. H. Davenport, *South Africa: A Modern History* (Johannesburg, 1977), p. 254. On the development of the concept of apartheid, see chap. 18.

3. See E. H. Brookes, *Apartheid: A Documentary Study of Modern South Africa* (Johannesburg, 1968).

4. *The Churches' Judgment on Apartheid* (Cape Town: The Civil Rights League, 1948), p. 13.

5. *Ibid.*, p. 11.

6. *Ibid.*, p. 7.

7. *Ibid.*, p. 6.

8. *Ibid.*, pp. 4f.

9. *Christian Citizen*, pp. 7f.

10. Lutuli, "The Christian and Political Issues," *ibid.*, p. 72.

11. *Christian Principles in a Multi-Racial South Africa,* a report of the DRC Conference of Church Leaders, Pretoria, November, 1953, pp. 176f.

12. *Ibid.*, pp. 17ff.

13. Cf. Davenport, *op. cit.*, chap. 14.

14. Cape Town, 1952.

15. Stellenbosch, 1956, p. 85.

16. London, 1957, p. 182.

17. "Open Letter to the Prime Minister," March 6, 1957; cf. Alan Paton, *Apartheid and the Archbishop, the Life and Times of Geoffrey Clayton* (Cape Town, 1973), p. 279.

18. Statement of the Executive of the Baptist Union of South Africa, March, 1957.

19. A Statement of Principles issued by the Council of the DRC, March, 1957.

20. Early in 1978, the government relaxed the law at the request of the DRC. Those churches which had refused to acknowledge it in the first place did not regard this as of great significance, for they had never obeyed it.
21. Quoted in the *Cape Times,* Cape Town, April 30, 1957.
22. Cf. Davenport, *op. cit.,* pp. 286f.
23. Cf. A. P. Walshe, *The Rise of African Nationalism in South Africa* (London, 1970).
24. Cf. A. H. Lückhoff, *Die Cottesloe-Kerkeberaad* (unpublished Ph.D. thesis, University of the Witwatersrand, Johannesburg, 1975), pp. 19f.
25. *Ibid.,* pp. 38f.
26. Quoted by Victor Charles Paine, *The Confrontation between the Archbishop of Cape Town, Joost de Blank, and the South African Government on Racial Policies, 1957-1963* (unpublished M.A. thesis, University of Cape Town, 1978), p. 204.
27. H. E. Fey, ed., *The Ecumenical Advance: A History of the Ecumenical Movement* (London, 1970), II, 245.
28. Leslie A. Hewson, ed., *Cottesloe Consultation: the Report of the Consultation* (Johannesburg, 1961), p. 74.
29. *Ibid.,* pp. 81f.
30. W. A. Visser 't Hooft, *Memoirs* (London, 1973), p. 287.
31. *Puritans in Africa,* p. 255.
32. Visser 't Hooft, *op. cit.*
33. The official periodicals, *Die Kerkbode* and *DRC Africa News,* reflect the position of the church.
34. English translation published by the DRC Information Bureau, 1966.
35. English translation published by the DRC Publishers, Cape Town, 1975.
36. Cf. "The Dutch Reformed Church and Non-Whites," Fact Paper 14, July, 1956, pp. 11f.
37. *Principle and Practice in Race Relations* (Stellenbosch, 1962), p. 28.
38. *Ibid.,* p. 11.
39. *Human Relations and the South African Scene,* p. 13.
40. *Ibid.,* pp. 25f.
41. *Ibid.,* p. 26.
42. *Ibid.,* pp. 30f.
43. *Ibid.,* pp. 32f.
44. *Ibid.,* p. 38.
45. *Ibid.,* pp. 63-99.
46. This position is reflected in all major DRC documents on the subject, at least since the DRC Congress held in Bloemfontein in 1950. Cf. *The Minutes of the Cape Synod,* 1961, pp. 271-72. It is certainly expressed in both the 1966 and 1974 reports on human relations. Indeed, even the DRC delegates at Cottesloe

had no difficulty in affirming the Cottesloe resolutions and declaring in a concluding statement: "We wish to confirm that, as stated in the preamble to the Consultation Statement, a policy of differentiation can be defended from the Christian point of view, that it provides the only realistic solution to the problems of race relations and is therefore in the best interests of the various population groups" (p. 80).

47. *Human Relations,* p. 100.
48. Cf. W. A. Landman, *A Plea for Understanding: A Reply to the Reformed Church in America* (Cape Town, 1968), p. 32.
49. *Ibid.,* p. 20.
50. Allan A. Boesak, *Farewell to Innocence: A Socio-Ethical Study on Black Theology and Power* (New York and Johannesburg, 1977), p. 36.
51. J. Alex van Wyk, "Latente motiewe in die Verklaring van die N. G. Kerk oor: Ras, Volk en Nasie en Volkereverhoudinge in die Lig van die Skrif," *Ned. Geref. Teologiese Tydskrif,* vol. XVII, no. 2 (March, 1976); J. J. F. Durand, "Bible and Race: the Problem of Hermeneutics," *Journal of Theology for Southern Africa,* no. 24 (September, 1978); Brian Johanson, "Race, Mission and Ecumenism: Reflections on the Landman Report," *Journal of Theology for Southern Africa,* no. 10 (March, 1975).
52. Durand, *op. cit.,* p. 4.
53. *Ibid.,* p. 6.
54. *Ibid.,* p. 8.
55. Johanson, *op. cit.,* p. 60.
56. Thomas Karis and Gwendolen M. Carter, eds., *From Protest to Challenge: A Documentary History of African Politics in South Africa, 1881-1964* (Stanford, 1972), I, 85.
57. J. H. Oldham, *Christianity and the Race Problem* (London, eighth edition, 1926), p. 192.
58. P. 72.
59. C. P. Mulder, "The Rationale of Separate Development," *South African Dialogue,* ed. Nic Rhoodie (Johannesburg, 1972), p. 49.
60. See n. 48.
61. Cf. Peter Berger, *Pyramids of Sacrifice* (New York, 1976). Berger evaluates two so-called model developmental societies. capitalist Brazil and communist China, in terms of "a calculus of pain and a calculus of meaning." He finds both systems wanting. They dehumanize, even though they promise a better future. We have not attempted an exhaustive analysis and critique of apartheid and separate development, but simply indicated some basic reasons why most churches in South Africa reject them. For a more detailed discussion, see, inter alia, Heribert Adam, *Modernizing Racial Domination: the Dynamics of South African Politics* (California, 1972). Adam includes a very useful bibliography. Chap. 4 of this book at-

tempts to express some of the 'gut level' feelings of blacks regarding government policy.

62. Cf. F. A. Wilson, *Migrant Labour in South Africa* (Spro-cas, Johannesburg, 1972), chap. 8.

63. Johanson, *op. cit.*

64. Cf. W. F. Nkomo, "An African's View of Apartheid," *South African Dialogue,* ed. Nic Rhoodie (Johannesburg, 1972), p. 352.

65. *Delayed Action* (Pretoria, 1961), p. 11.

66. An unpublished mimeographed paper, October 22, 1965, signed by Ds. W. J. Villiers, Dr. H. W. de Jager, Prof. I. H. Eybers, Prof. W. D. Jonker, Prof. J. A. Lombard, Dr. H. J. P. van Rooyen, Dr. A. J. Venter, and Mr. A. C. Viljoen.

67. March, 1968, p. 7; cf. *DRC African News* (March, 1977), p. 4.

68. *The Koinonia Declaration,* dated November 16, 1977, was drawn up by some members of the Gereformeerde Kerk in Potchefstroom together with members of a Calvinist study group in Germiston, a town in the Transvaal. It is not an official church document, but a very thorough attempt to apply Calvinist principles to the political situation in South Africa. The declaration has been warmly received by some English-speaking churches, becoming an official study document of the United Congregational Church. But it has received a cool reception from the DRC and the Gereformeerde Kerk. The declaration was privately circulated, but was subsequently published, inter alia, in the *Christian Leader,* the newspaper of the Presbyterian and Congregational Churches, in March, 1978, and the *Journal of Theology for Southern Africa,* September, 1978.

69. Keet, *op. cit.,* p. 83.

70. Cf. André Bieler, *The Social Humanism of Calvin* (Richmond, Va., 1964); W. Fred Graham, *The Constructive Revolutionary: John Calvin and his Socio-Economic Impact* (Richmond, Va., 1971).

71. In *Comparative Studies in Society and History* (June, 1972), p. 320.

72. Ben Marais, *Colour: Unsolved Problem of the West,* p. 70.

73. J. C. G. Kotzé, *Principle and Practice in Race Relations* (Stellenbosch, 1962), p. 29.

74. A documentary account of this ministry has been published by Karl Breyer, *My Brother's Keeper* (Johannesburg, 1977).

75. An editorial in *Die Kerkbode,* September 19, 1973.

76. Part of a resolution on dialogue with the DRC adopted by the SACC National Conference, July, 1975, published in *Ecunews* 23/75, appendix D; cf. *Ecunews,* 43/77, p. 1.

77. In *South African Dialogue,* ed. Nic Rhoodie (Johannesburg, 1972), p. 477.

78. The *Church Unity Commission* was established in 1967 by the Anglican, Congregational, Presbyterian, and Methodist Churches, to seek ways whereby these churches could form one church. Since then, considerable co-operation has developed, including intercommunion, but a proposed *Plan of Union* has been shelved for the present time. Instead, the churches will vote in 1978 on a *Covenant,* which includes the full recognition of ministries, and proposals for joint-ordination. Cf. *Journal of Theology for Southern Africa,* no. 23 (June, 1978).
79. Cf. Lesley Cawood, *The Churches and Race Relations in South Africa* (Johannesburg, 1964). More recent documentation can be found in the annual yearbooks of the churches, and in *Ecunews,* the weekly news bulletin of the SACC.
80. Cf. *Apartheid and the Church,* Spro-cas church report (Johannesburg, 1972), p. 6ff.
81. See chap. 4, p. 167.
82. Cf. *Human Relations,* p. 69.
83. Cf. *ibid.,* p. 70; see also *Human Relations in South Africa* (1966), p. 39, and Kotzé, *op. cit.,* p. 22.
84. *Human Relations,* p. 70.
85. See John W. de Gruchy, "The Relationship between the State and some Churches in South Africa, 1968-1975," *Journal of Church and State,* vol. 19, no. 3 (Autumn, 1977).
86. A full list of names would be too lengthy to include here, even if it were available. *Pro Veritate* carried documentation before it was banned. The Rev. Ben Ngidi, a former chairman of the United Congregational Church, was in prison without trial or reason given for almost a year. This is one example among many.
87. Cf. *The State vs. the Dean of Johannesburg,* S.A. Institute of Race Relations (Johannesburg, 1972).
88. Hinchliff, *Anglican Church,* p. 240.
89. Quoted in Cawood, *op. cit.,* p. 95.
90. Cf. n. 77.
91. André de Villiers, ed., *English-speaking South Africa Today* (Cape Town, 1976), pp. 11f.
92. Cf. *The Churches' Judgment on Apartheid,* p. 15. See above, n. 4.
93. Finbar Synnott, O. P., *Justice and Reconciliation in South Africa,* a report of the Southern African Catholic Bishops' Conference (Pretoria, n.d.), p. 11.
94. Early in the 1970s this led to such tension at St. Peter's Seminary, Hammanskraal, that the rector was forced to resign. A black priests' movement was established to remove discrimination from the life of the church. Cf. Drake Koka, "Open Letter on Day of Consecration," sent to Bishop P. J. Buthelezi on October 22, 1972, on behalf of the Black Justice and Peace

Vigilantes Committee. It is notable that in 1968 Bishop Buthelezi became the first black Catholic archbishop in South Africa.

95. Cf. Hans W. Florin, *Lutherans in South Africa* (report on a survey, 1964-65).

96. On contemporary Lutheran thinking in South Africa see, inter alia, the publications of the Lutheran Missiological Institute, Umpumulo, Natal. The Institute is held annually under the auspices of FELCSA to examine the socio-political situation in South Africa. See, for example, K. Nürnberger, ed., *Affluence, Poverty, and the Word of God* (Durban, 1978). J. Lukas de Vries, *Mission and Colonialism in Namibia* (Johannesburg, 1978), is a recent discussion of the issues by a black Lutheran theologian and Namibian church leader. While de Vries concentrates on Namibian issues, his position reflects that of many black Lutherans in South Africa.

Chapter Three: **The Growing Conflict**

1. International Commission of Jurists, eds., *The Trial of Beyers Naudé* (London and Johannesburg, 1975), pp. 68ff.

2. D. E. Hurley, OMI, "The Christian Institute," *South African Outlook* (November, 1977), p. 163.

3. See Beyers Naudé, "Die Tyd vir 'n 'Belydende Kerk' is Daar," *Pro Veritate*, vol. 4, no. 6 (July, 1965). Subsequent articles on the same theme by Dr. Naudé can be found in *Pro Veritate*, vol. 4, nos. 7 and 8.

4. See E. Bethge, "A Confessing Church in South Africa? Conclusions from a Visit," *Bonhoeffer: Exile and Martyr,* ed. John W. de Gruchy (London, 1975; New York, 1976). Although the title of our book may remind readers of the church struggle in Germany during the Third Reich, we have not attempted to relate our discussion to that situation. That there are illuminating parallels we do not wish to deny, but simply to equate the two distorts reality and clouds the issues. Cf. H. Adam, *Modernizing Racial Domination: The Dynamics of South African Politics* (California, 1972), esp. chap. 3. An attempt to draw out the similarities will be found in "An Open Letter Concerning Nationalism, National Socialism and Christianity," supplement to *Pro Veritate*, July, 1971.

5. Peter Walshe, "Church versus State in South Africa: the Christian Institute and the Resurgence of African Nationalism," *Journal of Church and State,* vol. 19, no. 3 (Autumn, 1977), p. 462.

6. See n. 1.

7. In his Preface to *The Trial of Beyers Naudé.*

8. During the last four years of its existence, the CI regularly

published details of political arrests, bannings, etc., in its *CI Newsletter.*

9. "Banning" means that action whereby a person, while not imprisoned, is virtually excluded from public life. Bannings prevent the affected persons from teaching, publishing, and speaking in public. They cannot meet with more than one person at a time, except their immediate family; they cannot leave their magisterial district; they cannot enter educational or publishing premises. On occasions, banned clergymen have preached, some regularly, but all charges against them for doing so have been dropped by the state.

10. Walshe, *op. cit.,* pp. 477f.

11. Jürgen Moltmann, *Theology of Hope* (London, 1967), p. 321.

12. Walshe, *op. cit.,* pp. 478f.

13. *Migrant Labour in South Africa* (Johannesburg, 1972). This volume is also recommended in the DRC 1974 report on *Human Relations;* see p. 75.

14. The SACC has published a monthly newspaper, *Kairos,* since 1968. Prior to that, the *Christian Council Quarterly* was its official mouthpiece. *Ecunews,* a weekly news service, was started in June, 1971.

15. "The Constitution of the SACC," Article 2(b), published in E. Strassberger, *Ecumenism in South Africa: 1936-1960* (Johannesburg, 1974), pp. 270ff. The membership of the SACC is extensive. Inter alia, it includes all the English-speaking churches. While none of the white Afrikaans churches is a member, the N. G. Kerk in Afrika is, and the Sendingkerk is an observer. The African Independent Church Association has recently joined, and the Roman Catholic Church has been an observer since Vatican II. The Baptist Union withdrew as an observer in 1975, having been a member up until 1973. "A Statement of Theological Principles" was adopted by the SACC in 1977; see *Kairos,* vol. 9, no. 8 (Sept., 1977).

16. Cf. *Christians in the Technical and Social Revolutions of our Time,* the official report of the World Conference on Church and Society, 1966 (Geneva, 1967).

17. Cf. *Church and Society,* a report on a national conference sponsored by the SACC and CI, February, 1968.

18. Cf. John W. de Gruchy and W. B. de Villiers, eds., *The Message in Perspective* (Johannesburg, 1969).

19. Cf. *Pseudo-Gospels in South Africa,* a report published in Johannesburg, 1968.

20. *Ibid.,* p. 35.

21. *Ibid.,* p. 31.

22. *Ibid.,* p. 34.

23. De Gruchy and de Villiers, *op. cit.,* pp. 39f.

24. Dietrich Bonhoeffer, *The Cost of Discipleship* (New York, 1963), p. 69.
25. Mimeographed document, 1969.
26. See chap. 2, n. 80.
27. The Spro-cas reports, edited by Peter Randall, were:
    Education Beyond Apartheid, 1971
    Towards Social Change, 1971
    Power, Privilege and Poverty, 1972
    Apartheid and the Church, 1972
    Law, Justice and Society, 1972
    South Africa's Political Alternatives, 1973
    A co-ordinated report, *A Taste of Power* (Johannesburg, 1973), was written by Mr. Randall.
28. Cf. Harold G. Fey, ed., *The Ecumenical Advance: A History of the Ecumenical Movement* (London, 1970), II, 244f.
29. "Comments by the South African Council of Churches' Executive on the Statement of the WCC Consultation on Racism," a mimeographed letter, August 6, 1969.
30. On the PCR, see "An Ecumenical Programme to Combat Racism," *Ecumenical Review,* vol. 21, no. 4 (October, 1969), pp. 348f.; "Programme to Combat Racism," *Ecumenical Review,* vol. 23, no. 2 (April, 1971), pp. 173f.; "Programme to Combat Racism: 1970–1973," *Ecumenical Review,* vol. 25, no. 4 (October, 1973), pp. 513f.; and Wolfram Weisse, *Süd-Afrika und das Anti-Rassismus Programm: Kirchen im Spannungsfeld einer Rassengesellschaft* (Frankfurt, 1975). The only South African on the PCR Committee was Dr. Alex Boraine. He withdrew early on when his pleas against the grants to liberation movements went unheeded. His position was stated in his presidential address to the Methodist Conference in 1971, "The Church and Society," in which he called for "revolutionary non-violence."
31. *Pro Veritate,* vol. 9, no. 6 (October, 1970), p. 7. This was a special issue on the PCR, containing, inter alia, South African church resolutions and responses.
32. John W. de Gruchy in *Kairos,* vol. 2, no. 9 (November, 1970), p. 1.
33. Letter of March 9, 1971, published in *Pro Veritate,* vol. 10, no. 3, (July, 1971), p. 14.
34. *Pro Veritate,* vol. 10, no. 3, contains all the correspondence on the proposed consultation. The correspondence of the planning committee of the South African member churches was written by Mr. Rees and the Revs. Alex Boraine and John de Gruchy.
35. Letter of May 8, 1971, to the Rev. John de Gruchy; cf. letter of March 16, 1971, from the Prime Minister to Mr. J. C. Rees.
36. Letters of Dr. Blake to Mr. Rees, April 2, 1971, and May 26, 1971.

37. Letter of May 26, 1971, to the Rev. Alex Boraine.
38. For the WCC reaction to the cancellation of the consultation, see *Ecumenical Review*, XXIII, no. 3 (July, 1971), pp. 320f.
39. Letter to Mr. J. Vorster, June 11, 1971.
40. Cf. D. Bax, "Hammanskraal ... A Vital Christian Witness to Fundamental Change," a letter in response to criticism, *Pro Veritate* (April, 1975), pp. 12f.
41. The full text was published in *Ecunews* (August 5, 1974), p. 6.
42. Cf. *Ecunews* (August 21, 1974), p. 4.
43. John Rawls, *A Theory of Justice* (Cambridge, Mass., 1971; Oxford, 1972), p. 382.
44. On the Parliamentary debates, cf. *Hansard* (1976), cols. 798–828; 1450–1486; 6749–6766; and 6809–6886. See also *Kairos*, vol. 6, nos. 10 and 11 (Nov./Dec., 1974), p. 11, for the views of the SACC on the Defense Further Amendment Bill.
45. *Seek* (September, 1974), p. 8. Cf. *Ecunews* (August 5, 1974), p. 6.
46. Section 121'(c) of the Defense Act, as amended on November 20, 1974.
47. D. Bax, *op. cit.*, p. 14.
48. *Conscientious Objection in South Africa*, a summary of South African law and a considered opinion by Dr. James Moulder, 1977. Mimeographed. Cf. the more detailed discussion by Dr. Moulder, "The Defense Act and Conscientious Objection," *Philosophical Papers* (Rhodes University), vol. 7, no. 1 (May, 1978), pp. 25–50.
49. *Ecunews*, 5/77 (February 11, 1977), p. 11.
50. *Ecunews*, 14/77 (April, 1977), p. 1. The Anglicans expressed total support of the Roman Catholic bishops by adopting the Catholic resolution. On the Catholic stand, cf. *Ecunews* 5/77 and September 4, 1974.
51. *Ecunews*, 38/77 (October 26, 1977), p. 5.
52. Cf. *Kairos*, vol. 9, nos. 9/10 (November, 1977).

Chapter Four: **Black Renaissance, Protest, and Challenge**

1. Manas Buthelezi, "The Challenge of Black Theology," an unpublished, mimeographed paper.
2. Allan Boesak, *Farewell to Innocence* (New York and Johannesburg, 1977), p. 1.
3. See James H. Cone, *Black Theology and Black Power* (New York, 1969).
4. Johannesburg, 1972. For the American edition, see Basil Moore, ed., *The Challenge of Black Theology in South Africa* (Atlanta, 1974).
5. Essays on black theology by a wide range of South African authors have appeared in *Pro Veritate, South African Outlook,*

Missionalia, the *Ned. Geref. Teologiese Tydskrif*, and the *Journal of Theology for Southern Africa*. There are extensive bibliographies in Ilse Tödt, ed., *Theologie im Konfliktfeld Süd Afrika: Dialog mit Manas Buthelezi* (Stuttgart, 1976), and Boesak, *op. cit.*

6. Cf. Manas Buthelezi, "An African or a Black Theology?" in Moore, *op. cit.*

7. Bonganjalo Goba, "Ancient Israel and Africa," in Moore, *op. cit.*, p. 29; cf. D. Tutu, "Some African Insights and the Old Testament," *Relevant Theology for Africa*, ed. Hans-Jürgen Becken (Durban, 1973).

8. Buthelezi, *op. cit.*, p. 29.

9. Elliot Mgojo, "Prolegomenon to the Study of Black Theology," *Journal of Theology for Southern Africa*, no. 21 (December, 1973), p. 27.

10. *Ibid.*, p. 28.

11. "The Relevance of Black Theology," published in a mimeographed booklet by the Christian Academy of Southern Africa, Johannesburg, 1974.

12. Boesak, *op. cit.*, p. 12.

13. Ephraim Mosothoane, "The Liberation of Peoples in the New Testament," *Missionalia*, vol. 5, no. 2 (August, 1977), p. 70.

14. Desmond Tutu, "God Intervening in Human Affairs," *Missionalia*, vol. 5, no. 2, p. 115.

15. "Toward Indigenous Theology in South Africa," *The Emergent Gospel*, ed. Sergio Torres and Virginia Fabella (Maryknoll, N.Y., 1978), p. 74; cf. Moore, *op. cit.*, p. 34.

16. "Six Theses: Theological Problems of Evangelism in the South African Context," *Journal of Theology for Southern Africa*, no. 3 (June, 1973), p. 55.

17. Tutu, *op. cit.*, p. 111.

18. Boesak, *op. cit.*, p. 23.

19. Boesak, *op. cit.*, p. 26.

20. Manas Buthelezi, "Mutual Acceptance from a Black Perspective," *Journal of Theology for Southern Africa*, no. 23 (June, 1978), p. 74.

21. Boesak, *op. cit.*, p. 9.

22. This is the major issue discussed by Boesak in his *Farewell to Innocence*, and "Civil Religion and the Black Community," *Journal of Theology for Southern Africa*, no. 19 (June, 1977).

23. Mgojo, *op. cit.*

24. In Moore, *op. cit.*, p. 29.

25. Buthelezi, "Challenge of Black Theology."

26. D. J. Bosch, "The Church and the Liberation of Peoples," *Missionalia*, vol. 5, no. 2, p. 334.

27. Cf. Boesak, *Farewell*, pp. 125ff.; "Civil Religion and the Black Community," pp. 35ff.

28. The earliest critique "from within" came from Bishop Al-
    phaeus Zulu; see his "Whither Black Theology?", *Pro Veritate*,
    vol. 11, no. 11 (March, 1973), pp. 11f.
29. Buthelezi, "The Relevance of Black Theology," p. 1.
30. *South African Outlook* (November, 1974).
31. The Cillie Commission of Inquiry began its work in July, 1976.
    This was concluded a year later. By May, 1978, the findings of
    the commission had not been presented to Parliament. The
    evidence presented to the Cillié Commission is to be found in
    South Africa in Travail: The Disturbances of 1976/7 (S. A.
    Institute of Race Relations, Johannesburg, 1978). A private
    survey was conducted by the Institute for Black Research;
    cf. Razia Timal and Tutuzile Mazibuko, ed., *Soweto: A
    People's Response,* Durban, n.d., but this only contains predict-
    able responses from a cross-section of the population. *South
    African Outlook*, July, 1976, and February, 1977, carried ex-
    tensive coverage of Soweto.
32. In an interview published in *To the Point*, February 4, 1977, p.
    46.
33. *Ecunews*, 21/76 (July 7, 1976), Appendix A; cf. "Soweto Dis-
    turbances: Attitude of the D.R. Church," *DRC Africa News*,
    vol. 2, no. 3 (March, 1977).
34. *Ecunews*, 20/76 (June 30, 1976), p. 8.
35. Cf. *Ecunews*, 20/76, 25/76, 36/76, and 37/76.
36. *Ecunews*, 28/76 (September 3, 1976), p. 9.
37. *Ecunews*, 34/76 (October 15, 1976), p. 8.
38. *Kairos,* vol. 9, no. 10, November, 1977.
39. Quoted by Arthur F. Christofersen in *Adventuring into God:
    the Story of the American Board Mission in South Africa*, ed.
    Richard Sales (Durban, 1967), p. 22.
40. Cf. Monica Wilson, *Missionaries: Conquerors or Servants of
    God*, an address published by the South African Missionary
    Museum (Kingwilliamstown, 1976); and Hinchliff, "The
    'English-Speaking Churches' and South Africa in the 19th cen-
    tury," *Journal of Theology for Southern Africa*, no. 9 (De-
    cember, 1974).
41. Quoted in *CHURCHSOC* (the Church and Society Report of
    the United Congregational Church of Southern Africa), no. 18
    (April, 1978).
42. Revelation Ntoula, "Church Must Reach out to Youth," *The
    Voice,* black newspaper founded by the South African Council of
    Churches (October/November, 1976), p. 16.
43. Dr. F. E. O'Brien Geldenhuys, "Appraisal: New Issues and
    Challenges Facing the Church in South Africa," *DRC NEWS*,
    vol. 1, no. 9 (October, 1976), p. 6.
44. Margaret McNally, "Portrait of a Black Youth," *The Argus,*
    Cape Town, November 6, 1976, p. 17.

45. A. B. M. Mafeje, "Religion, Class and Ideology in South Africa," *Religion and Social Change in Southern Africa*, ed. Michael G. Whisson and Martin West (Cape Town, 1975), p. 176.
46. Bengt Sundkler, *Bantu Prophets in South Africa* (Oxford, 1976), p. 237.
47. Mafeje, *op. cit.*, p. 183.
48. Cf. "Religion and Political Involvement: A Study of Black African Sects," *Journal for the Scientific Study of Religion*, vol. 13 (1974), p. 169.
49. J. Moltmann, "The Liberation of Oppressors," to be published in the *Journal of Theology for Southern Africa*, no. 26 (March, 1979).
50. Clark H. Pinnock, "A Call for the Liberation of North American Christians," *Evangelicals and Liberation*, ed. Carl E. Armerding (Presbyterian and Reformed, 1977), p. 128; "Liberation" was the theme of the January 1977 Congress of the S.A. Missiological Society; see *Missionalia,* vol. 5, no. 2 (August, 1977).
51. Alphaeus Zulu, *The Dilemma of the Black South African* (Cape Town, 1972), p. 4.
52. Cf. *Ecunews*, 34/77 (Sept. 6, 1977), p. 2.
53. *Ecunews*, 30/77, p. 18.
54. *Ibid.*, p. 20.
55. Desmond Tutu, "God-given Dignity and the Quest for Liberation in the Light of the South African Dilemma," *Liberation,* the papers of the Eighth National Conference of the SACC (July, 1976), p. 59.
56. Boesak, *Farewell*, p. 16.
57. "Coming in out of the Wilderness," Torres and Fabella, *op. cit.*, p. 93.
58. Dietrich Bonhoeffer, *Ethics* (New York, 1965), p. 72.
59. Quoted by Sheila Patterson, *Colour and Culture in South Africa* (London, 1953), p. 300, n. 19.
60. Peter Randall, ed., *Power, Privilege and Poverty* (Spro-cas report, 1972), p. 25.
61. *Ibid.*, p. 103.
62. Jan H. Hofmeyr, quoting Hoernlé in *Christian Principles and Race* (Johannesburg, 1945), p. 16.
63. John S. Cumpsty, "White Racism," an unpublished paper prepared for the SACC Commission on Ideologies, 1977.
64. H. Richard Niebuhr, *The Responsible Self* (New York, 1963), p. 99.
65. Boesak, *Farewell*, pp. 1f.
66. *Ecunews*, 30/76 (Sept. 17, 1976), p. 4.
67. Bonhoeffer, *Ethics*, p. 67.
68. Charles Dickens, *Complete Works* (London, 1967), III, 141.

69. Cf. Dietrich Bonhoeffer's reflections "After Ten Years" in his *Letters and Papers from Prison* (New York, 1972).

70. "From Apartheid to Afrocentrism," *South African Outlook*, vol. 107, no. 1278 (December, 1977), p. 181; cf. Nadine Gordimer, "What Being a South African Means to Me," *South African Outlook*, vol. 107, no. 1273 (June, 1977).

71. Quoted by Peter Hinchliff, "The 'English-Speaking Churches' and South Africa in the 19th century," *Journal of Theology for Southern Africa*, no. 9 (December, 1974), p. 34.

Chapter Five: **The Kingdom of God in South Africa**

1. H. Richard Niebuhr, *The Kingdom of God in America* (New York, 1937).

2. Walter Rauschenbusch, *A Theology for the Social Gospel* (New York, 1917), p. 5.

3. Cf. G. E. Ladd, *Jesus and the Kingdom* (New York, 1964), pp. 298f.

4. Langdon Gilkey, *Reaping the Whirlwind* (New York, 1976).

5. Cf. J. Jeremias, *New Testament Theology* (London, 1971), I, 96ff.; J. Moltmann, *Theology of Hope* (London, 1967); H. Berkhof, *Christ the Meaning of History* (London, 1966). By "eschatology" we mean interpreting the historical present in terms of the ultimate purpose of God. The end of history (eschaton) becomes the basis for determining present action and attitudes. "Apocalyptic" (literally "unveiling") is difficult to define satisfactorily. As used in this context, it refers to the imminence of God's "breaking into history" to vindicate his purposes and his people in the struggle between good and evil. It confronts people with the urgent need to choose sides and stresses the suffering, though ultimately triumphant, role of the church as a persecuted minority.

6. André Dumas, "The Christian's Secular Hope and his Ultimate Hope," *Technology and Social Justice*, ed. R. H. Preston (London, 1971), p. 167.

7. Ladd, *op. cit.*, p. 38.

8. W. Pannenberg, *Theology and the Kingdom of God* (Philadelphia, 1969), p. 73.

9. Bonhoeffer, *Ethics* (New York, 1965), p. 82.

10. Niebuhr, *op. cit.*, p. 198.

11. Charles C. West, "Puritans in Africa and America," *South African Outlook* (November, 1976), pp. 167f.

12. During the past few years there has been a gradual reawakening of social conscience among some white conservative evangelical groups in South Africa. This has been particularly true of the witness of *Africa Enterprise*, an evangelistic organization led by Michael Cassidy. It is also true of some evangelical university student organizations. Cf. Michael Cas-

sidy, *Prisoners of Hope: The Story of South African Christians at a Crossroad* (Pietermaritzburg, 1974).

13. It is important to remember that social concern and action in nineteenth-century America was not the prerogative of liberal Christians. Many of the leading evangelicals, including Charles G. Finney, were social activists. Cf. Donald W. Dayton, *Discovering an Evangelical Heritage* (New York, 1976).

14. For the contemporary debate on this issue, cf. T. Dunbar Moodie, *The Rise of Afrikanerdom* (California, 1975); André du Toit, "Ideological Change, Afrikaner Nationalism and Pragmatic Racial Domination in South Africa," *Change in Contemporary South Africa,* ed. L. Thompson and J. Butler (Berkeley, California, 1975); and Heribert Adam, "Ideologies of Dedication vs. Blueprints of Expedience," *Social Dynamics,* vol. 2, no. 2 (1976), pp. 83–91.

15. *The Providence of God* (Grand Rapids, 1961), p. 166.

16. Cf. *Church Dogmatics,* III/3, p. 33; *Dogmatics in Outline* (London, 1955), p. 48.

17. Cf. Jeremias, *op. cit.,* pp. 108ff.

18. Ladd, *op. cit.,* p. 61.

19. *The Church, the Gospel and Society* (London, 1962), pp. 108f.

20. T. F. Torrance, *Theology in Reconciliation* (London, 1975; Grand Rapids, 1976), p. 271.

21. Gilkey, *op. cit.,* p. 267.

22. *Ibid.,* p. 266.

23. Cf. Dietrich Bonhoeffer, *Letters and Papers from Prison* (New York, 1972), p. 17.

24. José Míguez Bonino, *Revolutionary Theology Comes of Age* (London, 1975); *Doing Theology in a Revolutionary Situation* (Philadelphia, 1975), p. 4.

25. *Ibid.,* p. 5.

26. *Ibid.,* p. 7.

27. *Ibid.,* p. 12.

28. *Ibid.,* p. 17.

29. Cf. José Míguez Bonino, *Christians and Marxists* (London and Grand Rapids, 1976), p. 19.

30. Míguez Bonino, *Revolutionary Theology,* p. 138.

31. New York, 1951, chap. 1.

32. Quoted by Paul Peachey in G. F. Hershberger, *The Recovery of the Anabaptist Vision* (Scottdale, 1957), p. 334.

33. Míguez Bonino, *Revolutionary Theology,* pp. 80f.; 146f.

34. Clifford Geertz, *The Interpretation of Cultures* (New York, 1973), p. 229.

35. Robert Bellah, "Civil Religion in America," *Daedalus,* vol. 96, no. 1.

36. Jean Luis Segundo, *The Liberation of Theology* (Maryknoll, N.Y., 1976), p. 102.

37. Gustavo Gutiérrez, *A Theology of Liberation* (Maryknoll, N.Y., 1973), p. 234.
38. Cf. André Bieler, *The Social Humanism of Calvin* (Richmond, Va., 1964), p. 75; Helmut Thielicke, *Theological Ethics: Politics* (Philadelphia, 1969), pp. 22ff.
39. J. Degenaar, "Philosophical Roots of Humanism," *Church and Nationalism in South Africa*, ed. T. Sundermeier (Johannesburg, 1975), p. 12.
40. Bonhoeffer, *Ethics*, p. 216.
41. Míguez Bonino, *Revolutionary Theology*, p. 163.
42. Cf. André du Toit, *op. cit.*; Heribert Adam, *op. cit.*
43. Cf. K. Barth, *The Humanity of God* (Atlanta, 1960).
44. Bieler, *op. cit.*
45. Cf. Andrew Kirk, "The Meaning of Man in the Debate between Christianity and Marxism," *Themelios,* vol. 1, nos. 2 and 3 (1976). In our discussion we have not attempted to make all the necessary qualifications about types of Marxism. By Marxism, we have primarily meant Marxist-Leninism. Neo-Marxism is far too much of an academic position to have much political significance in southern Africa. Communism refers primarily to the socio-political systems of Russia and its East European satellites.
46. Míguez Bonino, *Christians and Marxists*, p. 117.
47. H. Gollwitzer, *The Christian Faith and the Marxist Critique of Religion* (Edinburgh, 1970), p. 151; cf. Karl Barth, *Theology and Church* (London, 1962), p. 234.
48. E.g., Cyrus (Isaiah 41:5-7; 44:28; 45:1f.).
49. Edward K. Smith, "Challenge to the Church from Mozambique," *Ecunews,* 35/75 (November 5, 1975).
50. Míguez Bonino, *op. cit.*, p. 123.
51. Cf. John 16:8f.
52. Bonhoeffer, *Ethics*, p. 116.
53. Bonhoeffer, *Letters and Papers,* pp. 361f.
54. Yoder, *Politics of Jesus* (Grand Rapids, 1972), p. 13.
55. John Gladwin, "Politics, Providence and the Kingdom," *Churchman,* vol. 91, no. 1 (January, 1977), p. 48.
56. Berger, *Pyramids of Sacrifice* (New York, 1976), pp. xi-xiv.
57. Cf. Colossians 2:15.
58. Jürgen Moltmann, "The Cross and Civil Religion," *Religion and Political Society* (New York, 1974), p. 35.
59. Cf. Ephesians 6:10ff.
60. Cf. G. B. Caird, *Principalities and Powers* (Oxford, 1956); H. Berkhof, *Christ and the Powers* (Scottdale, 1962); Richard J. Mouw, *Politics and the Biblical Drama* (Grand Rapids, 1976), chap. 5.
61. Yoder, *op. cit.*, p. 156.
62. Bonhoeffer, *Letters and Papers*, p. 14.
63. Quoted by René Padilla in "The Class Struggle," an unpub-

lished address to PACLA, Nairobi, 1976. Cf. "Christians should take a stronger stand in favor of the weak rather than consider the possible right of the strong." D. Bonhoeffer, *Gesammelte Schriften* (Munich, 1975), IV, 181; see also K. Barth, *Church Dogmatics*, II/1, p. 386.

64. Cf. Psalm 146:6-10; James 1:27-2:8; to say nothing of the Gospels themselves.

65. Yoder, *The Christian Witness to the State* (Newton, Kans., 1964), p. 77.

66. Book IV, ch. 20, para. 32. This position fully accords with a proper exegesis of Mark 12:13-17 and Romans 13:1-7. Cf. James Moulder, "Romans 13 and Conscientious Disobedience," in *Journal of Theology for Southern Africa*, no. 21 (December, 1977).

67. Cf. C. F. A. Borchardt, "Afrikaanse Kerke en die Rebellie, 1914-1915," *Teologie en Vernieuwing*, ed. I. H. Eybers, A. König and C. F. A. Borchardt (Pretoria, 1975). The statement was a resolution of the Afrikaans Council of Reformed Churches.

68. Inter alia, this point is made very strongly in the 1974 report of the DRC, p. 70; cf. the *Koinonia Declaration*.

69. Herbert W. Richardson, "What Makes a Society Political?", *Religion and Political Society*, p. 120.

70. Caird, *op. cit.*, p. 101.

71. Jürgen Moltmann, "An Open Letter to José Míguez Bonino," *Christianity and Crisis*, March 29, 1976.

72. David Bosch, *op. cit.*, p. 27.

73. Cf. K. Barth, *Church Dogmatics*, II/2, p. 721.

74. Bonhoeffer, *Ethics*, p. 315.

75. Bonhoeffer, *Letters and Papers*, pp. 15, 384.

76. J. Verkuyl, *The Message of Liberation Today* (Johannesburg, 1971), p. 29.

77. Cf. Luke 7:18ff.

78. Bonhoeffer, *Ethics*, p. 232.

79. Moltmann, "An Open Letter to José Míguez Bonino."

80. Bonhoeffer, *op. cit.*, p. 14. Cf. K. Barth, *Church Dogmatics*, IV/3, p. 938.

81. J. H. Yoder, "Fuller Definition of 'Violence'" (an unpublished mimeographed paper, March 28, 1973). Apart from the many studies on the problem of violence and nonviolence published during the past decade, including very useful treatments of it by Míguez Bonino, see Martin Hengel, *Victory over Violence* (Philadelphia, 1973), and *Non-Violent Action*, a report commissioned for the United Reformed Church in England (London, 1973).

82. "God Intervening in Human Affairs," *Missionalia*, vol. 5, no. 2, pp. 116f.

83. E.g., the comment by Mrs. Jael Mbogo, Deputy General Secretary of the All Africa Conference of Churches, that the armed struggle in southern Africa is a holy war, *Ecunews,* 39/76, December 10, 1976; and the comments of the DRC regarding the Gereformeerde Kerken support for the PCR, *DRC Africa News,* vol. 3, no. 3 (March, 1978).

84. "The Bondage of Liberation: A Pacifist Reflection," *Worldview* (March, 1977), p. 24.

85. T. F. Torrance, *op. cit.,* p. 276.

86. Cf. *DRC Africa News*, vol. 2, no. 6 (June, 1977); *Reformed World,* no. 34 (1976), pp. 50-57; Allen O. Miller, ed., *A Christian Declaration on Human Rights* (Grand Rapids, 1977).

87. The "charismatic renewal" in South Africa, as in other parts of the world, is rapidly growing within the English-speaking churches, notably the Anglican, about a third of whose bishops would identify with it. About 2,300 people of all races and many denominations participated in the S.A. Renewal Conference held in Johannesburg in September, 1977. Also of note, but not as part of the "charismatic renewal" as such, is the proposed S.A. Christian Leaders Assembly scheduled for mid-1979, a development out of PACLA, held in Nairobi in 1976 under the auspices of Africa Enterprise.

88. Bonhoeffer, *Letters and Papers*, p. 300.

89. *The Passion for Life* (Philadelphia, 1978), p. 47.

90. *Library of Christian Classics,* Wilhelm Pauck, ed., Westminster, Philadelphia, 1961, XV, 413. Cf. Moltmann, "The Cross and Civil Religion."

91. "Why We're Hoping Against Hope," *Sunday Tribune*, Durban (March 6, 1977).

Postscript: **A Response to Major Criticisms**

1. James R. Cochrane, *Servants of Power: the Role of the English-speaking Churches in South Africa* (Johannesburg: Ravan, 1986).

2. See my essay "Theologies in conflict: the South African debate" in Charles Villa-Vicencio and John W. de Gruchy, eds., *Resistance and Hope* (Cape Town: David Philip; Grand Rapids: Eerdmans, 1985).

3. See esp. the discussion in *Social Dynamics,* a journal of the Centre for African Studies at the University of Cape Town, vol. 9, no. 1 (1983).

4. See Buti Tlhagale, "Towards a black theology of labour," and James R. Cochrane, "The churches and the trade unions," in Villa-Vicencio and de Gruchy, *op. cit.*

5. Bob Clarke, "A Review of 'The Church Struggle in South Africa,'" in *Reality* (November, 1979), p. 17.

6. *Social Dynamics,* vol. 5, no. 1 (1979).

7. See my essay "Theologies in conflict" in Villa-Vicencio and de Gruchy, *op. cit.*

8. See John W. de Gruchy and Charles Villa-Vicencio, eds., *Apartheid is a Heresy* (Cape Town: David Philip; Grand Rapids: Eerdmans, 1983); see also my article "The Revitalization of Calvinism," in the *Journal for Religious Ethics* (Spring, 1986).

9. *The Reformed Journal* (February, 1981), p. 28.

10. See my article "Christians in Conflict: the Social Reality of the South African Church," in the *Journal of Theology for Southern Africa,* no. 51 (June, 1985), pp. 16ff.

11. *The Kairos Document* was reprinted in the *Journal of Theology for Southern Africa,* no. 53 (September, 1985), and in *The Challenge to the Church* (Grand Rapids: Eerdmans, 1986).

12. The best discussion of this issue in the South African context is David Russell, *A Theological Critique of the Christian Pacifist Perspective with Special Reference to the Position of John Howard Yoder,* Ph.D. Thesis, University of Cape Town, 1985.

13. See Allan Boesak and Charles Villa-Vicencio, eds., *When Prayer Makes News* (Philadelphia: Westminster, 1986).

Index of Subjects

271

Index of Names

Bibliography

The select bibliography (which did not appear in the original U.S. edition) has been revised for this new edition of *The Church Struggle in South Africa*. It therefore contains many titles that were published after the book was written. Although some titles pertaining to the 19th and early 20th centuries are included, the list is by no means exhaustive but rather is a sample which should provide a way into the material. There is a vast literature on the social history of South Africa both past and present which needs to be consulted in order to locate the church in its proper context. A few pertinent titles have been included in this area, but only by way of introduction. The reader should also consult the *Annual Survey of Race Relations* published each year by the South African Institute of Race Relations, Johannesburg. Although the material here has been separated into various categories (Historical, Theological, Documentary), there is considerable overlapping of subjects.

Historical

Adonis, J. C. *Die Afgebreekte Skeidsmuur Weer Opgebou.* Amsterdam: Rodopi, 1982.

Briggs, D. R., and J. Wing. *The Harvest and the Hope: The Story of Congregationalism in Southern Africa.* Johannesburg: United Congregational Church of Southern Africa, 1970.

Brown, W. E. *The Catholic Church in South Africa, from its Origin to the Present Day.* London: Burns & Oates, 1960.

Bryan, G. McLeod. *Naudé: Prophet to South Africa.* Atlanta: John Knox, 1978.

Clarke, R. G. *For God or Caesar? An Historical Study of Christian Resistance to Apartheid by the Church of the Province of South Africa, 1946–1957.* 2 vols. Ph.D. thesis, University of Natal, Pietermaritzburg, 1983.

Clayton, Geoffrey. *Where We Stand: Archbishop Clayton's Charges, 1948–1957.* Ed. C. T. Wood. Cape Town: Oxford University Press, 1960.

Davies, Horton. *Great South African Christians.* Cape Town: Oxford University Press, 1951

de Klerk, W. A. *The Puritans in Africa: A History of Afrikanerdom.* Harmondsworth: Penguin, 1976.

Dreyer, A. *Boustowwe vir die Geskiedenis van die Nederduitse Gereformeerde Kerke in Suid-Afrika, 1804–1836.* Kaapstad: Nasionale Pers, 1936.

du Plessis, J. *A History of Christian Missions in South Africa.* London: Longmans, Green & Co., 1911; repr. Cape Town: C. Struik, 1965.

————. *Life of Andrew Murray.* London: Marshall Bros., 1919.

du Toit, Andre, and Hermann Giliomee. *Afrikaner Political Thought: Analysis and Documents.* Vol. 1, 1780–1850. Cape Town: David Philip, 1983.

Engelbrecht, S. P. *Geskiedenis van die Nederduitsch Hervormde Kerk van Afrika.* Cape Town, 1953.

Ffrench-Beytagh, G. A. *Encountering Darkness.* London: Collins, 1973.

_____. *Encountering Light.* London: Collins, 1975.

Florin, Hans W. *Lutherans in South Africa.* Durban: Lutheran Publishing House, 1967.

Gerdener, G. B. A. *Recent Developments in the South African Mission Field.* London: Marshall, Morgan & Scott, 1958.

Gerhart, Gail. *Black Power in South Africa: The Evolution of an Ideology.* Berkeley: University of California Press, 1978.

Guy, Jeff. *The Heretic: A Study of the Life of John William Colenso, 1814–1883.* Johannesburg: Ravan, 1983.

Hexham, Irving. *The Irony of Apartheid: The Struggle for National Independence of Afrikaner Calvinism against British Imperialism.* New York: Edwin Mellen Press, 1981.

Hewson, Leslie A. *An Introduction to South African Methodists.* Cape Town: Methodist Publishing House, 1951.

Hinchliff, Peter. *The Anglican Church in South Africa.* London: Darton, Longman and Todd, 1963.

_____. *The Church in South Africa.* London: SPCK, 1968.

Hope, Marjorie, and James Young. *The South African Churches in a Revolutionary Situation.* Maryknoll: Orbis, 1981.

Huddleston, Trevor. *Naught for Your Comfort.* London: Collins, Fontana, 1956.

Hudson-Reed, Sydney, John Jonsson, and Christopher Parnell. *Together for a Century: The History of the Baptist Union of South Africa, 1877–1977.* Pietermaritzburg: Baptist Historical Society, 1977.

Hudson-Reed, Sydney, ed. *By Taking Heed: The History of the Baptists in Southern Africa, 1820–1977.* Roodeport, Transvaal: Baptist Publishing House, 1983.

Jooste, J. P. *Die Geskiedenis van die Gereformeerde Kerk in Suid-Afrika, 1859–1959.* Potchefstroom, 1959.

Kruger, Bernhard. *The Pear Tree Blossoms: The History of the Moravian Church in South Africa, 1837–1869.* Genadendal: Moravian Church Board, 1967.

le Feuvre, P. *Cultural and Theological Factors affecting Relations between the Nederduitse Gereformeerde Kerk and the Anglican Church of the Province of South Africa in the Cape Colony, 1806–1910.* Ph.D. thesis, University of Cape Town, 1980.

Lewis, Cecil, and G. E. Edwards. *Historical Records of the Church of the Province of South Africa.* London: SPCK, 1934.

Lodge, Tom. *Black Politics in South Africa since 1945.* Johannesburg: Ravan; London: Longman, 1983.

Lombard, R. T. L. *Die Nederduitse Gereformeerde Kerke en Rasse-politiek met verwysing na die jare 1884–1961.* Silverton, Transvaal: Promedia, 1981.

Luckhoff, A. H. *Cottesloe.* Cape Town: Tafelberg, 1978.

Luthuli, Albert. *Let my People Go.* London: Collins, 1962.

Matthew, Z. K. *Freedom for my People.* Cape Town: David Philip, 1981.

Moorreess, A. *Die Nederduitse Gereformeerde Kerk in Suid Afrika, 1652–1873.* Cape Town: Bible Society, 1937.

Nash, Margaret. *Black Uprooting from "White" South Africa.* Johannesburg: SACC, 1980.

Norman, Edward. *Christianity in the Southern Hemisphere: The Churches in Latin America and South Africa.* Oxford: Clarendon Press, 1981.

Odendaal, Andre. *Vukani Bantu! The Beginnings of Black Protest Politics in South Africa to 1912.* Cape Town: David Philip, 1983.

Paine, V. *The Confrontation between the Archbishop of Cape Town, Joost de Blank, and the South African Government on Racial Policies.* M.A. thesis, University of Cape Town, 1978.

Paton, Alan. *Apartheid and the Archbishop: The Life and Times of Geoffrey Clayton.* Cape Town: David Philip, 1973.

Randall, Peter, ed. *Not Without Honour: Tribute to Beyers Naude.* Johannesburg: Ravan, 1981.

Reeves, A. *Shooting at Sharpeville: The Agony of South Africa.* London: Gollancz, 1961.

―――. *South Africa—Yesterday and Tomorrow: A Challenge to Christians.* London: Gollancz, 1962.

Regehr, E. *Perceptions of Apartheid: The Churches and Political Change in South Africa.* Scottdale, Pa.: Herald Press, 1979.

Sales, Jane M. *The Planting of the Churches in South Africa.* Grand Rapids: Eerdmans, 1971.

Serfontein, J. H. P. *Apartheid, Change and the NG Kerk.* Johannesburg: Taurus, 1982.

Spoelstra, C. *Bouwstoffen voor de Geschiedenis der Nederduitsch-Gereformeerde Kerken in Zuid-Afrika, 1652–1804.* Parts 1 and 2. Amsterdam and Cape Town: Jacques Dusseau, 1907.

Stoker, H. G., and F. J. M. Potgieter, eds. *Koers in die Krisis.* Vol. 1. Stellenbosch: Pro Ecclesia, 1935.

Stoker, H. G., and J. D. Vorster, eds. *Koers in die Krisis.* Vol. 2. Stellenbosch: Pro Ecclesia, n.d.

———. *Koers in die Krisis.* Vol. 3. Stellenbosch: Pro Ecclesia, 1941.

Strassberger, E. *Ecumenism in South Africa: 1936–1960.* Johannesburg: SACC, 1974.

———. *The Rhenish Mission Society in South Africa, 1830–1950.* Cape Town: C. Struik, 1969.

Thomas, David. *Councils in the Ecumenical Movement.* Johannesburg: SACC, 1979.

Verryn, Trevor. *A History of the Order of Ethiopia.* Cleveland, Transvaal: Central Mission Press, 1972.

Walshe, Peter. *Church Versus State in South Africa: The Case of the Christian Institute.* Maryknoll: Orbis; London: Hurst, 1983.

Weisse, Wolfram. *Südafrika und das Antirassismusprogramm.* Frankfurt am Main: Peter Lang, 1975.

Theological

Bax, Douglas S. *A Different Gospel: A Critique of the Theology Behind Apartheid.* Johannesburg: Presbyterian Church of Southern Africa, 1979.

Becken, Hans-Jürgen, ed. *Relevant Theology for Africa.* Durban: Lutheran Publishing House, 1973.

Boesak, Allan A. *Farewell to Innocence: A Social-Ethical Study of Black Theology and Black Power.* Maryknoll: Orbis; Johannesburg: Ravan, 1977.

Bosch, David, Adrio Konig, and Willem Nicol, eds. *Perspektief Op Die Ope Brief.* Cape Town: Human & Rouseau, 1982.

Botha, A. J. *Die Evolusie van 'n Volksteologie.* Ph.D. thesis, University of the Western Cape, 1984.

Cloete, G. D., and D. J. Smit, eds. *A Moment of Truth: The Confession of the Dutch Reformed Mission Church, 1982.* Grand Rapids: Eerdmans, 1984.

Cochrane, J. R. *The Role of English-speaking Churches in South Africa: A Critical Historical Analysis and Theological Evaluation with Special Reference to the Church of the Province and the Methodist Church, 1903–1930.* Ph.D. thesis, University of Cape Town, 1982. Rev. and published as *Servants of Power: The Role of the English-speaking Churches in South Africa.* Johannesburg: Ravan, 1986.

de Gruchy, John W. *Bonhoeffer and South Africa: Theology in Dialogue.* Grand Rapids: Eerdmans; Exeter: Paternoster, 1984.

————. *Cry Justice! Prayers, Meditations and Readings from South Africa.* London: Collins; Maryknoll: Orbis, 1986.

de Gruchy, John W., and W. B. de Villiers, eds. *The Message in Perspective.* Johannesburg: SACC, 1969.

de Gruchy, John W., and Charles Villa-Vicencio, eds. *Apartheid is a Heresy.* Cape Town: David Philip; Grand Rapids: Eerdmans; London: SPCK, 1983.

Desmond, Cosmas. *Christians or Capitalists? Christianity and Politics in South Africa.* London: Bowerdean, 1978.

Eybers, I. H., A. Konig, and C. F. A. Borchardt. *Teologie en Vernuwing.* Pretoria: UNISA, 1975.

Geyser, A. S., et al. *Delayed Action.* Pretoria: NG Kerk Boekhandel, 1961.

Govender, Shun, ed. *Unity and Justice: The Witness of the Belydende Kring.* Braamfontein: The Belydende Kring, 1984.

Hofmeyr, J. W., and W. S. Vorster, eds. *New Faces of Africa: Essays in Honour of Ben Marais.* Pretoria: UNISA, 1984.

Hurley, D. E. *State and Church: An Approach to Political Action by Christians.* London: Geoffrey Chapman, 1966.

Jabavu, D. D. T. *An African Indigenous Church: A Plea for its Establishment in South Africa.* Lovedale: Lovedale Press, 1942.

Johanson, Brian, ed. *The Church in South Africa—Today and Tomorrow.* Johannesburg: SACC, 1975.

Keet, B. B. *Whither South Africa?* Stellenbosch: University Publishers, 1956.

Kotze, C. S. *Die NG Kerk en die Ekumene.* Pretoria: NG Kerk Boekhandel, 1984.

Kotze, J. C. G. *Principle and Practice in Race Relations.* Stellenbosch: SCA Publishers, 1962.

Leatt, James, Theo Kneifel, and Klaus Nurnberger, eds. *Contending Ideologies in South Africa.* Cape Town: David Philip; Grand Rapids: Eerdmans, 1986.

Mosala, I., and B. Tlhagale, eds. *The Unquestionable Right to be Free: Essays on Black Theology.* Johannesburg: Skotaville, 1986.

Motlhabi, Mokgethi. *The Theory and Practice of Black Resistance to Apartheid: A Social-Ethical Analysis.* Johannesburg: Skotaville, 1984.

Moodie, T. Dunbar. *The Rise of Afrikanerdom: Power, Apartheid and the Afrikaner Civil Religion.* Berkeley: University of California Press, 1975.

Moore, Basil, ed. *The Challenge of Black Theology in South Africa.* Atlanta: John Knox, 1973.

Nash, M. *Christians Make Peace.* Durban: Diakonia/PACSA, 1982.

_____. *Ecumenical Movements in the 1960's.* Braamfontein: SACC, 1975.

Nolan, Albert. *Jesus before Christianity: The Gospel of Liberation.* London: Darton, Longman and Todd; Maryknoll: Orbis, 1977.

Nurnberger, Klaus, ed. *Affluence, Poverty and the Word of God.* Durban: Lutheran Publishing House, 1978.

_____. *Ideologies of Change in South Africa and the Power of the Gospel.* Durban: Lutheran Publishing House, 1979.

Oosthuizen, G. C. *Pentecostal Penetration into the Indian Community in South Africa.* Pretoria: HSRC, 1975.

Oosthuizen, G. C., J. K. Coetzee, J. W. de Gruchy, J. H. Hofmeyr, and B. C. Lategan. *Religion, Intergroup Relations and Social Change in South Africa.* Pretoria: HSRC, 1985.

Paton, David. *Church and Race in South Africa.* London: SCM, 1958.

Pauw, B. A. *Christianity and Xhosa Tradition.* Cape Town: Oxford University Press, 1975.

Prior, Andrew, ed. *Catholics in Apartheid Society.* Cape Town: David Philip, 1982.

Setiloane, G. *The Image of God among the Sotho-Tswana.* Rotterdam: Balkema, 1976.

Smith, N. J. *Die Planting van Afsonderlike Kerke vie Nie-Blanke Bevolkingsgroepe deur die Nederduitse Gereformeerde Kerk in Suid Afrika.* Stellenbosch: University of Stellenbosch, 1973.

Smith, J. J., F. E. O'B. Geldenhuys, and P. Meiring. *Stormkompas.* Kaapstad: Tafelberg, 1973.

Stevens, R. J. *Community Beyond Division.* New York: Vantage Press, 1984.

Storey, Peter. *Here We Stand: Submission to the Commission of Inquiry into the South African Council of Churches.* Johannesburg: SACC, 1983.

Sundermeier, T., ed. *Church and Nationalism in South Africa.* Johannesburg: Ravan, 1973.

Sundlker, Bengt. *Bantu Prophets in South Africa.* London: Lutterworth, 1948.

————. *Zulu Zion and Some Swazi Zionists.* London: Oxford University Press, 1976.

Templin, J. Alton. *Ideology on a Frontier: The Theological Foundation of Afrikaner Nationalism, 1652–1910.* Westport, Conn.: Greenwood Press, 1984.

Theology—Confession—Politics. The Papers and Responses of the Conference of the South African Theological Society, 1984. Ed. D. J. Smit. Bellville: University of the Western Cape, 1985.

Truernicht, A. P. *Credo van 'n Afrikaner.* Kaapstad: Tafelberg, 1975.

Turner, R. *The Eye of the Needle: Toward Participatory Democracy in South Africa.* Johannesburg: SPRO-CAS, 1972; Johannesburg: Ravan, 1980.

Tutu, Desmond. *Crying in the Wilderness.* London: Mowbray; Grand Rapids: Eerdmans, 1982.

————. *The Divine Intention: Presentation to the Eloff Commission of Enquiry.* Johannesburg: SACC, 1982.

_____. *Hope and Suffering.* Johannesburg: Skotaville, 1983; London: Collins; Grand Rapids: Eerdmans, 1984.

Villa-Vicencio, Charles. *Race and Class in the English Speaking Churches.* Bellville: University of the Western Cape, 1985.

_____. *The Theology of Apartheid.* Cape Town: Methodist Publishing House, n.d.

_____. *Saints and Citizens.* Grand Rapids: Eerdmans; Cape Town: David Philip, 1986.

Villa-Vicencio, Charles, and J. W. de Gruchy. *Resistance and Hope: South African Essays in Honour of Beyers Naudé.* Cape Town: David Philip; Grand Rapids: Eerdmans, 1985.

Viljoen, A. C. *Ekumene onder die Suiderkruis.* Pretoria: UNISA, 1979.

von Allmen, Daniel. *Theology—Advocate or Critic of Apartheid? A critical study of the "Landman Report" (1974) of the Dutch Reformed Church (South Africa).* Bern: Swiss Federation of Protestant Churches, 1977.

Vorster, W. S., ed. *Church and Society.* Pretoria: UNISA, 1978.

_____. *Church Unity and Diversity in the Southern African Context.* Pretoria: UNISA, 1979.

West, Charles. *Perspective on South Africa.* Princeton: Princeton Theological Seminary, 1985.

West, Martin. *Bishops and Prophets in a Black City: African Independent Churches in Soweto, Johannesburg.* Cape Town: David Philip, 1975.

Wilmore, G. S., and J. H. Cone, eds. *Black Theology: A Documentary History.* Maryknoll: Orbis, 1979.

Documentation

Apartheid and the Church: Report of the SPRO-CAS Church Commission. Johannesburg: SPRO-CAS, 1972.

Cassidy, Michael, ed. *I Will Heal their Land.* The Content of the South African Congress on Mission and Evangelism, Durban, 1973. Pietermaritzburg: Africa Enterprise, 1974.

Cawood, Lesley. *The Church and Race Relations in South Africa.* Johannesburg: Institute of Race Relations, 1964.

The Christian Citizen in a Multi-Racial Society. A Report of the

Rosettenville Conference, July, 1949.

Christian Principles in Multi-Racial South Africa. A Report on the Dutch Reformed Conference of Church Leaders, Pretoria, 17-19 November, 1953.

Christian Reconstruction in South Africa. A Report of the Fort Hare Conference, July, 1942. Lovedale: Lovedale Press, 1942.

Cottesloe Consultation. The Report of the Consultation Among South African Member Churches of the World Council of Churches, 7-14 December, 1960.

The Future of South Africa. A Study by British Christians. London: SCM, 1964.

God's Kingdom in Multi-Racial South Africa. A Report on the Inter-Racial Conference of Church Leaders, Johannesburg, 7-10 December, 1954.

Human Relations in South Africa. A Report adopted by the General Synod of the Dutch Reformed Church, 1966.

Human Relations and the South African Scene in the Light of Scripture. A Report adopted by the General Synod of the Dutch Reformed Church, October, 1974. Cape Town: NG Kerk Boekhandel, 1976.

International Commission of Jurists, Geneva, eds. *The Trial of Beyers Naude.* London: Search Press; Johannesburg: Ravan, 1975.

The Kairos Document: Challenge to the Church. A Theological Comment on the Political Crisis in South Africa. Johannesburg: The Kairos Theologians, 1985.

Landman, W. A. *A Plea for Understanding.* Cape Town: NG Kerk Uitgewers, 1968.

Nash, Margaret. *Your Kingdom Come.* Papers and Resolutions of the Twelfth National Conference of the SACC, 1980. Johannesburg: SACC, 1980.

Paton, D. M. *Church and Race in South Africa: Papers from South Africa, 1952–57.* London: SCM, 1958.

Randall, Peter. *A Taste of Power: The Final SPRO-CAS Report.* Johannesburg: SPRO-CAS, 1973.

Thomas, David, ed. *Liberation.* The Papers and Resolutions of the Eighth National Conference of the SACC, 1976. Johannesburg: SACC, 1976.

World Council of Churches. *Report on the WCC Mission in South Africa, April–December 1960*. Geneva: WCC, 1961.

Journals and Periodicals

The following selection of South African journals and periodicals should be consulted for articles and essays on the church and theology in South Africa.

ABRECSA Newsletter. Published by the Alliance of Black Reformed Christians in Southern Africa.

Diakonia News. Published by Diakonia, Durban, Natal.

Die Kerkbode. Newspaper of the Dutch Reformed Church.

Dimension. Newspaper of the Methodist Church of Southern Africa.

Ecunews. The Monthly News Bulletin of the South African Council of Churches.

Grace and Truth. A Catholic theological journal published by the Dominican Order in South Africa.

ICT News. Newsletter of the Institute for Contextual Theology.

Missionalia. Journal of the Southern Africa Missiological Society.

Ned. Geref. Teologiese Tydsrif. Theological journal of the Dutch Reformed Church in South Africa.

Religion in Southern Africa. Published by the Association for the Study of Religion (Southern Africa).

Seek. The newspaper of the Church of the Province of South Africa (Anglican).

South African Outlook. An Independent Ecumenical Monthly journal concerned with political, racial, and economic issues.

Southern Cross. The newspaper of the Roman Catholic Church in South Africa.

The Journal of Theology for Southern Africa. An ecumenical theological journal.

Theologia Evangelica. Journal of the Faculty of Theology, University of South Africa.

Witness. Published by Africa Enterprise, Pietermaritzburg.

Woord en Daad. An independent journal dealing with socio-political issues from a Reformed perspective.

Bibliographies

For further detailed references of articles and essays see:

Borchardt, C. F. A. and W. S. Vorster, eds. *South African Theological Bibliography.* Vols. 1 and 2. Pretoria: University of South Africa, 1980, 1983.

DATE DUE